Harmless lovers?

This book reconstructs a decisive and neglected aspect of modern social thought: the evolution of modern gender theory from Mary Wollstonecraft at the end of the eighteenth century to the beginning of the twentieth century and Max Weber. It examines the responses of major intellectual figures – Comte, Marx, Engels, Mill, Durkheim, Enfantin and Nietzsche – to the 'new' woman and 'women's emancipation' in the period immediately following the French Revolution and the Declaration of the Rights of Man. The pressure for social equality between men and women, and the fact that writers like Mary Wollstonecraft actually produced first-class political and social theory, created new tensions within both the private lives of the theorists and social theory itself. The crisis was suppressed in the writing and lives of Marx and Durkheim, who remained attached to the traditional framework, but all the other men examined in this book sought to evolve new ways of living in gender relations. Some of these variations involved a neo-conservatism (Comte), others a new liberalism (Mill), others a version of a new communism (Enfantin, Engels) while some sought pure transcendence (Nietzsche). This book seeks to develop a fresh look at these writers by examining some of the continuities and discontinuities between theory and lived practice. The book will appeal to a general readership as well as to students in theory, gender, women's studies and the history of ideas.

Mike Gane is Senior Lecturer in Social Science at Loughborough University.

Harmless lovers?

Gender, theory and personal relationships

Mike Gane

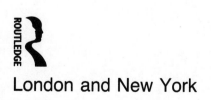

London and New York

First published 1993
by Routledge
11 New Fetter Lane, London EC4P 4EE

Simultaneously published in the USA and Canada
by Routledge
29 West 35th Street, New York, NY 10001

© 1993 Mike Gane

Phototypeset in Times by Intype, London
Printed and bound in Great Britain by
TJ Press (Padstow) Ltd, Padstow, Cornwall

British Library Cataloguing in Publication Data
A catalogue record for this book is available from the British Library.

Library of Congress Cataloging in Publication Data
A catalogue record for this book is available from the Library of Congress.

ISBN 0–415–09448–8
      0–415–09449–6 (pbk)

For M. H. A.

What miracles we harmless lovers wrought . . .
John Donne

Contents

Acknowledgements

This book was initially contracted with Gordon Smith of Unwin Hyman Publishers. Subsequently Unwin Hyman passed into the domain of Routledge, and this project to the sphere of Chris Rojek. I would like to thank both Gordon Smith and Chris Rojek for their interest and support. I have benefited greatly from discussions with many people over issues raised in this book and I would like to thank in particular some members of the board of *Economy and Society* with whom I have discussed relevant issues; Beverley Brown, Maxine Molyneux, Ali Rattansi and Keith Tribe. *Economy and Society* has published some of my related papers on gender, and I thank the board for permission to use material from those papers in this book. I have discussed themes from the book with a number of members and students of the Department of Social Sciences at Loughborough University, some of whom have kindly commented on earlier drafts of chapters of the book: Michael Billig, Alan Bryman, Anna Dempsey, Teresa Keil, Jane Littlewood, Alan Radley. I am also indebted to groups of students on both undergraduate courses (Sociology of Gender) and postgraduate courses (Women's Studies) at Loughborough, and would like to thank the many students who have contributed to the debates. I have also presented a seminar at Leicester University's Department of Sociology, and would like to thank Terry Johnson and Sallie Westwood for their discussion. I have discussed issues concerning Durkheim with W. S. F. Pickering and Herminio Martins at the Centre for Durkheim Studies at Oxford. I have also been helped on these issues by the women's group at Toulouse University (Le Mirail), *Simone*, and would particularly like to thank Marie-France Brive for her assistance. Some of the chapters of this book were written while I was on study leave at Toulouse University (Le Mirail), and I would like to thank Professor Jean-Michel Berthelot for his hospitality and for his critical comments on the project. I have benefited from discussions with Jeff Hearn who has also commented in detail on parts of the draft manuscript, and I would like to thank Sara Mills, who commented on the whole manuscript. I am also indebted for discussions on all these issues to Monique Arnaud. I should

emphasize however that in this work the final responsibility for the interpretations developed, and any deficiencies, is ultimately my own.

Mike Gane

Introduction

The arrangement of this book, which examines the heterosexual attitudes (often claimed scientific) of selected leading social theorists from 1792 to 1920, requires something of an explanation: why begin with Durkheim and end (via Wollstonecraft, Marx, Godwin, Enfantin, Comte, Mill, Engels and Weber), with Nietzsche? There are a number of reasons. The chapter on Emile Durkheim was first published ten years ago in 1983. It was then the first attempt to excavate and try to examine fully Durkheim's position on the question of women. Since then there have been other efforts to do this (notably Rosalind Sydie (1987: 13–49), and Terry Kandal (1988: 79–88)). Today however, this chapter (and, for me, also the comparable chapters in Sydie and Kandal) remain more of a puzzle than an answer. This book does not resolve the puzzle but it does work towards a statement of its nature.

First, to begin with Durkheim's response to the crisis which opened after the French Revolution, is to start with a writer who, today, is still regarded, but in a language which itself is very much in question, as a 'founding father' of sociology (alongside Marx and Weber).[1] A modern discipline which starts with Durkheim (and Marx and Weber) has consequences for the way gender issues are constituted and considered, for Durkheim wrote about gender matters only indirectly, his position on women (unlike his approach to other problems (Gane 1992)) is also explicitly anti-radical. The major 'gender radicals' in the early period of sociology were Enfantin and the Saint-Simonians, Comte, Mill, Engels and Nietzsche; I use the word radical in the sense that it was these individuals who tried to create new, imaginative solutions to the new problems of gender relations in the era dominated by the promise of universal liberty and equality. Of all the sociologists considered here, it is Durkheim who provides the most thoroughgoing 'scientific' argument (though it has to be teased out of his writings) *against* civic equality for women and provides systematic intellectual grounds for the urgent need to refuse the demand for women's emancipation. In this sense Durkheim is a problem and also a puzzle.

Second, there are severe problems in trying to relate Durkheim's writings to the way he lived as a person. Some, notably Greenberg (1976), Lacroix (1981), and Mestrovic (1988), have tried to think about this problem and have had to resort to speculation in the absence of evidence. Durkheim's papers were lost in World War Two (see Mestrovic 1988: 19), and few accounts of his life have survived. One will search in vain, for example, even for the dates of birth of his two children (not given in the standard intellectual biography by Lukes (1973) nor indeed in the genealogical family tree in the unpublished part of Lukes' thesis on Durkheim). It is known that Durkheim had two children and something is known of his son André, since an obituary written by Durkheim exists. Little is reported in the literature about his daughter or Durkheim's own relation to her. Unlike the evidence which exists for Marx or Freud and their relations with their wives, virtually nothing exists in comparable form for Durkheim. We know that Durkheim's father died in 1896, and we know that at around the time Durkheim was in considerable emotional turmoil and in the process of a dramatic recasting of his general theory to include the force of the sacred. Are the two events connected?

The chapter on Durkheim presented here not only attempts to provide a detailed discussion of his ideas on gender issues, particularly on the position of women, it also argues that Durkheim's gender theory underwent considerable modification at the same time as his own personal crisis between 1893 and 1898. His later theory makes the connection between the sacred and emergence of the sexual divisions in society. Durkheim talks of the fact that he faced the necessity of having to rethink his whole theory in the light of his new recognition of the decisive importance of religion and sacred phenomena. But how and under what intellectual and extra-intellectual pressures did this occur? He also talks of becoming aware, in the process of research, of the importance of sexual relations in human culture: he says he can even remember the moment the idea occurred to him. The notion is current among commentators on Durkheim that his life was extremely ascetic, and that he did not experience very strongly the forces of Eros (Tiryakian 1981: 1026). All one can say is that evidence for this, for or against in the form of letters or diary does not exist. But as Mestrovic has pointed out (1988) not all sources have been investigated in France, and it is known that a considerable as yet unpublished stock of letters does exist. Could it be true that Durkheim did not experience the turbulence felt by others such as Marx or Freud, or Comte, Nietzsche or Weber? Or have the traces been erased or lost?

The question of the relation between the individual and theory has long been debated. My own point of departure was the debate which raged in the 1960s between the Sartrean and the Althusserian positions. During the years 1966–7, as the full impact of the Althusserian critique of existentialism emerged, I became aware of the dangers of both a reduction of thought to experience and the hidden acceptance of essential categories in an 'expressive totality' (that is where each individual part possesses and expresses the homogeneous quality of the whole itself). After this transition the idea that it would be necessary to look at personal experience in the analysis of theoretical development was regarded with great suspicion. However, even Althusser himself did not hold to this extreme form for very long, and when he developed his concept of the Ideological State Apparatuses in 1969 he immediately linked this to the explanation of the way that Marx's thought itself had developed: the development of Marx's theory was not purely an intellectual process occurring in and motivated by pure logic, but a social and individual project meeting head on the ideological apparatuses of several states. In an essay of 1980, I criticized Althusser's 'apparent regression' suggesting that 'returning as Althusser does to Marx's experiences merely acts to resurrect the sanctity of authoriality' (in Gane, 1989a: 146). In separating knowledge and experience in this way I wanted to hold on to the vital distinction between subjective representations within lived experience and adequate objective understanding, to resist the temptation to claim legitimacy or veracity for an idea by an appeal to the status of its author's status or experience. I still regard this as an important objective.

In 1992, Althusser's autobiography was published posthumously in France.[2] Something of the life of Althusser has already been widely known since the episode which ended his career, the tragic uxoricide in his apartment at the Ecole Normale in 1980. There was never an open trial; the case was judged officially 'non-lieu' (as in cases where there are insufficient grounds for prosecution), but in this instance with supplementary conditions: he was denied the right publicly to explain the event; he was clinically interned and his civil rights were annulled; the medical documentation of his prolonged treatment and his mental state have been kept secret (Althusser 1992: 20–1): the autopsy confirmed that she died of strangulation. In 1985 he was functioning sufficiently to write an account of his life. This account goes much further than anything Althusser had said before about the interconnection of experience and theory: the self-psychoanalytic components and conceptual development are closely interwoven. Although there is much about his relations with his mother and to other women, especially his wife Hélène Legotien, there is a remarkable absence of theoretical reflection on the condition of women or on the politics of the relations between the sexes.[3] What emerges is the story of a turbulent and passionate relationship which tends to glorify Hélène Legotien (in Chapter 12 of his book (1992) he suggests that her writing, her style, was greater than that of Joyce,[4] etc. just as Mill claimed that Harriet Taylor's poetry was greater than Shelley's); but the account tries to reflect on his own intellectual projects, and their 'deep and profound – conscious and above all unconscious motives' (1992: 161).

In fact Althusser had long supported the cause of psychoanalysis, and evidently been under psychoanalytic treatment. His work supported a close relation between the two forms of analysis (Marxist and psychoanalytic) as epistemological allies. His final position was to see an aspect of a complete combination of the two projects, which, in a strange way, mirrors the existentialist project of Sartre who wanted to achieve a complete psycho-social analysis of writers like Flaubert, Genet, etc. The tendency towards this analytic position seemed apparent in Althusser's writing as soon as doubts began to emerge as to the genuinely scientific nature of Marx's works and Marxism in general, and as soon as a critical evaluation of the nature of extreme philosophical rationalism within Marxism began to occur. Althusser also became more critical of the function of the working-class organizations and replaced the proletariat as the decisive historical agent with broader popular movements. While he remained strictly communist in orientation and materialist in philosophy, he placed less importance on high theory, especially a theory developing under its own logic, though he did not abandon his thesis that it was important not to avoid treating theory as a form of human intersubjectivity, and he continued to hold to his position of anti-humanism in theory.

But for the tragic event of the death of Hélène Legotien and the way in which the Althusser case was dealt with as a 'non-lieu' it may be possible to doubt whether Louis Althusser's account would have been written. Ironically of course this itself is evidence of the force of circumstance. Ironically, also, from the contrary point of view it did not give rise, it appears, to any direct, focused reflection in the autobiography on the problems of the oppression of women though he had considered and written briefly on this subject in two periods of his life in relation to debates on feminism (see Boutang 1992: 328), the latter also at the time his thought was widening to embrace the theory of social movements (presumably also the women's movement). Althusser himself writes as victim. He is even victim of the 'non-lieu'. What is perhaps somewhat surprising is that there exists a genre or tradition of Althusserian-influenced feminism (see Assiter 1990). Yet there is such a current and one clearly polarized towards a specific kind of alliance with (Lacanian) psychoanalysis, the kind of psychoanalysis which influenced Althusser theoretically. Although this feminism is highly effective in its own terms, and it obviously includes psychoanalysts it does not seem to have generated analyses of the fusion of the personal, experiential and the political and theoretical to which in the end even Althusser himself was led. This is, in my opinion, because the femininst element in this tradition does not emerge within the tradition, the tradition is imposed on and merges with it. There has never been an Althusserian *appel de la femme* just as there was never one from Marx.

There has nonetheless, particularly outside France, been a huge development of interest in the relation of gender issues and theory within the sphere of sociology, literature and philosophy. Titles like *The Sexism of Social and Political Theory* (Clark and Lange 1979) and *Feminist Theory and the Philosophies of Man* (Nye 1988) are now very common. Unlike their French counterparts, bookshops in Britain have large sections devoted to women's issues and gender theory. There are now special sections in some bookshops devoted specifically to men, masculinity and theory. The collection *Men, Masculinities and Social Theory* (Hearn and Morgan (eds) 1990) brings together papers taken from the first important conference on masculinity in Britain in 1988.[5]

I have here tended to connect the categories of lived experience and gender theory quite spontaneously. I certainly do not wish to re-establish a new sort of synthetic essentialism, or conceptual reductionism, what Warner calls biographical reductionism (1986: 30). In the study undertaken here I do not claim that the theories of gender which are the object of study simply 'express' the biographies of the individual thinkers concerned. I do not claim either that there is a politically correct way to think about these issues in some absolute, timeless sense.[6]

The aim of this book is not, again, to produce a single definitive account or theory of patriarchy or masculinity. The aim is much more modest: to begin to explore some of the obvious and available pieces of evidence of the way certain gender theories have been produced. The study in this book is part of a larger investigation, and is restricted to a study of selection of key formative writers. The fact that it begins with a study of Emile Durkheim (written in 1983) which does not try to make these connections is thus in part a benchmark for the way in which social theory has itself been changing over the last decade.

But it would perhaps be quite out of keeping with the general line of argument adopted in this book if I were to hold that this book was simply and purely part of the changing intellectual and theoretical *zeitgeist* of sociologists, though I have been greatly influenced by certain currents of theoretical feminism. In this area I am entirely without experience of 'men's consciousness-raising' groups: I know nothing about them directly, and cannot really praise them or criticize them. My experience of men's groups (for example some departments of sociology, some editorial boards) is that they are, even if they claim to be left wing and radical, the most difficult of terrains to try to 'raise consciousness' on the question of gender. I have a deep-seated distrust of quasi-critical self-analyses presented as revelatory renewals of self-consciousness; they are generally ludicrous processes of self-deception. As Nietzsche once said: 'Whenever a person permits something to become visible, one can ask "what does

it hide? From what does it wish to divert someone's gaze? What precon-
ception should it arouse? And further: to what extreme does the subtlety
of this disguise go? And, does he misperceive himself in all that?" ' (cited
in Salomé 1988: 10).

It might be thought surprising that it could ever be fashionable for
men to suffer humiliation before women either in order to be reborn as
men or as a means to reach a new position or new truth. However, the
idea is certainly not new, in one way or another there are many writers
examined in this book who do say this: perhaps most evidently Comte,
Marx and Mill. The problem is that many of these writers also believe
that their own masculinity, their own being as men is born in love, in
homage to, in the arms of, a woman. Marx says this explicitly, and it is
interesting that Althusser does also (1992: 121). Out of this (awakened)
masculinity comes the strength to go out into the world; but in the end
this strength creates a world where the feminine is a secondary agency.
Clearly Comte sought to humble men by advocating that they literally
worship women. But, to remain on the safe side, he retained all the
levers of power (institutions, property) in the hands of men. Thus any
attempt by men alone to modify or sacrifice the hegemony of men, just
as any attempt by a political party to serve the people, will be looked
upon with considerable suspicion as another attempt to invent power.
The position occupied by Marx and Durkheim, that the traditional form
of male domination is the best does have at least one merit: it is open
about its policy of segregation and its strategy of power. But at the
same time in its theoretical strategy masculinity is rendered invisible, for
everything happens explicitly only in the domain of men themselves, or
only in the realm of pure logic. For those who find this unacceptable,
the problem is to discover effective critiques and alternatives to the
traditional pattern: in effect, apart from Marx and Durkheim, this is what
the writers examined in this book attempted to do.

This still leaves a question as to the logic of the order of the writers
considered here. After a look at Durkheim's sociology, I go back to the
emergence of the modern problem with a consideration of the work of
Mary Wollstonecraft (1759–97), the new woman *par excellence*. If her
language resonates with the concepts which dominated the discourse of the
eighteenth century, her intellectual and political positions burst through
the limits of that discourse into that of the modern period. After Wollstonecraft I examine the romantic patriarchalism of Karl Marx as a refusal
to take up the revolutionary challenge in gender relations. I then turn to
those who did take up the challenge in various very different ways. On
Wollstonecraft's death William Godwin, symptomatically, dramatically
recast his theory on central issues as a result of her influence. The major
influence at the birth of social sciences in continental Europe was undoubtedly that of Saint-Simon. Here I focus the discussion on the key variations

in the way the Saint-Simonian collective, Comte, Mill, and then Engels, Weber and Nietzsche tried to adjust themselves to the new systemic disturbances in the conjugal milieu. Weber is treated as a crucial contrast to Emile Durkheim, and the existence of letters relating to his personal life is used to discuss the important connection between personal and theoretical developments, and his specific forms of accommodation to the new situation. The final place is given to Nietzsche, as it is Nietzsche who has now clearly become the focus of discussion of the opposition to modernity, and has become the central intellectual source of 'postmodernity'. The position of Nietzsche in the current debate is curious. For long considered racist and misogynist, the assessment now is more nuanced, but still unresolved. Nietzsche forms the crucial inspiration for postmodernism, and there is no need to question this. What is relevant to ask here is just how far Nietzsche provides the basis for thinking about forms of masculinity which transcend the modernist variations discussed elsewhere in this book. In the reading I present here I argue that his key text is *Thus Spake Zarathustra*, the first sections of which can be read as a chronical of the journey to the specifically Nietzschean, that is to say postmodern, new man as Übermensch, superman. In the conclusion I examine some of the curious responses to the question: who, where is the partner to Zarathustra?

I want to turn to some of the immediate theoretical problems involved in this study. First of all, to repeat, I do not wish to suggest that theorizing can be reduced to the personal experience or mode of life of the theorist concerned. This would be to overlook general social and cultural milieux, and the political conjunctures which often intervene in the discussion of problems as controversial as the position of women in society – the 'woman question' – and also the complex creative forces of abstract thought itself. In the perspective developed in this book, the period discussed is precisely that of the aftermath of the French Revolution of 1789, the declarations of the rights of man and the 'vindication' of the rights of woman immediately after. The period is that of the gradual emergence of the women's movement, feminism, the appearance both of the 'new woman' and of the 'new man'. The male radicals often made specific declarations or interpellations which called for the new woman to make her appearance, and which, courteously, provided a distinct place for her alongside the 'new man'; some even claimed dramatically to have found her and indeed even presented her as such to others as an ideal and exemplar. But even those who regard themselves as radicals in some spheres do not necessarily push this radicalism in the sphere of gender; there are influential male writers who resist the call for the 'new woman' even though they advocate a new society based on formal equality: in this case instead of appealing to and waiting for the new woman to emerge, woman, it is insisted, must herself wait for the new society to be made for her by men in order that she may then appear in a new form. Others suggest that the new woman is perhaps a completely mistaken idea, and that the feminine, a primary symbolic power, will always and necessarily be of secondary social status and function. But this latter conservative, even now reactionary, position has curiously given rise to radical postmodern feminist theories of gender difference.

I suggest, fundamentally, that these positions are not developed randomly or accidentally. Two quite different immediate processes are involved. First is the personal and ideological formation of the individual writer which plays its role in predisposing the person to a particular ideological orientation: towards a radical reorganization of sexual and gender relations in one direction or another, or to a new defence of the old regime. The second is the decisive effect of such situations themselves, of the relation between the theorist and the significant partner (or partners) concerned, here specifically the woman (or women) who is the direct object of the theory and who often plays a crucial role in the formulation of the theory itself. It seems to me that William Godwin's theories were decisively influenced by Mary Wollstonecraft and his own intense experience of the encounter with her, to develop in a certain direction, and that Godwin was conscious of becoming a 'new man' in the process. The immense influence of Saint-Simon extended to a reconstruction of the masculine in the efforts of both Enfantin and his rival Comte, developing in different ways out of different ideological preconceptions and in relation to very different women. J. S. Mill was certainly predisposed to find an intellectual like Harriet Taylor intriguing. When he 'found' her she was of course no *tabula rasa* but already a strong intellectual personality and she decisively influenced the way his theory of gender and emancipation was finally constructed in detail. Marx and Engels each became involved with women from two quite different backgrounds, indeed two distinctly different social-class statuses from their own. It was Engels, not Marx who finally developed a revolutionary theory of sexual emancipation through the new proletarian woman outside bourgeois marriage. Despite a commitment to the struggle for the new society, Durkheim like Marx, found a companion who was devoted to providing a traditional domestic *menage*.

Max Weber, who married a feminist intellectual, was initially committed to strict monogamy, but after his encounters with two women with whom he had secret and intense affairs he restructured his theory in order to indicate the value and meaning of the extra-marital affair and the erotic sphere. Comte came from a Catholic background and his later positivism gave birth to a positivist church and a cult of the virgin mother modelled on his partner Clotilde de Vaux. Engels, Weber and Nietzsche came from Protestant (Pietist, or Lutheran) backgrounds and their ideal was one of equality and partnership, though often with strong elements of complementarity rather than identity of spheres. Godwin and Mill were decisively influenced by English Protestantism and develop a highly rationalistic culture into one which attempts to embrace the feminine sphere of emotion. It might be thought that Nietzsche too was predisposed to establish a relationship based on the recognition of separate spheres, even to find a model *hausfrau* as partner – but he fell in love with Lou Salomé, an intellectual determined to remain independent and sexually active but not in marriage. Her refusal to become his partner pushed him into the project of self-overcoming.

If we count as radical those who attempted not only to provide a new theory of gender but who also tried to live in a new way, it is clear that this category would apply to Godwin, the Saint-Simonians, Comte, Mill, Engels, Weber and Nietzsche. For the most part the individuals concerned here tried to establish new codes of living, new practices based on a new evaluation of 'woman', and were in fact childless. The writers who held to the traditional conjugal divisions and statuses, those who refused the challenge of the new woman, were Marx, Durkheim (and Freud); these were also all family men, fathers (all, incidentally, originating from and breaking with – or continuing the break with – a Jewish ethnic background). Of course the Jewish culture is not homogeneous, but there are within it 'cultures' – rituals, practices, statuses, etc. – which are strongly patriarchal while at the same time providing the mother with important symbolic and emotional functions in 'a body of practices minutely governing all the details of life and leaving little free room for individual judgement' (Durkheim, in Lukes 1973: 40).

It is clear that some of these writers had an intensely difficult relationship with one or other of their parents, or with other members of the family over issues directly concerning their gender identity. Comte with the intervention of his mother at a crucial period; Engels with the demands of his family for a conventional marriage; Nietzsche with the intervention of his mother and sister over the choice of partner; Weber with the crude patriarchal mode of domination of his father. Of these family conflicts it is clear that there is an uneven record of evidence, though more and more is now becoming available and is due to become available (in the cases of Weber and Durkheim in particular). In such a scenario therefore, the investigation is in no sense an attempt at a definitive assessment; it is intended as an initial exploration, an attempt to outline the nature of the relationships which appear with the available evidence as a series of biographical profiles. It is therefore highly instructive to see that at the very origins of sociology, the problem of gender in the context of the promise of *les droits de la femme*, of the emancipation of women, a promise opened by the declaration of the rights of man (liberty, fraternity, equality) seemed to form a basic and fundamental issue for practice and theory. But intense family conflicts, be they inter-

or intra-generational, seem to be articulated around the problem of the correct and appropriate gender mode of behaviour (Weber criticized his father for being too much of the patriarch), or not adhering to proper gender practices (Comte's mother insisted on a Catholic wedding etc.), or the correct choice of partner (Nietzsche's sister fundamentally objected to Nietzsche's choice of the unconventional Lou Salomé). Sometimes the issue of conflict arises in a group of friends: Jenny Marx refused to accept the partner of Friedrich Engels, Mary Burns, on a number of grounds – Mary Burns was illiterate, from the working class, was not married to Engels, and yet was presented to the communist group as the model new woman, woman as she ought to be.

It is possible therefore to establish, relative to the communities concerned, the norm, the conventions of the traditional patriarchal pattern up to the end of the eighteeth century: a separation of spheres and responsibilities, the dominance of the law of the father over the family. A very clear pattern of dominant sex and second sex, though inflected in various important ways for Protestant, Catholic and Jewish communities (see Moses 1984: 1–16). In the eighteenth century, social structure in Europe was decisively influenced by the pattern of absolute monarchy, aristocracy and estates. With the French Revolution and the declaration of the rights of man, a completely different principle of social organization was announced, and there may also have been a form of 'sexual revolution' in customs (see Shorter 1977: 86–112). The political implication of the declaration was grasped immediately by the gender radicals in France and other countries and given the most universal significance. Mary Wollstonecraft's *Vindication of the Rights of Woman* of 1792, the first long and theoretically original reflection on the immediate consequences for gender of the Revolution. As she noted, she often felt herself a virile spirit in a female frame. But she incarnated, and in this she was not alone, the spirit of the new woman: intellectual, independent, and unwilling to accept 'tradition' as a justification for a pattern of inequality. If there was to be inequality, even in the family, there had to be, if it was to be accepted as legitimate, she insisted, an adequate reason.

For many, about this time in particular, the fact that the conjugal division traditionally involved the separation of reason and emotion became more and more problematic: was it a simple, natural division or had it to be socially reproduced and maintained? If it was natural why should there be any necessity for institutional codes of exclusion of women? Rousseau's educational theory segregated Emile and Sophie: the latter was to learn to seduce and to serve the male. It was possible to argue that the two sexes were essentially different, and that the complementarity was for the advantage of all. By the end of the eighteenth century the strength of the egalitarian argument had certainly been felt across Europe (see Brown 1987), and it became clear that arguments were beginning to be developed around the proposition that the division of conjugal labour was politically determined. Burke, Hegel, Schopenhauer and then Durkheim and others began to deploy renewed arguments in favour of the traditional order, the order of the patriarchs. However, the basic ambiguity of the phrase 'rights of man' remained: were women equals and to be included, or inferior and different in essence and to remain outsiders? The problem of a woman like Mary Wollstonecraft was critical: a woman who revealed evidence of a wide culture and intelligence, even genius. In her case, because of her unconventional, even immoral lifestyle, she could be and was stigmatized and dismissed as a deviant case. But the case was nevertheless a cause for a certain anxiety.

It is difficult to identify, of course, just when severe instability began to affect the conjugal system in Europe (I am not talking about earlier sporadic 'crises of masculinity' which certainly did occur (see Kimmel in Brod 1987: 121–54), or the periods of revolutionary questioning (see Hill 1972), or changes in sexual customs (Shorter 1977) or indeed changes in subjectivity (Foucault in Martin, Gutman and Hutton 1988: 49)) but in contrast to, say, specific working-class communities, it is clear that in certain milieux, particularly groups of radical intellectuals, it was felt very strongly as a cultural dislocation at the end of the eighteenth century. I am convinced that the roots for this go very deep into the eighteenth century, even earlier, but in order to follow them it would be necessary to investigate the dominant theoretical vocabulary in detail, especially the problematic of moral science and the concept of virtue. In this book the central questions concern social science and the concepts of truth and power. Although there was widespread questioning of the conjugal relation at the beginning of the nineteenth century (for Britain see the discussion in Taylor (1983) for example), curiously, as this question has been encoded by the group of men known by the quaint and questionable term 'founding fathers' of the discipline (sociology is very much a patrology) the problem of gender, especially the sociology of gender was finally pushed to the margins and expelled from sociology when the main traditions were established around Marx, Durkheim and Weber in the twentieth century. At the end of the twentieth century there is considerable talk of the 'new man' and masculinity, even in sociology. It is certainly salutary to realize that the 'new man' has made many appearances in history and none more important for sociology than at the origins of the discipline, at the end of the eighteenth century and the beginning of the nineteenth century. In one sense this book is about that 'new man' and is part of the study of the genealogy of the 'new man' with the focus of interest turned to sociologists themselves.

But what of the theory of gender that this account implies? In my view there is little that is adequate in the social theory of gender. On the other hand it is very important to be careful about key concepts. Certainly there is still merit in the critical use of the term patriarchy, or oppression. But as will become apparent, there is an obvious and glaring gap in vocabulary concerning the gender system as a form of social stratification. Discussions tend very quickly to use terminology brought in from outside: class, caste, estate, and anything else that can be useful, including Mill's astonishing but necessary recourse to the use of the term 'slave' system. It is clearly symptomatic that the great era of social theory did not produce a specific concept even for sexual or gender exploitation and oppression. We talk of the dominant sex, or 'hegemonic' masculinity.[7] It is true that there are the terms patrimonial and patriarchal, but their use, unsurprisingly, has not been predominantly to analyse gender. There has been some discussion of androcracy, fratriarchy and viriarchy recently as possible alternative terms.[8] But the basic problem it seems to me is that these terms often appear to be simply added on to a ready-made analysis which focuses on production, class stratification, dominant culture, state – the question becomes 'how can we fit gender in somehow?'. This practice is complementary to the now infamous proposition, current among French thinkers, that woman does not exist and that there is only one libido, and that is masculine (see Lacan 1982; Kristeva 1983; Guattari 1984; Baudrillard 1990; Lyotard 1989). This problem of theory is reflected in French-influenced feminist writers like Alice Jardine, who presents the term gynesis as a process of putting 'woman' into discourse to produce *gynema*, conceived as 'a reading effect, a woman-in-effect that is never stable and has no identity. Its appearance in a written text is perhaps noticed only by the feminist reader' (Jardine 1985: 25).

I am ready to admit the importance of such effects, and especially in the light of the dangers of over- or misplaced generalization, stereotyping, reification, essentialism and reductionism when it comes to gender analysis. However it seems important to recognize the physical basis of sexual reproduction (primary and secondary sexual differentiation of female and male characteristics), while acknowledging variations (see Kaplan and Rogers in Gunew 1990: 205–28), and to acknowledge at the same time that the function or even the physical existence of sexual organs may not be known at all until puberty (on the differences in maturation see for instance the Freudian ontogenetic table constructed by Fliess (1950: 254–5)): a recognition simply of the existence of human consciousness *and* the human body. In this domain it is very difficult to argue that the process of physical motherhood is somehow unimportant for gender, or ambiguous. It does not make good theory to suggest that physical maternity is anything other than something experienced by women, and here it is important to note, for example, the secondary differences of emphasis which appear to arise out of this in the psychoanalytic writing of men as compared with women (see Sayers 1991: 2–20). The problem arises in relation to individual identities, for as de Beauvoir said, to become a mature woman, or man, is not purely a physical process. If human ontology is symbolic, social, psychological, political, strategic etc., then it is necessary to insist that it is by symbolic means that it occurs, means which are not reducible to physiological processes. If identities are constructed, as is suggested by basic sociological propositions, then they vary according to the modes and contexts of their construction or seduction, in relation to others (if the child is fathered and mothered, the parents are also 'fathered' and 'mothered' in the process). It is not good theory here, either, to look for absolute essences, and it is not plausible, either, to say that such constructions are aleatoric or 'never stable'. The problem is that social processes seem able to convert symbolic processes into apparently obvious essential and physical facts (within limits since it is almost always the case that these 'facts' already exist).

The immediate solution to many of these issues is to recognize that the symbolic and semiotic orders of gender are not epiphenomenal processes to be added on to already existing social forms, or to be added on later as an afterthought to the neutral persona or 'self' of individual writers. On the contrary, they should be recognized as primary and fundamental forms to which other (neutralized) social formations are erected or correspond. This is of immediate importance to the examination of social theory itself. The disappearance of the author (into the text) is one way in which a (very masculine) illusion is created, an illusion which can suggest, simplistically, that 'there is no outside of the text', or that the text inhabits a realm of pure logic, pure thought that is totally alienated from experience. As Marx said in a parallel argument, this allows one to forget that the author who is gendered has to be born, engendered, (as son, daughter, nephew, niece, father, mother). When a 'woman' appears in discourse, does she not have a father or mother? If not, she is either superhuman, or there is something about her which is not acceptable to consciousness. In Rousseau's *Emile* it is clear that Sophie must be educated to learn to serve in a seductive way. In Kierkegaard's 'Diary of a seducer' (1971), Cordelia is naturally seductive. But in either case there is no question of instability of meaning or status. Such education of males and females has been the object of considerable stable organizational and ideological effort, just as have been the specific elaborations of the legal dependent status of women in society. Women are not born as wives, however the constructed status of wife is stable yet not static (only very recently in Britain have wives achieved some legal protection from rape in marriage). In the same way 'men' are not born fathers, and the status of men changes in relation to that of women. Workers, however, have to be already formed men or women; it is men and women who go out to work, it is not workers who go out to the family to become men and women (as is usually assumed by sociology textbooks which start with the productive system and only reach the discussion of gender, if at all, many chapters later).

The perspective which lies at the base of this particular book, then, starts from the point of view that the crucial processes are intimately associated with the life-cycle, and the social construction and organization of the symbolic processes of birth and death. It is necessary to acknowledge, as the Freudians have always done, the importance of the processes of sexual maturation at both a physical and symbolic level, even if Freud was not completely consistent in applying his own principles to himself, or able to evolve a theory which escaped his patriarchal cultural matrix. Creative and intellectually fertile Freudian and modern psychoanalytic theory has to be approached, in my view, extremely critically in view of the deeply interwoven patriarchal assumptions and attitudes woven into its fundamental conceptual apparatus of the Oedipal theory (Coward 1983). (This book is certainly influenced by psychoanalysis, and originally I intended to include a chapter on Freud as one of the 'founding' social theorists. Certainly, in relation to the question of the way in which his theory was influenced by his relation with significant women has yet to be fully and convincingly analysed, though much more is known about Freud[9] than is known about Durkheim.)

Thus the individual is 'socialized', to use a term that is far too passive, into a kinship group and community in which gender roles and statuses are challenged by fundamental changes in ideology and culture. At certain times and places, severe and chronic tensions afflict the definitions and workings of these roles and statuses. In the case of some of the writers considered here, notably Marx and Durkheim, there was a marked process of letting go, even rejection, of ethnicity, a secularization and a prolonged attempt to integrate into the wider community. But here I have no intention of trying to elaborate an account of this complex secularization process, I only note that certain possibly unconscious hierarchical structures of kinship orientation, as in all such radical processes, seem to have been conserved. But even if this conservation occurs the process is certainly open to considerable individual variation. The career events and significant others encountered and understood in relation to these structures, often appear as fortuitous and chance events. William Warner (1986) has tried to elaborate the principles of a 'biographical reading' of such authors. Writing of texts which ignore or suppress the biographical evidence, he observes, aim at creating a specific illusion of textual mastery. Chance personal events and uncharacteristic and unexpected reactions to them often threaten this illusion and hence are omitted from the account. The ramifications of this possibility are manifold.

Warner (1986: 25) discusses the difficulty of rendering the texts of the 'genius' into an intelligible flesh and blood account:

the author who receives the accolade of 'genius' becomes strangely difficult to know. The sense grows among an interpretive community that the architectonic greatness of his text cannot be explained by reading the traces of life in the writing, whether they are etched there by consciousness, the unconscious, ideology, the structure of institutions the person inhabits, the *zeitgeist*, or some overdetermined combination of these.

Warner provides one of the better attempts to work out a way of trying to connect theoretical and experiential biographic events to what he calls 'life-writing'. By taking the evidence of the writer's life and, more specifically, supplementary writings (letters, diaries etc.), the aim is to improve the status of the lived context as a way of establishing a corpus for a new kind of reading (a form of intertextuality), and in so doing attack the exclusion and stigmatization of such 'other' writing to 'anecdotal footnotes' (1986: 30). One could recall with profit Derrida's (1981: 202–3) remark on textual grafts, on 'the functioning of footnotes, for example, or epigraphs, and in what way, to the one who knows how to read, these are sometimes more important than the so-called principal or capital text. And when the capital title itself becomes a scion, one can no longer choose between the presence or absence of the title'.

Warner (1986: 28) thus wants to take the risk of 'reading biographically' so that it might be possible to 'explore the way the contingencies of the personal life are not some incidental added term, but a pivotal factor in the production of the texts. . . . I call these readings "conceptual narratives" '.

The advantage, says Warner, is that the authors concerned respond to what could be conceived as chance events and the appearance of significant others. These situations and encounters are not under the control of the writer, indeed the writing which appears to arrive as a single homogeneous message from a single donor author is actually often 'a collaboration with significant other people, which is only partly voluntary, partly controlled'. Warner (1986: 29) concludes:

> because in the 'life' there is no innocent state of being apart for the person, and because for the 'writing' there is no condition of standing apart in the mode of pure consciousness to express an idea, life and writing are always already inscribed in the traces of a complex historical formation. . . . Life-writing often seems to be written to, for, with, and/or against another person.

Although Warner does not make the connection, this project is in many important respects parallel to that of dialogic inquiry (associated with Bakhtin (1981) and rhetoric (Gane 1989b)), which in other ways seeks to establish the contextualization of writing through the 'resurrection' of the invisible other, to whom the voices in the text are in opposition or argument.

It is important to make the case for a critical perspective both to science and art. In one important sense the turn towards rhetoric and the examination of experience has as one of its conditions the gradual fading of the acknowledgement that what was once claimed as social science was successful science. Social science (Marxism or early Comtean positivism for example) started by simulating the methods and expositional forms of natural or life science. In this enterprise it was important to suppress dialogue and to celebrate monologue. It is not necessary to attempt dogmatically to define science and non-science (it may well be for example that most 'science' is negative experimentation and hence social science should not be judged simply on its effectiveness as truth). Whenever something is claimed as truth because it is scientific, because it is presented in expositional forms that appear to simulate scientific ones closely, it is necessary to approach it in the most critical manner. Mill's famous critique of Comte, and his rejection of misogynist pseudo-scientific conceptions of women, simply refused the legitimizing veil of scientificity (Durkheim, on the contrary, always had 'faith' in what was 'scientific'). On the other hand the rejection of positivism could lead to attempts to establish truths in more mystical and poetic forms as if they were established by revelation, or through the superior sensitivity of the artist who had transcended bad faith (as in Nietzsche). Much of Nietzsche's own philosophical and poetic vision could be manipulated into racial and elitist doctrines (as they were by his sister, Elizabeth, after Nietzsche's death (MacIntyre 1992)), perhaps partly because of their very poetic and aphoristic forms of exposition. What is attempted here is a consideration of the often forgotten or suppressed side of the origins of social thought, in order to raise questions about the gendered complexion of that thought itself, whether scientific or artistic, in order to establish a *prima facie* case that gender as a topic was essential at the moment modern sociology was constituted, its later marginalization was the result of the way sociological knowledge was canonized around the writings of Marx, Durkheim and Weber.

This book, then, examines some of the variations of accommodation to the conjugal crisis of the nineteenth century (see Buci-Glucksman in Gallagher and Laqueur 1987: 220–9). These variations reveal a number of the key dimensions of the way that men accommodated themselves to the new situation opened by the call for liberty, equality and fraternity. In this case change was closely related to direct experience. Almost immediately, the power and sovereignty of Reason was brought into question, though it had been the forces of Reason which had played a large part in the critique of the *ancien régime*. The age of pure reason, the illusion that social progress could be determined by pure reason, lasted a very short time amongst those who were prepared to see where the full practical implications led: some remained in the apparently secure framework of traditional forms, others tried to open new paths. In exploring equality in the field of sexuality and gender relations, it became very quickly apparent that the Enlightenment concept of Reason had been developed almost exclusively by men in the public sphere. As a consequence, men had also been divorced from the domains of emotion, sympathy and affection, which had been developed by women in the private sphere. The old pattern, the traditional patriarchal system, not only, it appeared, reproduced separation, hierarchy and superstition, it also reproduced and hypocritically acquiesced in the fact of prostitution (increasingly regarded, within the context of a socialist critique, as part of a wider system of dehumanizing exploitation).

But what could be the structure of relations in the new order, once 'the imagination was let loose'? (Burke 1883). Godwin's notion of free unions dictated by the demands of pure reason gave way immediately to marriage, family and the rule of the heart. The radical dissenting tradition is clearly continued in Mill: Reason again is envisaged as serving the heart, and again it is the idea of liberty which is seen to be the key to equality. Even though everything comes to the bar of Reason in one way or another, Mill provides an essential place for the adoration of woman. On the continent, the impetus for the sovereignty of secular logic soon gave way to the recognition of the need for religion in some form. The attempt to work out new forms of sexual relation and gender identities in France seemed both more collective and more authoritarian. The Saint-Simonian experimentation attempted to work out a collective sexual de-sublimation under the control of a 'papal' couple, prepared to legitimate the formation of temporary liaisons. The Comtean experiment insisted on eternal liaisons under the authority of the positivist 'pope'. Comte required a strict segregation of male and female spheres in a project which would make the latter sovereign and formally the object of an organized cult, while all the others accepted the new woman legitimately possessed both heart and mind.

Evidently, if the ideas of liberty and equality were to be extended to include women then there were several possible ways in which this could be envisaged: the basis could be the individual, the couple or the group. The division of labour and division of human attributes could be maintained as being based on essential gender divisions but developed in a new form, or one could attempt to break the links between sex, gender and social role and status. The evolution could be organized as a social project, or it could be envisaged as essentially removing the institutions of segregation and control. There was also the dilemma as to whether this liberation could be eroticized, or whether it would be essentially sexually repressive, cultivating the idea of chaste relations. Whatever the form of the evolution it was clear that it would inevitably involve the modification of patterns of masculinity and femininity. Where the ideal of segregation was maintained, the principal form of the modification of masculinity was in the direction of chaste relations and the elevation of 'pure woman' in to a cult object; where the evolution involved the project of de-segregation, the break-up of separate spheres, this led to a period of reconstruction of identity for both the 'new men' and the 'new women'; where there was both de-segregation and the development of the elements of a cult of woman, there was the readjustment of component elements of reason and emotion, as well as the process of the humiliation of both masculine presumption and of feminine submission.

Part I
The crisis

Chapter 1

Emile Durkheim: woman as outsider

Women have been burdened . . . by a long history of deeply unsettling, mystifying, mixed messages about themselves.

(J. Ochshorn 1981: 243)

INTRODUCTORY REMARKS

Durkheim's sociology, it has quite often been said, reflects a tension created by the action of two quite distinct principles. On the one hand, it suggests the idea that social forces exercise an external constraint over the individual (thus producing a conception of an external logos as emblematology); on the other, it posits the thesis that in society 'individuals' are themselves hierarchically organized by the action of these forces (and therefore reflect differential levels of civilization). The former principle has in effect tended to dominate interpretations of his sociology so that the application of the principle of constraint has not been developed as inter- caste or class, or sex domination. Thus the Durkheimian proposition that certain individuals are constrained in a certain way and to a certain degree by social facts, a constraint which then enables them to form a dominant social group, has been ignored though it is at the heart of his sociology (of religion, of law, of education, etc.). The primary categories of Durkheim's sociology – men, women and children – reflect the action of social constraint but also stand in unequal relationship to each other as an order of domination. In presentations of Durkheim's work, relations of this second type (social hierarchy, power, moral domination) have been neglected, even as politics, while the elements of methodology have upstaged them.[1]

Durkheim's sociology appears to be caught up also in a tangle of political currents that has, again, bemused critics. Conservatives, particularly of the Catholic right, saw his sociology as a grave threat to the moral order he sought to defend, while the revolutionary left has either regarded his sociology as irrelevant or as an obstacle to the formation of class analysis and politics (see Bottomore 1981). Feminists have had even less time for him. It is clear however that neither Durkheim's own work nor his influence has been consistent in its orientations. To illustrate this, and to illustrate the fact that his positions cannot be thought of simply as the prejudices of a previous era, the problem of inequality between the sexes can be represented clearly by two writers, who, in their own ways state the two sides of the dilemma in a clearly Durkheimian mode. The conservative position was expressed particularly clearly by E. E. Evans-Pritchard in 1955:

> the problems of the relations of the sexes are not just those of sex as such, but of authority, leadership, control, co-operation, and competition . . . and they cannot be solved by an insistence on absolute equality but rather by recognition of differences, exercise of charity, and acknowledgement of authority.
>
> (Evans-Pritchard 1965: 37–57)

This argument suggests that in primitive society women recognize the differences and inequality of the sexes and 'do not want to be like men', and that it is only comparatively recently that women have become the objects of a male debate on equality which has spilt over into the female camp. Much of this debate, however, according to Evans-Pritchard, is entirely fanciful: there can be no radical alteration in the relative positions of the sexes since 'men are always in the ascendency, and this is perhaps the more evident the higher the civilization'.

On the other hand Robert Hertz's argument concerning the preeminence of the right side (1909 in Needham 1973), suggests that the opposition to women's equality is too often posed as a simple recognition of necessity just as have been the privileges of the right hand over the left. The relative 'paralysis' of the left side Hertz saw as a kind of sacrificial 'mutilation' required for the supremacy of the sacred over the profane:

> (but) the dream of humanity gifted with two 'right hands' is not at all chimeric. But from the fact that ambidexterity is possible it does not follow that it is desirable. . . . However, the evolution we are now witnessing . . . is not an isolated or abnormal fact in our culture. . . . The ancient ideas which . . . founded the exclusive preponderance of the right hand, are today in full retreat.
>
> (Ibid.: 22)

Hertz, though indirectly, presents the egalitarian view that an appeal to nature, biological givens in the debate on inequality, cannot be accepted as a closure of the argument by fiat. Hertz's essay points to the irony that the Durkheimian principle of the explanation of social fact by social facts alone is severely compromised if the terrain of the social fact is ambiguous, or itself a matter of political dispute, even a means of moral domination. This is particularly the problem insofar as the primary groups of the social substratum are conceived as beings which span the biological-social boundary in different ways and to different degrees. The theory seems to risk grave embarrassment at the boundary between the external constraints of the facts of instinct (determined by heredity) and the internal constraints produced by social forces as somatic phenomena (as determined for example by the division of labour). The problem becomes even more acute if, as happens in Durkheim's theory, the social takes up and utilizes 'natural differences' between individuals while producing at the same time, through occupational specialization, an unequal distri-bution of 'civilization' determining somatic and psychological character-istics of subjects. Insofar as 'civilization' is a male possession in Durkheim-ian sociology, women come to stand between the generations as creatures whose function is primarily biological and whose self regulation is gover-ned by facts of instinct. Instead of castigating this 'barbarian' status, like Hertz, and other sociologists like Veblen, Durkheim for a number of reasons, took the view that this 'barbarian' status reflected women's true nature.

But what is this 'society', as an order of life that emerges out of the effects of the relations of individual consciences and comes to constrain them, if not a 'vitalism'? But a vitalism of a specific genre: a relative of the 'heroic vitalism' of Carlyle, Nietzsche and others (see Bentley 1947). Durkheim is not reluctant to displace the charisma of the superman onto its true support, social authority (Durkheim 1973: 91); a social body which suffers all the processes of life and death and rebirth. Nor is it an accident that Durkheim's emblematology should resemble so closely that of Carlyle's Teufelsdröckh. This strand of vitalism also commonly places women at a certain distance and they then become the object of an extreme ambivalence: despised on the one hand ('women are born wor-shippers' says Teufelsdröckh; 'with a few devotional practices and some animals to care for, the old unmarried woman's life is full' says Durk-heim), but the objects of a violent desire on the other, is reflected by Durkheim as a mark of the superiority of men. Durkheim's specific vitalism and its paradoxical nature arises out of the fact that while the conservatives were attempting to revive dead heroes or defunct gods (his own apostasy is symptomatic) and the revolutionaries dreaming up utopian schemes (it should not be forgotten that he suggested that Saint-Simon's remedies simply 'aggravated the evil' they sought to cure (Durk-heim 1962: 245)), which could only make matters worse, his own position faced the humbling prospect that because for him the 1789 revolution was only half-born, its completion had to await a genuine creative effer-vescence. Meanwhile the cause was best served by a liberal practice of strengthening the emergent being and protecting it from the past and the future. This could best be achieved by attempting to identify the real elements of social solidarity and defending them against the illusions of a current 'morbid' effervescence. Opposition to this current also involved opposition to all impractical utopian schemes such as that developed by the women's movement. Durkheim's position here seemed to lead him to conceive of social evolution as moving at its own natural (i.e., inevitably slow) pace.

These remarks of Durkheim on women have been regarded by sociologists, with rare exceptions, as a minor blemish, a superficial reflection of a dominant ideology and a mistaken biology. No doubt one of the reasons why little of the exegetical and critical literature concerns itself with his conception of the relations between the sexes is a consequence of the fact that these three basic subjects, 'men', 'women' and 'children', are not constituted as objects in their own right but appear as one of a series of primary divisions against which are projected the more obviously constructed foreground topics. It is 'law', 'suicide', 'religion' etc., which organize commentaries in relation to problems of moral integration and social density. It may be seen that the general avoidance of his ideas on this subject – so complete incidentally that neither of two recent presentations, Giddens (1978) and Thompson (1982) pays any attention to them at all – stem from at least two tendencies. The first, most apparent among sociologists, relies on the idea that this aspect of Durkheim's work is compromised by an inconsistent incorporation of the male supremacist ideology of his period. Edward Tiryakian expresses this idea in a recent essay to the effect that he was simply 'operating within the frame of reference of the bourgeois male-centred late Victorian or pre-World War I context' (1982: 288), and that 'in good male chauvinist fashion' he produced a sociological image of the prejudice of his time. It is this ideology which Durkheim uses to shore up an edifice troubled by its own findings. Caught up in this reactionary ideology Durkheim appears as a Cicero or Bonald trying to halt the inevitable forces of progress by clinging to out-moded forms of absolute marriage. Untypically, however, while holding on to this prop, Tiryakian goes beyond the *ne plus ultra* of others, to lift the veil of Durkheim's writing on sexuality, and finds material to develop the concept of sexual anomie. In fact Tiryakian fashions this concept out of Durkheim's more limited 'conjugal anomie', and recommends its application to the contemporary period of transition in the relations between the sexes in the widest sense. The equalization of the sexes is, against the background of Durkheim's own writing on sexual relations, one of the most profound movements in human evolution, accompanied, says Tiryakian, by a change in the representations of the divine itself in the direction of androgyny. Even the political and cultural episodes of the 1960s can be regarded as aspects of a more profound 'sexual revolution', mirroring the more radical formulation of Durkheim which, Tiryakian argues, sees the sexual order as 'a constitutive feature of social organisation' (1981: 1035). Tiryakian's article thus holds on to the conventional view that the ideological political superstructure can be brushed off as a minor blemish while taking up a more radical and unconventional stance on the question of the significance of Durkheim's other writings on sexual relations.

In assessing Tiryakian's views it must first be noted that Durkheim himself must have been keenly aware of the differences within the ideological matrix of male supremacist ideology which could hardly be called homogeneous. In his discussion of sexual education he points out sharply that his defence of the recognition of the necessarily mysterious nature of sexual relations should not be taken as 'giving in to bourgeois prudery' (1979: 143), and insists in relation to more general questions that his position is not derived from male chauvinism (in this respect see his reviews collected in Durkheim 1980, esp: 179–83, 251–2, 163–305). Durkheim's conception of the forms of collective representation of the social being also embraces a strong element of androgynism, for the social is always represented as an authority with two sides, whether in the anonymous forms of totemism or the personified being of a later religion: a male side which 'blocks us when we would trespass' and a female side, 'the nourishing mother from whom we gain the whole of our moral and intellectual substance' (1973: 92). Durkheim disconnects these two aspects from the form of representation, while Tiryakian's cult of a personified form looks distinctly antiquated in conception, even if androgynous. Durkheim's position leads to a qualified support for Saint-Simon's 'religion without a God' strongly situated in the tradition of Spinozism. The problem is not the form of the representation, as Hertz has shown, but the relative values accorded to functions distributed in society. Finally, Tiryakian's target, the concept of anomie is not without its own problems. In Durkheim's work it has a curiously ambiguous meaning, for it is both a condition (of insufficient regulation) and a current of opinion (of despair and pessimism) which arises in relation to that condition. France, in contrast to Germany and England, according to Durkheim, suffered the effects of this current to an excessive degree because the segmental structures were most destroyed there without the compensating construction of new organic forms of solidarity. Tiryakian wants from Durkheim a conception of anomie as a condition and not as a social force, for as far as the latter is concerned Durkheim is explicit: it is a force of rejection, despair, pessimism, irrationalism, mysticism, i.e., is deeply reactionary. Tiryakian half acknowledges this by referring to Durkheim's use of the term to describe the wave of terrorism in Europe in the 1890s (1981: 1049–50).

The second paradoxical tendency which leads to the same half-avoidance of Durkheim's ideas can be found among anthropologists. Here it is more generally recognized that a large portion of Durkheim's work was taken up with problems of kinship and sexual relations, but it is these writings which have found least favour and suffered an eclipse under the influence of Lévi-Strauss. It is thus curious that it is precisely from the anthropologists that these writings have nonetheless been rather grudgingly praised. Lévi-Strauss, while criticizing Durkheim's theory of incest prohibitions, says it is the theory 'most conscientious and systematic from purely social causes' (Lévi-Strauss 1969: 20). Rodney Needham describes the same essay as 'one of the most signal advances in the history of prescriptive alliance (if unaccountably ignored by certain much later writers) an admirable feat of structural analysis' (Needham 1966: 162–3). The essay on incest is now apparently so deeply buried that Robin Fox (1980) makes not the slightest reference to it in his recent book on incest, preferring to debate with Lévi-Strauss, whom he criticizes as adopting a Durkheimian approach, though he might have added: not Durkheim's. Lévi-Strauss's anthropology leans heavily on a Durkheimianism purged of its concern with domination, and Marxism purged of its concern with class struggle: the norm of reciprocity even dominated the exceptional cases of non-reciprocity through balanced non-reciprocity.[2] Gouldner's attempt to extricate himself from this problem is instructive (Gouldner 1973: 260–99).

If Lévi-Strauss attempted to claim a bond with Marxism through Engels, it is also quite possible to attempt to situate Durkheimian sociology in this way, and in this way also, incidentally, to attempt to situate some elements of contemporary Marxism, notably that of Althusser (1971), Hirst (1979), Hirst and Woolley (1982). Therborn (1980) etc. Although the following remark of Engels's concerns the theory of ideology, its relevance to the very object of Durkheim's sociology is striking. Engels writes, in the late 1870s:

> All religion is nothing but the phantastic reflection in men's minds of those external forces which control their daily life. . . . The phantastic personifications, which at first only reflected the mysterious forces of nature acquire social attributes, become representatives of the forces of history . . . in existing bourgeois society men are dominated by the economic conditions created by themselves, by the means of production which they have produced, as if by an extraneous force. The actual basis of religious reflex action therefore continues to exist, and with it the reflex itself . . . man proposes and God (that is, the extraneous force of the capitalist mode of production) disposes.
>
> (Engels 1936: 346–7)

Whereas Engels goes on to talk of the end of religion and the beginning reign of conscious control over social forces brought about by a social 'act', Althusser, in the tradition of Durkheim, rejects this conclusion, making ideology, in a 'new form . . . which will depend on a science' (Althusser and Balibar 1970: 131), a necessary element of all social formations. Althusser's conception of the ideological state apparatuses adopts the Durkheimian formulation of social reproduction as the function of ritual and education, and the relation between the social subject and individual subject as the basis of a theory of ideology as interpellation. It is ironic that a number of Althusserians find themselves as anti-Durkheimians in this Durkheimian problematic (especially Hirst and Therborn). No doubt they would pose it as a question not of Durkheim but of Engels, or more precisely the 'transitional' Marx rather than the 'mature' Marx. Therborn has demonstrated convincingly that Durkheim's sociology represents a liberal-bourgeois variation of certain elements of the problematic of Marx's 'transitional' period (Therborn 1976) but could have noted also that it is one into which more than one Marxist has been tempted to stray. Durkheim's specific variation consists in inverting the Marxist thesis that bourgeois society is an alienated 'monstrous' force into a necessarily beneficent one. If society is essentially the source of all that is sustaining in the individual then it will be so represented whether as an anonymous force or a personified being. Durkheim inverts Engels's proposition that the social force is alienated and thus external to the individual, into a formal recognition that social forces are to be defined by being external to the individual and as a transcendent being will always be so represented in collective practices and representations. But Engels only continues a line of thought which perhaps in Marx reached its height in the *Grundrisse* where capital is regarded as that 'animated monster' an 'alien will and an alien intelligence' an 'external' force relative to the 'individual' (Marx 1973: 94, 158, 164, 226, 470, 487, etc.) For Durkheim this dark side is stigmatized as a temporary abnormality since society is and must always be the primary source of that life which raises the individual beyond the animal level. Veneration of society in Durkheim does not always appear as the cult of a God, as has been pointed out; the theory of ideological 'interpellation' is thus apparently wider than Althusser's. (Note the difficulties encountered on this point of the non-human subject in Hirst (1979: 61–2).) Indeed, in Durkheim's consideration of the teacher-pupil relationship, the teacher interpellates the individual as subject in a certain objective language (the social voice) appropriate to the hypnosis of the subject (Durkheim 1956: 85; 1973: 139–41); but in speaking in the name of this specific God (society) the teacher must recognize that it is 'quite impersonal' for reasons that are directly political, to counteract all tendency to meek subservience (thus Durkheim rejects all suggestions that education be carried out by a single teacher) and 'to evoke a sentiment that . . . (is required for) . . . a democratic society . . . the respect for legality, the respect for impersonal law deriving its ascendency from impersonality itself' (Durkheim 1973: 155–6). Education is the primary mechanism by which the individual comes to form attachments outside himself, and is 'above all the means by which society perpetually recreates the conditions of its very existence (Durkheim 1956: 123, cf. Althusser 1971: 123–9).[3]

Durkheim's respect for the social and for the generative powers of ritual also stands in marked contrast to Freud's. Although Durkheim's notion of the social has been quite rightly likened by Parsons and others to the super-ego, it is the comparison of a whole group of issues – the way in which the concept of ritual is analysed in relation to the totem and taboo complex – which is illuminating. For Freud the elements of ritual were conceived ultimately as being connected with a series of pathological phenomena in individuals which could be compared with ritualized social life. Whereas Durkheim regarded ritual as productive of social energies, Freud took the opportunity to locate them as obsessional forms, and eventually as 'compulsions to repeat' driven by Thanatos. In writing *Totem and Taboo* he sought to align his findings of 'totemic' behaviour among children with the anthropological materials on totemism in early society. Durkheim too constantly compared childhood with primitive social experience but conceived the tendency to ritual behaviour as the basis of civilized discipline and good habits. Freud's conception, which treated 'obsessional neurosis as a pathological counterpart of the formation of a religion', and described that 'neurosis as an individual religiosity and religion as a universal obsessional neurosis' (Freud 1907, S.E.ix: 126–7) was developed at considerable length by his disciples Reik (1931) and Roheim (1930). The latter even attempted a full-scale analysis of the Australian materials used by Durkheim: whereas Durkheim formulated a theory of the socio-genesis of the sacred as an absolute category, Roheim formulated a theory of primitive society organized 'on the basis of castration anxiety' (Roheim 1930). Just as Durkheim envisaged a dynamic of the production and disciplining of a sacred substance, Roheim envisaged social evolution as dominated by stages of sexual organization articulated as models of control of sexual fluids.[4] Again, although they appear as two sides of the same coin, the tendency of both theories is towards an analysis of social domination, a tendency notably absent in the Lévi-Strauss fusion of Marx, Freud and Mauss.

The analysis of Durkheim's own views is complicated by the fact that his own discovery of the importance of the sexual order played a crucial role in the reorganization of his conception of primitive society. The initial synthesis of 1893 (1964b) proposed a progressive evolution from societies based on mechanical solidarities to complex societies based on organic solidarities. The relation of the sexes faithfully reflected this evolution; thus it was conceived of as being entirely revolutionized in the course of social development. At first the ties between the adults were based on bonds of similitude requiring no great moral solidarity. Specialization and the divison of labour in society then brought about an entirely new relation between the sexes based on the principle of mutual need.

This had the effect however, over millenia, of forming two quite different beings, mirrored in increasing dimorphism. The sphere of women's specialization became the vital formative institution of the conjugal family.

The familiar ring of this argument reflects the fact that Durkheim reproduces in many ways the common position of sociologists of the nineteenth century: Saint-Simon, Comte, the later Spencer, Schaeffle, etc. After 1893, however, Durkheim began to publish a number of papers which, culminating in *The Elementary Forms* of 1912, suggested that primitive society far from being characterized by sexual communism was characterized by an extreme, even chronic, segregation of the sexes. At first this segregation might even have favoured women, but ideas of purity and veneration turned into fear and loathing, as women became subjects *minoris resistentiae*, scapegoats of the collective wrath. His researches into the separation of the sexes were pivotal in the reorganization of the general theory. The absence of any sustained examination of his work in this area in general accounts of his sociology have thus led, particularly in the case of Parsons, to a severely imbalanced account of the evolution of his thought. What is even more surprising is that the importance of these ideas was signalled more than once by Durkheim himself:

> the dark, mysterious and awe-inspiring nature of the sexual act was revealed to me through historical and ethnographic research, and I even know the exact moment I was struck by the extremely general nature of the fact and how wide its implications were.
>
> (Durkheim (1911) 1979: 144)

This must surely be linked with his comment that:

> it was only in 1895 that I had a clear idea of the capital role played by religion in social life . . . it was a revelation to me . . . all my previous research had to be started all over again so as to be harmonised with these new views.
>
> (Durkheim (1907) 1982: 259)

In the light of these comments, Tiryakian's remark that 'when it came to sex, Durkheim was far more ascetic than Max Weber who experienced first hand the force of eros' (Tiryakian 1981: 1026) might be said to have missed the point.[5]

The reorganization of the theory had the wider effect of placing the sacred as an absolute at the heart of the beginning of the social. If the social was born in the revolutionary upsurge of effervescence in which the social logos inscribes itself deliriously on the bodies of individuals, the business of man's relation with the sacred becomes, as Parsons has noted, also the beginning of the serious moral life which produces the enduring inscription of somatic effects on two social orders: men and women. But the serious bubbles over into play, the frivolous into games and into the moral-aesthetic sphere. The sacred is the origin of these forms and dominates them. In the introduction to *The Division of Labour* of 1893, subsequently deleted from following editions, he argued that the moral aesthetic sphere is the inferior sphere since it is the sphere of the gratuitous, and is inherently without obligation (Durkheim 1964b: 431); and this survived into the essay on incest where it is the realm of familial duty which dominated that of sexual aesthetics, and which links passion to the imagination.[6] And it is women, as we shall see, who are to be the subjects of this sphere in more ways than one.

Thus women have a unique position in Durkheim's theory: they become the primary occupational caste, *sub specie aeternitatis*. Caste establishes its hierarchical effects on the body and utilizes its effects in its own functioning. The emergence of the class system, and its more subtle accommodation of aptitude and function, manifest in the development of contractual law which more and more tends to repress external inequalities of constraint on contractual parties, is erected alongside this caste, standing in an absolute distance from men, and their society. Some of the elements of Durkheim's elaboration of a defence of this position are examined in the following sections of this chapter.

DURKHEIM'S INITIAL THEORY

> In segmental society 'female functions are not very clearly distinguished from male. Rather the two sexes lead almost the same existence'.
>
> (Durkheim (1893) 1964b: 58)

Durkheim's initial approach presents the view that segmental societies are characterized above all by similarities between individuals who are thus 'absorbed' into the group. This provides the basic form of cohesion in primitive society and the basis of primitive 'communism' (Durkheim 1964b: 179) also called 'mechanical solidarity'. And this solidarity is extended to the relation of the sexes so that 'the further we look back to the past, the smaller becomes [the] difference between man and woman' (ibid.: 57). Because the adult sexes were relatively undifferentiated, the conjugal tie was weak so that 'sexual relations were entered into and broken at will without any juridical obligations linking the union'. This era of promiscuity, and absence of contractual marriage was also associated with the egalitarian nature of the relation of the sexes, 'there is, even now, a great number of savage people where the woman mingles in political life', and, he adds in the same vein, 'we very often observe women accompanying men to war, urging them on to battle and even taking a very active part'. Durkheim's evident enthusiasm for this stage of affairs is reflected in his admiration of the fact that, he notes, all the major human attributes appear equally dispersed between the adult sexes and, specifically, 'one of the distinctive contemporary qualities of women, gentility, does not appear to pertain to her in primitive society' (ibid.: 58).

The relation of the sexes is presented in terms of a remarkable dialectic of images (no doubt a precursor of his concept of 'representations'). In mechanical solidarity, given of course an irreducible difference in sexual function, the unity of the sexes, through the attraction of like for like, is a relation of interiority: the image of each sex is not distinct from the other. Thus, when they come together they 'confound' each other, for, 'when the union results from resemblances of two images, it consists in agglutination . . . being indistinct, totally or in part . . . they become no more than one' (ibid.: 62). No new quality or property is thus created in this union and so 'the state of marriage in society where the two sexes are only weakly differentiated thus evinces conjugal solidarity which is itself very weak' (ibid.: 59).

In great contrast to the 'agglutination' of images which occurs in segmental society, the division of labour brings about another form of solidarity and a different relation between images: 'they are outside each other and are linked only because they are distinct' (ibid.: 62). The number of definite ties and obligations between the sexes grows, and the conditions under which the union can take place are restricted. Under these changed circumstances 'the duty of fidelity gains order; first imposed on women only, it later becomes reciprocal'; the emergence of the dowry gives rise to 'very complex rule [which] fix the respective rights of each person . . . the union has ceased to be ephemeral' (ibid.: 59). With the increasing division of labour in society the sexes could not but be affected:

> it is certain at the same time [as the division of labour proceeds generally] sexual labour is more and more divided . . . limited at first only to sexual functions it slowly becomes extended to others. Long ago, woman retired from warfare and public affairs, and consecrated her entire life to her family. Since then her role has become even more specialised. Today woman leads a completely different existence from that of man. One might say that the two great functions of the psychic life are thus dissociated, that one of the sexes takes care of the affective functions and the other of intellectual functions.
>
> (Ibid.: 60)

Durkheim thus joins the tradition which established innumerable basic consequences of the division of labour (cf. manual and mental labour, productive and unproductive labour, etc.) and establishes a primary division between what might be called affective and intellectual labour in the tradition of Comte. In relation to this specialization a whole series of physical consequences followed: a differentiation of the size of the brain, and in the dimensions of the body generally, between the two sexes. Social evolution had as its raw material the 'female form [which] was the one and only type from which the masculine variety slowly detached itself' (ibid.: 57). Fully accepting the findings and inferences of craniometry and physical anthropology as suggesting evolutionary dimophism, he concluded that with the division of labour in society there is 'a considerable development of masculine crania and a stationary or even regressive state of female crania' (ibid.: 60). To this was added the regression in physique or pedomorphism, so that woman had become a pathetically 'weak creature'.[7]

But if there had been costs in social evolution there had also been gains: the differentiation of the sexes with its consequent externally differentiated imagery is productive of a new order of solidarity. Organic solidarity rests on difference and separation and 'if the sexes were not separated an entire category of social life would be absent' (ibid.: 61): the order of conjugal solidarity. Mutual interdependence, caused by functional differentiation, produces a complex conjugal solidarity which carries ramifications throughout society: 'conjugal solidarity . . . as it exists among the most cultivated people makes its action felt at each moment and in all the details of life' (ibid.). Both sexes are now dependent on each other and are two sides 'of the same concrete universal which they reform when they unite' (ibid.: 56); and, although this union might be reflected in terms of the images of exchange, this 'is only the superficial expression of an internal and very deep state . . . a continuity which exchange does not possess.' Interdependence thus means that each part has become the 'natural complement' of the other. And if each image is completed by the other, the other 'thus becomes an integral and permanent part of our conscience, to such a point that we can no longer separate ourselves from it.' Each becomes dependent not only on the definition of the image reflected in the other but also on the energy which is transferred, so 'we . . . suffer from all circumstances which, like absence or death, may have as effect the barring of its return or the diminishing of its vivacity' (ibid.: 61–2).

The division of labour then is a single progressively preponderant principle, producing through its differentiating organ an ever-readjusted unity between them. Effects, which enter into relations with one another, contribute to each other in an exchange of energy which comes to sustain them. By so entering into these secondary relations the effects themselves call secondary phenomena into existence. This necessary, if constantly changing harmony between social elements, produces at each stage a relative 'functional equilibrium' (ibid.: 271). It is in this framework that Durkheim introduces his theory of human desire. Between the impulse and the desire there is a gap: sexual desire, the result of an impulsion, can exist 'only after having entered into relations' with its object, which is in no way inevitable since 'these indeterminate aspirations can rather easily deviate' (ibid.: 274). The 'normal' object, itself the product of evolution, is already waiting to be found so 'at the very moment when man is in a position to taste these new enjoyments and calls for them, even unconsciously, he finds them within his reach' (ibid.). In opposition to the principle of pre-established harmony, says Durkheim, these two orders of fact meet, simply because they are effects of the same causes: the division of of labour. The apparent teleological super-imposition of cultural ends reflects a more profound unity of causation. The two sexes, reflecting the forces of the division of labour, are 'impelled towards' each other but come to *desire* each other only under determinate circumstances, 'only after having entered into relations' with one another.

Evident here in the theory of the staged functional equilibria is the underlying evolutionist matrix of Durkheim's whole initial theory. If it is true that at times he is at pains to point out that with respect to ideas of social evolution, 'in a literal sense the terms superior and inferior . . . have no scientific meaning' (Durkheim (1888) 1978: 219), it is clear that Durkheim's whole objective is not posed passively or apolitically: the analysis of the progression of the division of labour is linked to the aim of effective social intervention in modern society in order to facilitate such functional equilibria. The initial approach thus begins both to elaborate principles by which abnormal and pathological forms can be identified and to proceed to identify them. Theoretically and politically, therefore a link is established between the search for the normal course of social evolution, and the understanding of its rhythm, and the elaboration of specific proposals to remedy abnormalities. The totalizing ambition of *The Division of Labour* represents a search for origins in order to complement a prospective political vision.

It is the action of this evolutionary 'grid' which produces the 'harmony' of the theory and its elements. An important moment is therefore the construction of a table of social types. The first, no longer existing, but deducible from the existing lower forms, were the primal hordes. The existing lower forms are made up 'by the simple aggregation' of such masses: 'an almost pure example . . . the Iroquois [reveals that] the adults of both sexes are on the plane of equality . . . kinship is not organised'. Hordes that have thus ceased to be independent are thus transformed into the clan elements of segmental society. The coherence of these clans is the 'external criterion which generally consists in using the same name': strangers are admitted easily. The evolution of clan society is marked by the organization of either matriarchal or patriarchal authority which with the development of the division of labour develops along patriarchal lines alone, as the sexes differentiate, eventually leading to the modern conjugal family as the specialized unit of reproduction and affective relations. In developing this evolutionary perspective Durkheim erects a trail of societies with ever-increasing moral complexity. The following comment illustrates both the method and the content:

> Among the Iroquois, we sometimes see a part of a clan leave to go off to join a neighbouring clan. Among the Slavs, a member of the Zadrugua who is tired of the common life can separate himself from the rest of the family and become a juridical stranger to it, even as he is excluded by it. Among the Germans, a ceremony of some slight complexity permitted every Frank who so desired completely to drop off all kinship obligations. In Rome, the son could not leave the family of his own will, and by his sign we recognise a more elevated type social. But the tie that the son could not break could be broken by the father. . . . Today neither the father nor the son can alter the natural state of domestic relations.
>
> (Durkheim 1964b: 209–10)

The hierarchy of social forms here displays the progression of domestic structures which are shown to be of increasing definition and obligation. In the case of the attachment of a sibling to the domestic group, Durkheim argues that it is not a question of the elaboration of contractual ties, but the bond becomes more absolute with the assumption that our own societies are the highest form. It is thus the allocation of the whole society to its place in the hierarchy which determines the value placed on any one element: the revolutionary will judge the family, he remarked in 1888, 'according to the way they treat women. But the privileged situation of women, far from being a sure index of progress, is sometimes caused by a still rudimentary domestic organisation' (Durkheim 1978: 213). Durkheim's holistic sociology is intransigent: an evaluation of the part has to take its cue from the whole, to which it may have been sacrificed.

The survey of the evolution of the family thus extracts from the societies placed in the known hierarchy, specific aspects from which an evolutionary tendency is deduced. As Durkheim is concerned with the changing complex of moral and legal bonds he attempts to show that there is an evolutionary tendency which moves from repressive to restitute law and which reflects a changing structure of power and authority in the family and society. Thus at the level of the whole, the increasing size and complexity of the society is reflected in the rise of powerful authority figures, the state, and patriarchal authority in the family: the division of labour makes its presence felt in the context of a displacement of mechanical solidarity: 'in this case the tie which binds the individual to the chief is identical with that which in our day attaches the thing to the person'; this mechanical solidarity as domination is reflected in the 'relations of a barbarous despot with his subjects . . . a master with his slaves, of a father of a Roman family with his children' (Durkheim 1964b: 180). The preponderance of the division of labour eventually brings a new type of solidarity which tends to equalize the relations in society and in the family, but this must not be confused with earlier communal forms, such as the Zadruga form which, although egalitarian, is a more primitive form tending to 'neutralize' the progress of the division of labour (ibid.: 284). This progress is more surely embodied in the growth of complexity of the moral bond of marriage itself: at first a purely 'private affair', a 'sale, real among primitive people, later fictive [requiring] neither solemn formalities of any kind nor intervention by some authority'. Later, in Europe, Christian forms intervened in this process and from then on 'marriage ceased to be freely contracted', the church establishing a monopoly over the juridical contract while only later still did the civil authority intervene; the same process is evident in the dissolution of the contract (ibid.: 207). The tendencies at work, says Durkheim, can also be seen in the changing rules of adoption: first it is open and unrestricted, eventually it becomes so highly defined that it hardly occurs at all.

In fact, therefore, Durkheim's conception of evolution in the domestic sphere involves a number of different, even contrary movements. The changing elements of authority and power combine with the changing nature of sanction: in the decalogue the death penalty for infraction of the domestic code has wide scope; in Greece and Rome there is a narrowing of scope (in Greece penal law embraces relations between parents, parents and offspring, and others; whereas in Rome it covered relations solely between client and patron); and today it covers only bigamy and adultery. The same tendency, he says, is evident in sanctions involved in the regulation of sexual relations: today there are only two offences, acts which offend the public decency and attacks on minors. He places rape and violation, not under the rubric of sexual regulation but under that controlling acts of violence, thus saving the evolutionary hypothesis. This aspect of the argument is clear: out of the initially strong and repressive *conscience collective* there develops a society with extensive administrative responsibilities over the family but with a 'regression of collective sentiments concerning the family' (ibid.: 157). But in opposition to the formation of conjugal society as a moral sphere based on contract of two free parties, the role of the state begins to insist upon obligations which are not in any way contractual, in fact they appear to become more absolute: 'as domestic obligations become more numerous, they take on . . . a public character. Not only in early times do they not have a contractual origin, but the role which contract plays in them becomes smaller'. The social tendency seems to consist in an increasing state involvement: 'social control over the manner in which they form, break down, and are modified, becomes greater' (ibid.: 210).

Durkheim's conception of the forces at work in the evolution of the domestic milieu is twofold. As a 'product of a secondary segmentation of the clan' (ibid.), the family's evolution is itself a sphere of the action of the division of labour: 'from its very origins [it] is only an uninterrupted movement of dissociation . . . of functions . . . separated, constituted apart' within the domestic milieu so as to make 'relatives . . . and relations of dependence . . . each of them a special functionary'. And this internal division, Durkheim stresses, 'dominates the entire development of the family' (ibid.: 123); but it does not determine it, since this sphere is articulated within a whole so that 'the family becomes one of the organs . . . and, accordingly everything that happens within it is capable of general repercussions'. If, as happened, the course of evolution in the family is out of synchrony with the development of the wider society 'the regulative organs of society are forced to intervene in order to exercise a moderating influence' (ibid.: 210). Together these two forces had the combined effect of bringing into existence a functional differentiation of the sexes and a series of stages of their functional equilibrium. The new concrete universal of the human being became divided into two incomplete parts. But woman's specialization led her to 'retire' or 'withdraw' from society, and thereby to a physical and mental stagnation or decline thus giving her character the appearance today of a primitive nature as contrasted with man's rise to civilization: 'in the same way as the happiness of man is not that of woman, according to Pascal, that of lower societies cannot be ours' (ibid.: 250). But on the other hand it is man who has to pay the price, as he remarks in anticipation of his study of suicide:

> classes . . . furnish suicide a quota proportionate to their degree of civilisation. Everywhere the liberal professions are hardest hit. . . . It is the same with the sexes. Woman has had less part than man in the movement of civilisation. She participates less and derives less profit. She recalls, moreover, certain characteristics of primitive natures. Thus, there is about one fourth the suicides among women as among men.
>
> (Ibid.: 247)

This passage is significant because it links the evolutionary progression of civilization, as both a specific kind of moral entity and an increase in its extent, with the problem of the internal stratification of modern society. It is now possible to turn to Durkheim's conception of the social as it emerges into the era of greater organic complexity, and to consider the place of this gap between the sexes in its light.

A large and important section of *The Division of Labour* is thus taken up with a consideration of the relation between social and biological facts, in which Durkheim attempts to define the sphere of the social, and thus of civilization, as both being beyond the action of biological facts (indeed it moulds them to its own ends) while itself having the character of a determined structure (giving rise to the possibility of liberty in the Durkheimian sense). The political import of the problem is clearly evident from the start of the discussion to its conclusion: 'liberty is the subordination of external forces to social forces'; society is a sphere of life *sui generis* beyond 'nature'. Indeed the subordination of nature deprives things of their 'fortuitous, absurd, amoral character' for man 'can escape nature only by creating another world where he dominates nature' (ibid.: 387). The higher the social form the more complete is the process of the subjection of the external natural conditions to social ones. But in the phases of transition, the qualities of civilization are developed by the dominant strata who become beings of a more elevated type, whose mode of domination is by very virtue of their possessing moral superiority. At the basis of this discussion is a very simple evolutionary scheme: a primary communism followed in a succession by caste and class society, followed perhaps by a higher society, a pure organic society. The evolutionary tendency is the movement towards meritocracy combined with charity which becomes increasingly obligatory.

The sphere of this new social order, this 'new life, *sui generis*' is beyond the instincts and is 'imposed on the body'. Thus it follows that 'the progress of conscience is in inverse ratio to that of instinct'. Durkheim's assessment here carefully works towards the idea that it is 'not the first which breaks up the second'. By becoming conscious, instinct may indeed be given 'a much greater resistive force to dissolution'. This leads to an important formulation that 'conscience does not make instinct recede; it only fills the space instinct leaves free' (ibid.: 347). Thus the argument suggests that it is outside and beyond the shackles of the facts of instinct that social life begins to establish itself: it is not from the 'psychological nature of man in general, but from the manner in which men once associated mutually affect each other' that social forms are determined (ibid.: 350). But such a development is uneven: at first the division of labour established fixed orders of caste occupations; but even with class divisions the social hierarchy is reflected in somatic differentiation. In order for organic solidarity to have evolved the effects of such differentiation could not have been irreversible, 'that is not to say that heredity is without influence, but that it transmits very general faculties and not a particular aptitude' (ibid.: 315). The apparent difference in intelligence between classes (ibid.: 273) reflects social needs, and the fact that in relation to the brain 'the functional indifference . . . if not absolute, is nevertheless great . . . cerebral functions are the last to assume immutable form . . . thus their evolution is prolonged much later with the learned man than with the uncultivated' (ibid.: 336). No class has a monopoly of intelligence and it is no surprise to find working-class children 'surpassing' children from middle-class backgrounds; even if aptitudes are not allocated through social-class transmission they are none the less unevenly transmitted and 'each will have his own nature' developed under different circumstances. The development of the division of labour and its specializations submits the general faculty to 'active elaboration' (ibid.: 320). Thus in opposition to elitism of a directly biological kind:

> civilisation can be fixed in the organism only through the most general foundations on which it rests. The more elevated it is, the more, consequently, it is free of the body. It becomes less and less an organic thing, more and more a social thing.
>
> (Ibid.: 321)

In relation to the problem of the relation of the sexes these arguments bear directly only on the possibility of social development for men. For although Durkheim appears to be talking throughout about all human beings, it is evident that women are excluded from these comments. This fact makes his remarks appear in a rather different light, for the 'general faculty' which is the basis of elaboration by society is not found in women. Although Durkheim writes that it is not from the 'psychological nature of man' that society is constructed, it must be noted that it is precisely the 'psychological nature of *men*' which is a condition of its creation, for even if society is constructed beyond and outside of the instincts, somehow this is only possible on the basis of a particularly male 'faculty'. The first observation which can be made is that in the midst of modern organic relations there appears to be installed a very specific mechanical caste whose character seems precisely to be transmitted by heredity, and which has fixed psychological faculties which disable it from participating in the movement of civilization, although it is civilization which also appears to have created the disability. Secondly, the overwhelming tendency, described by Durkheim, which finds in organic society the spontaneous mechanism by which 'social inequalities exactly express natural inequalities' (ibid.: 377) is not permitted to extend to half the adult population, although Durkheim writes explicitly that 'all external inequality compromises organic solidarity' (ibid.: 379), even, 'it ignores and denies any special merit in gifts of mental capacity acquired by heredity' (Durkheim 1957: 220). What this 'externality' is in this case is elsewhere described as a 'supplement' and is strictly admonished:

> the situation is no longer the same if some receive supplementary energy from some other source, for that necessarily results in displacing the point of equilibrium, and it is clear that this displacement is independent of the social value of things. . . . If then it does not derive from the persons of the individuals, from their social services, it falsifies the moral conditions of exchange.
>
> (Durkheim 1964b: 384)

Considering the weight Durkheim gave to the significance of the evolutionary tendency and to the radiance of organic moral solidarity, it appears that his reluctance to admit the validity of the demand for the extension of organic solidarity in society to women must have been prompted either by profound fears for the consequences or by a deeply irrational misogyny.

Some evidence that it was perhaps the former, coupled with an ambiguous paternalism, might be found in his remarks on the problems of previous transitions of social adjustment; the case of class struggle in Rome:

> moral contagion manifests itself only on predisposed ground. For needs to flow from one class to another, differences which originally separated these classes must have disappeared or grown less. Through changes produced in society, some must have become apt at functions which were at first beyond them. . . . When the plebians aimed to dispute the right to religious and administrative functions . . . it was because they had become more intelligent, richer and more numerous, and their tastes and ambitions had in consequence been modified.[7]

The link between aptitude and function was broken and only continued through 'more or less violent' constraint alone (Durkheim 1964b: 375–6). The superiority of the higher, ruling classes supported by their moral distinctiveness, became weakened by contact with a new class which had developed the capacity to support the higher moral principle, but development towards more fluid forms was blocked by reversion to an 'abnormal' form of control. This passage provides a hint that Durkheimian sociology contained not only a theory of moral domination but also a theory of violence both as a phenomenon of transitional periods when normal moral control was lost (see also the section on the forced division of labour (ibid.: 374–88)) but also (as I shall discuss later) as a phenomenon of normal superiority under certain conditions. If not developed during the writing up to 1893, there is ample evidence afterwards that Durkheim moved to a position which began to interpret the position of women as that which had long been under threat from this second kind of violence.

WOMEN BECOME MINOR SUBJECTS

> It is not only on solemn occasions that men and women must avoid each other; even in the most ordinary circumstances of daily life, the least contact is severely forbidden.
>
> (Durkheim [1898] 1963: 78)

Completely new elements are introduced into the discussion of the relations between the sexes in segmental society in Durkheim's essay of

1898 on the incest taboo. Gone are the egalitarian societies based solely on mechanical bonds. Into the theory of elementary solidarity is inserted the 'totem and taboo' nexus. This complex of issues retains the evolutionary framework of the transition from the primal hordes to clans (which remain 'amorphous groups') but, increasingly, they appear to be organized, not at the level of the family but at the level of the fusion of clan kinship with the principles of sacred and profane hierarchical classification. The totemic complex is presented as the most simple, the earliest form of human society properly speaking. The relations between phratries, clans and marriage groups function to fuse the sacred phenomena with exogamy (without producing conjugal society). The incest taboo is the primary form of the action of the sacred law in the sphere of kinship relations. In the absence of the conjugal bond it is the organic mother-child relation which forms the primary bond (ibid.: 41–2). In this new scheme the productivity of the sacred in relation to sexual division which is raised to the first rank: in place of the former relative equality of the sexes, Durkheim now recognizes an extreme segregation and inequality. The action of the primary religious complex in relation to the phenomena formed in primitive thought places women, universally, in a position that is at a distance from society and also profoundly ambiguous.

The power of this prohibition suggests to Durkheim that it relates to phenomena that are seen not simply as devastating in their power but also immediate in their effects. Long-term physical deterioration of men and women could not have produced this effect, and thus he concludes that the eugenic argument for the incest taboo is likely to be a modern rationalization of the practice. Indeed he argues that incest is not universally prohibited, what is universal is the application of the sacred/profane dichotomy to human blood and sexual practices, and sexual relations are deeply affected by this tendency.[8] Exogamous practices are now seen as fused with the principle of sacred blood through the actions of totemic ritual: the object of these rituals is 'to avert the dangerous effect of magical contagion' by preventing contact between two orders of phenomena (ibid.: 70). Durkheim is able to retain the principle of similitude and resemblance as a force creating the unity of the clan: the reality of common blood, as each clan has its own unique blood and is 'a homogenous and compact mass . . . where each resembles all'. Cohesion is represented in segmental society as the unity of the blood and the soul, since blood is the vehicle of life. This is why in the first societies the forms are matrilineal, a fact which also indicates the weakness of the conjugal tie. Durkheim's argument is that the incest taboo originated in conditions which were unmarked by anything resembling modern domestic morality and eugenic theory: no moral sentiments entered into the formation of the incest taboo other than those relating directly to the ambiguous sacred status of blood; initially women, as the sex directly associated with blood, were perhaps venerated because of it, but this veneration turned into disgust and loathing. Durkheim's conjecture is remarkable not for the elements it embraces but for its rigorous anti-teleological form, and for the order it introduces into the revamped evolutionary scheme.

Clear indications are given of Durkheim's emerging conception of the nature of primitive thought, but still in the framework of the integrative forces of the *conscience collective*: the repressive penal sanctions are now focused on the infractions of taboos derived from sacred forces identified as the unifying life substances of the clan segment. The action of the taboo on blood 'repulses any contact' with it and thus 'creates a vacuum' (ibid.: 83), the vacuum that is created between men and women. The epistemological principle is that of the *pars totalis* or sympathetic magic, the severed limb continues to live, just as the individual blood contains the group blood. The totemic unity is thus immanent in the clan as its soul. But because women are the natural 'theatre' of blood all the fears of blood are condensed, 'all the more easily since the rudimentary consciences are a terrain of predilection of all the phenomena of psychic transfer; the emotional states pass instantly from one object to another provided that, between the first and the second there is even the slightest relationship of resemblance or even neighbourliness' (ibid.: 91). Separated by the action of the category of the sacred, the divine object is subjected to the forces of the primal ambivalence of the pure versus the impure. The locus of the action of the substance is identified and its contagious actions disciplined by ritual; the perceived influence vacillates between the beneficient and the malign. Both ambivalent reactions are based on a common substratum of fear characteristic of all rituals governing both the boundary of the sacred and the profane, and the internal boundary between the pure and the impure. This class of prohibitions 'seems absolutely indiscernible from other customs which concern some manifestly privileged and truly divine beings' (ibid.: 93). Separation, the creation of social distance, a vacuum, combined with fear, is the primary ideological condition of social stratification: the initial condition of women is thus the direct precursor of royal blood castes, and the ritual separation of the priest or chief or instrument of a cult is of the same order since 'in these elite subjects, there inhabits a god, a force so superior to that of humanity that an ordinary man cannot come into contact with it without tragic consequences' (ibid.: 70). Because these forces here at work are conceived as immensely powerful the vessel containing or supporting the force has to be capable of sustaining its influence, a vessel that is unprepared 'would be destroyed by its contents' (ibid.: 71). Rituals aim therefore to avert such consequences arising from the proximity of unequal subjects and the dangers of contagion: marriage and sexual rites are a prime example of such a social prophylactic.

Durkheim's development of these ideas leads to the proposition established in *The Elementary Forms of the Religious Life* (1912), that women thus became subjects *minoris resistentiae*; in the exasperation of group mourning, anger is either turned inwards or finds an object of least resistance:

> Naturally this victim is sought outside the group; a stranger is a subject *minoris resistentiae*; as he is not protected by the sentiments of sympathy inspired by a relative or neighbour, there is nothing in him which subdues or neutralises the evil and destructive sentiments aroused. . . . It is undoubtedly for this same reason that women serve more frequently than men as the passive objects of the cruellest rites of mourning; since they have smaller social value, they are more obviously designated as scapegoats.
>
> (Durkheim 1961: 447)

Mauss emphasized that same point, adding that this tendency was strengthened by the fact that women were also considered the carriers of malign forces which rendered them dangerous (Mauss 1969 vol. III: 274). In the developed conception the fundamental process of primitive thought is not simply organized as a process of thought association, although principles of proximity and similarity do come into play, but the action of the principle of contagion is itself placed in a dominant position, not as a fundamental force of irrationality, but as a principle of representation of the sacred. Durkheim says in criticism of Lévy-Bruhl: 'conceiving is not simply isolating and grouping . . . it is relating the variable to the permanent, the individual to the social. And since logical thought commences with the concept, it follows that it has always existed; there is no period when men have lived in chronic confusion and contradiction' (Durkheim 1961: 487). The sacred is conceived in the mode of a liquid, a fluid force, and 'contagion is not a sort of secondary process by which sacredness is propagated . . . it is the very process by which it is acquired' (ibid.: 364); but it either consecrates or stains, sanctifies or contaminates. The emergence of this principle into the field of resemblances organizes and dominates it: the 'confusion' of men, animals, plants, and stars in the totemic system is not really a confusion at all, it is a reflection of the idea of sacred causation so that 'beings having one and the same religious principle ought to pass as having the same essence. . . . This is why it seemed quite natural to arrange them in a single category . . . transmutable into one another' (ibid.: 365). In the field of the relation between the sexes the principle of contagion becomes the object of ritual practices constitutive of primary stratification: insiders and outsiders. The object: prevention of contagion.

This relation is, however, evidently one of separation and of hierarchy, of hierarchical classification (the subject Durkheim had investigated with

Mauss (Durkheim and Mauss 1963b)). The model for primitive classification, they argued, with its arrangements of dominant and subordinate
elements could only have been society itself, and this classification is
intimately interwoven into the functioning of society: 'the whole universe
is divided up among the totems thus constituted in such a way that the
same object is not to be found in two different clans, the cults of the
different totems are adjusted to each other, since they complete each
other' (Durkheim 1961: 181).[9] Thus the totemic complex also entails a
subordination of the principle of mechanical solidarity through likenesses
to that of organic solidarity through differences and hierarchy, though
Durkheim hesitates to announce this reversal. But the new 'harmony' of
The Elementary Forms goes further: to reduce the opposition between
the sacred and the profane to social causation. Thus 'the two poles of
the religious life correspond to the two opposed states through which all
social life passes' (ibid.: 460). The birth of the sacred is coeval with that
of society: they are born outside of the individual in an ecstatic (ibid.:
259) social effervescence, *in foro externo* (ibid.: 472). The individual loses
himself in such delirium and no longer recognizes himself while the
external objective logos inscribes itself, automatically, on the bodies of
the individuals. Social dispersal on the other hand represents a loss of
this energy and excitement, the social begins to die and the force of its
logos is weakened (only to be rekindled in the renewal of social energy
in the reproductive rituals, whether in propitious or unpropitious circumstances). So society makes its action felt, indeed 'action dominates the
religious life, because it is society which is its source' (ibid.: 466). It is
in this sense that Durkheim's claim that 'all the great social institutions
have been born in religion' now comes to include the division of the
sexes: women, through their passive proximity to the sacred force of
blood, find themselves excluded from the sacred male rituals, which
actively elaborate collective sacred objects. These contain a symbolic
substance which mirrors that of blood, but outside the body. In the
processes of the valorization of these objects the cult 'produces a man
who is stronger, [who] feels within himself more force, either to endure
the trials of existence or to conquer them' (ibid.: 464).

In comparison with the later theory the article on incest appears far
more as a search for absolute origins than as a search for the principle
of the genesis of the social. In the earlier essays, Durkheim suggested
that 'at the beginning the women had a religious life of their own', but
this 'duality ended with the result that the woman found herself to a
large extent excluded from religion' (Durkheim 1963: 78). In defending
the argument of this essay in 1902 (in: 'Sur le Totémisme', 1902: 99, and
see Moret and Davy 1970: 30–1), he insisted that as against the view
of 1893, the matrilineal origins in no way now implied 'matriarchy or
gynaeocracy', but that 'whenever it is in force the woman enjoys if not

supremacy, at least a relatively high social condition';[10] and all the most primitive of tribes exhibit a collective memory of a time of such an egalitarian state. The tendency for society to switch to patrilineal forms with the progressive masculinization of social authority, is directly associated with the progressive exclusion of woman from religion and her annexation to the domestic circle.[11] Thus among the long-term effects of the incest taboo was the formation of two quite distinct social milieux: the internal domestic milieu which developed into the specialized organ of conjugal solidarity in later society, and the external milieu of free sexual relations outside of the family but subject to its influence. Once created – as an effect of the taboo – each of these milieux came to maintain themselves and their specific moral relations through the period of decline of clan exogamy. Modern rationalizations of the taboo are thus false as explanations of the origins of the practice, but alongside these rationalizations there is, he suggests, an 'obscure thought' that if the taboo on incest were relinquished 'the family would not be the family' (Durkheim 1963: 99); it is thereby recognized that these two opposed milieux are essential to the moral and cultural life of the modern community yet nothing in them makes their existence essential. The difference which these two milieux themselves create and perpetuate is between, on the one hand the pleasure principle and free volition, and on the other the principle of duty and obligation. Once established these two orders of cultural facts, which are in no way the development of a single logical category, may not again be conflated 'without creating a veritable moral chaos' (ibid.: 103). If these two milieux are not the natural product of instinctual feelings for Durkheim, their formation could only have been achieved by considerable forces, for the 'line of least resistance' (ibid.: 108) was in social terms, internal incestuous promiscuity. He presents an account of the practical difficulties of establishing exchange relations between clans as a conjectural history consisting of a picture of long and arduous negotiations and feuds. Thus the obstacle to the assimilation of the two milieux, which was the ever-present tendency, must have been, he concludes, no 'vague whim of desire' (ibid.: 106) but the powerful force of the sacred, the only force capable of overwhelming the painful separations of close kin and the endless complications of maintaining control of property (ibid.: 107–8).

Over the course of social evolution the sacred becomes again attached to elements of the domestic milieu and the conjugal moral sphere, the terrain of duty, obligation and maternal sanctity. The profane, the lesser of the two influences, is attached to the external sexual sphere, a sphere of 'activity and sensitivity' freed from the 'suffocating' atmosphere of the family, and indeed eventually this

sensitivity found itself in opposition to familial morality . . . it became complex and spiritualised . . . [and came to dominate] all the individual or collective manifestations where the imagination plays the largest part. That is why woman has so long been considered the centre of the aesthetic life.

(Ibid.: 110)

A consideration of Durkheim's ideas on the development of the relation between the sexes in society dominated by organic solidarity can be made through an examination of his writing on suicide, religion and education.

THE DIVISON OF THE SEXES IN ADVANCED SOCIETIES

The mystery with which . . . we like to surround the woman . . . and which imparts the principal charm to [the] relationship . . . would be difficult to maintain if men and women mingled their lives more completely.

(Durkheim 1963: 114–15)

Then, suddenly, as if born out of nothingness there appears before the portal of this hellish labyrinth, only a few fathoms distant – a great sailing-ship gliding silently along like a ghost . . . calm enchanted beings glide past him, for whose happiness and retirement he longs – *they are women*. He almost thinks that there with the women dwells his better self.

(Nietzsche 1960: 99)[12]

The development of organic solidarity and the division of labour alters the site of the sacred in society. More and more the particularized element of the social soul becomes significant, reflected in different practices as an increasing respect for the individual and the body; thus in education corporal punishment is opposed on the grounds that the body of the individual should be respected, and in sexual education such a valuation is the basis of the contemporary dilemma which reflects the:

respect that man generates in his fellows. As a consequence of such respect, we keep our distance from our fellows and they keep their distance from us . . . we hide and isolate ourselves from others, and this isolation is at once the token and the consequence of the sacred character which has been invested in us.

(Durkheim 1979: 146)

But the forces of separation and distantiation cannot go too far, for taken beyond certain limits they have disastrous consequences. These effects are examined in *Suicide*, and *inter alia*, the position of women in different milieux of contemporary society, and Durkheim's sociologically-based objections to the women's movement. The central idea of this theory of suicide is that suicide rates vary according to the forms of moral and social solidarity generated in different milieux. As against the interpretations of suicide as a supremely individual act, Durkheim insists that while a suicide only occurs where an individual acknowledges that it is a moment of a known sequence of individual events, and is in that sense an act, the social element in the causation of rates of suicide completely escapes the awareness of the individual. It is the suicide rate which 'must be taken as the object of analysis' (Durkheim 1970: 148), for 'human deliberations, in fact, so far as reflective consciousness affects them are often only purely formal, with no object but confirmation of a resolve previously formed for reasons unknown to consciousness' (ibid.: 297). Indeed, as far as knowledge of social causation is concerned 'facts show only too clearly the incompetence of consciousness in this matter' (ibid.: 311). Suicide is also important for Durkheim as a highpoint of two polar oppositions: moral over- or under-social determination, of self-sacrifice and self-punishment. The study of suicide furnished an opportunity to investigate another aspect of the abnormal moral condition of contemporary society, since 'without even knowing exactly of what they [the increased rates: MG] consist, we may begin by affirming that they result not from a regular evolution but from a morbid disturbance . . . a state of crisis and perturbation not to be prolonged with impunity' (ibid.: 369).

Durkheim's approach rests on the proposition that social life exists in the confluence of a number of social and moral currents; in its normal state these currents are held in a stable equilibrium: 'there is no people among whom these . . . currents . . . do not exist. . . . Where they offset one another, the moral agent is in a state of equilibrium which shelters him. . . . But let one of them exceed a certain strength to the detriment of the others and . . . it become suicidogenic. . . .' (ibid.: 321). Durkheim has no need of a contrary Eros and Thanatos, for each of his social currents are currents of life which may pass into the opposite after a certain threshold, a theory well in tune with a certain tradition of bourgeois political theory which approaches the idea of normal government through checks and balances. The very terms used by Durkheim include the idea of moral chaos as *anomia* close to Schaeffle's *paranomen* (1892: 174).

Two pairs of dichotomies are elaborated: at the level of moral integration, anomie against altruism, and at the level of social integration, egoism against fatalism. The 'true' suicide or modern suicide is egoistic-anomie which increases with civilization. The predominant forms of suicide in segmental societies reflect the generally lower value of human life and the specific forms of social subordination: the obligatory suicide of the widow in caste India, and the obligatory suicide of subordinates on the death of a leader in Gaul (Durkheim 1979: 220). In modern society these sacrificial forms give way to the 'sad' forms of egoism and anomie.

Anomic suicide arises out of conditions of moral indetermination and insufficiency of moral regulation. Rapid deterioration of material conditions gives rise to the illusion that suicide only results from worsening of the standard of life. In fact, Durkheim argues, rapid improvement in the conditions of life have the same effect: a too-rapid change in the moral equilibrium. This idea is linked to the specifically human form of regulation of desire through cultural forms as outlined in 1893. Levels of economic consumption are culturally conditioned so that 'in no society are they equally satisfied in the different stages of the social hierarchy' (Durkheim 1970: 247). In modern society, with its inbuilt tendency to change, there are normal rates of anomic suicide which vary according to position in the social hierarchy: and the strata with 'independent means . . . the possessors of the most comfort suffer most', while on the other hand 'everything that enforces subordination attenuates the effect of this state' (ibid.: 257), for this brings sense of place and recognition of limits. The symptoms of moral chaos are evidenced in the formation of currents of deep pessimism, 'of hatred and disgust for the existing order', are found in 'the anarchist, the aesthete, the mystic and the socialist revolutionary' (ibid.: 370), and reflect the 'great void' which has opened up in social existence (ibid.: 377). The one thing which seems a bulwark against such tendencies is the family, but the family, though offering resistance, has itself suffered, while it has retained its relative prophylactic function: Durkheim gives figures for the increase between 1863 and 1887 of married persons as being from 154 per million to 242 per million, and for unmarried persons from 173 to 289 per million (ibid.: 376–7). More than one critic has noted the perilously minute differences being considered here and has questioned the value of treating such a change in the suicide rate as a traumatic increase of 57 per cent, especially in this area where the data is open to wide variation of construction, as he himself admitted. Nevertheless from the point of view of the general argument here, such claims might be put aside for the moment. The specific changes in these rates, then, are held to indicate a deterioration in the protective effects of marriage, evincing an emergence of *conjugal anomie*. Before examining this directly it is worth looking at Durkheim's analysis of the beneficial effects of marriage.

Marriage is a sphere of moral obligation and of social integration, but affects the sexes differently. Marriage 'regulates the life of passion, and monogamic marriages more strictly than any other' (ibid.: 270). In relation to the sexes, men are more complex and dependent on many conditions beyond himself, thus marriage plays the role of confining desire and fixing it in one unique object: it fixes the desire while providing the means for its satisfaction, 'if his passion is forbidden to stray, its fixed object is forbidden to fail him' (ibid.: 270): 'Si ses jouissances sont définies, elles sont assurées' (Durkheim 1960: 304).[13] Now the position of the unmarried man appears to be one of liberty and freedom with regard to the choice of partner and mode of involvement. Durkheim, however, suggests this leads not to a single anomic but to a double anomic condition. The absence of a fixed eternal partner with fixed obligations leads, in its turn, to an indetermination of the individual himself. The lack of determination of the desire, reflected in impossible dreams of the infinite or non-existent, is mirrored in the subject's own non-existence: 'just as [he] makes no definitive gift of himself, he has definitive title to nothing' (Durkheim 1970: 271). This affects men far more than women: her needs 'have less of a mental character . . . [they] are more closely related to the needs of the organism' (ibid.: 272). This also explains the protection women seem to enjoy against egoism, for here also the difference between the sexes is marked.

Egoism is the tendency towards the relaxation of social integration and is reflected in states where the degree of social density of relations is low.

> When a widow is seen to endure her condition much better than a widower and desires marriage less passionately . . . it is said that woman's affective faculties, being very intense, are easily employed outside the domestic circle, while her devotion is indispensible to man to help him endure life. Actually if this is her privilege it is because her sensibility is rudimentary rather than highly developed.
>
> [The argument is consistent:] As she lives outside of community existence more than man, she is less penetrated by it; society is less necessary to her because she is less impregnated with sociability. She has few needs in this direction and satisfies them easily. With a few devotional practices and some animals to care for, the old unmarried woman's life is full . . . these very simple social forms satisfy all her needs.'
>
> (Ibid.: 215)

When Durkheim later argues that 'we are only preserved from egoistic suicide in so far as we are socialised' (ibid.: 376) it must be acknowledged that the 'we' is quite particular. And when he argues that social facts must only be explained relative to other social facts the specificity of the conception of the *social* must also be acknowledged. Women are outside of the activity of these forces *to a greater extent* than men. The lower suicide rates for women in general testify directly to the fact that, (as is the case in their way with children,) the action of social forces affects them only by about a quarter of the extent it affects men, who are thereby seen to be complex since their 'moral balance depends on a larger number of conditions' (ibid.: 216).[14] If the family is one form in which the protection against egoism is realized, Durkheim again indicates that this protection is weakening in this respect as well, since the former traditional permanence and stability, associated with a family continuity and personality with a well-defined existence, is giving way to family units which exist in social conditions which tend towards relatively ephemeral forms.

Taken together, therefore, the joint forces of increasing anomie and egoism lead to disturbance of the social and moral equilibrium. Investigating the various aspects of the relation of the domestic milieu to suicide, his persistence led him to investigate the different effects on the sexes of the suicide rates relative to the state of marriage itself: by comparing the rates of suicide of the sexes relative to the degree to which the marriage rule was absolute, he suggested the existence of an interesting difference between the two sexes: 'from the standpoint of suicide, marriage is more favourable to the wife the more widely practiced divorce is; and vice versa' (ibid.: 269). This issues directly in a problem, since divorce leads to a weakening of the moral value of marriage itself and to the interests of men in maintaining absolute marriage. In *Suicide* there is no attempt to hide the implications: 'we now have the cause of that antagonism of the sexes which prevents marriage favouring them equally: their interests are contrary; one needs restraint and the other liberty' (ibid.: 274). If there is however a polarity between anomie on the one hand, and fatalism (over-arching control) on the other, Durkheim was not inclined to develop this to account for the discrepancy, even though he suggests the suicides of slaves fall into this category (ibid.: 276). Later, in 1906, in the article 'Divorce by Mutual Consent', Durkheim (1978: 240–52) sought to prevent any weakening of the marriage vow, and in so doing returned to the findings of *Suicide* and reversed them:

> in taking up this question once again. . . . I perceived that the advantage enjoyed by married Parisian women is purely apparent and arises not from the fact that the married woman is in better moral conditions in Paris . . . but from the fact that unmarried women of about 20 to 35 years of age are in more unfavourable moral conditions (ibid.: 246). [Durkheim then takes the opportunity to formulate a surprising law:] the state of marriage has only a weak effect on the moral constitution of women . . . she stands somewhat beyond the moral effects of marriage.
>
> (Ibid.: 247)

Durkheim can then safely return to the conclusions of *Suicide* that taken in the broad outline the decrease in the total number of female suicides is 'imperceptible in the whole and does not balance the increase of male suicides' due to divorce (Durkheim 1970: 273). The emphasis is clear throughout, that it is men alone who benefit from absolute marriage although it is 'represented as a sacrifice made by man of his polygamous instincts, to raise and improve women's condition' (ibid.: 275).[15]

It is now possible to appreciate Durkheim's judgement on the idea of women's emancipation:

the two sexes do not share equally in social life. Man is actively involved in it, while woman does little more than look on from a distance. Consequently man is much more highly socialised than woman. . . . His needs, therefore are quite different from hers. . . . But it is by no means certain that this opposition must necessarily be maintained. Of course, in one sense it was originally less marked than now, but from this we cannot conclude that it must develop indefinitely. . . . To be sure, we have no reason to suppose that woman may ever be able to fulfil the same functions in society as man; but she will be able to play a part in society which while particularly her own, may yet be more active and important than that of today. The female sex will not again become more similar to the male; on the contrary, we may forsee that it will become more different. But these differences will become of greater social use than in the past. Why, for instance, should not aesthetic functions become woman's as man, more and more absorbed in functions of utility, has to renounce them? Both sexes would thus approximate each other by their very differences. (*Les deux sexes se rapprocheraient ainsi tout en se différenciant*). . . . As for the champions today of equal rights for women with those of men, they forget that the work of centuries cannot be instantly abolished; that juridical equality cannot be legitimate so long as psychological inequality is so flagrant. Our efforts must be bent to reduce the latter.

(Ibid.: 385–6)

Durkheim's conclusions in this way rejoin those of Comte (and Spencer's second thoughts of *The Study of Sociology* (1880)) where the argument is precisely that the obstacle to equality is a general psychological differentiation. What seems to characterize this other being is a specific function located in a definite moral milieu which in its turn seems to have no moral effect on her; 'fundamentally traditionalist by nature, they govern their conduct by fixed beliefs and have no great intellectual needs' (Durkheim 1970: 166); 'being a more instinctive creature than man, woman has only to follow her instincts to find calmness and peace' (ibid.: 272). Durkheim thus continues the themes of phrenology and pedomorphism established in 1893, with a misogynist psychology. The sociological remedy for this acknowledged inequality is well prepared: the aesthetic realm, already stigmatized as the inessential, but also, paradoxically, as the gratuitous, frivolous, even the terrain of 'the essentially *anomic*' (Durkheim 1964b: 431), of which woman is the preeminent *object*, is now to be her place as *subject*.

But there is a basic tension in the very construction of the idea of anomie; between, on the one hand, the element of disintegration and chaos, and on the other hand, the acceptance that this can be found organized, 'co-ordinated and systematized, and [which] then become complete theories of life . . . the formation of such great systems is therefore an indication that the current of pessimism has reached a degree of abnormal intensity' (Durkheim 1970: 370). This idea is not isolated, it appears several times in *Suicide*, for example in relation to egoism: 'currents of depression and disillusionment . . . reflect the relaxation of social bonds, a sort of collective asthenia, or social malaise . . . metaphysical and religious systems spring up which, by reducing these obscure sentiments to formulae, attempt to prove to men the senselessness of life. . .' (ibid.: 214). The evidently uncritical conflation of all movements opposing the existing state of affairs as egoistic-anomic, places the whole of the Durkheimian project itself in an acute contradiction, since it too is opposed to the existing state of affairs of society, as was pointed out many times by conservative Catholics, who regarded his theory as 'le plus grave péril' (Swart 1964: 20).

These remarks in *Suicide* are complemented by his reviews in the *Année*. For example, in his 1910 review of Marianne Weber's book on women he argues that it is precisely the sanctity of the domestic milieu which is women's basic strength in society:

> the feelings of respect that have directed her way and have become more and more pronounced . . . originate in large part, in the religious respect inspired by hearth and home. [And this has political consequences, for if the organic nature of the family ceases, if there is nothing other than] the partnership in which each have their centre of interest and concerns, it will be difficult for such a religion to survive. And woman's stature will be diminished because of it . . . the gains she will settle for . . . will be offset by important losses.
>
> (Durkheim 1980: 288–9)

This continues the theme of the article on the incest taboo which defined the home as the 'nerve centre of all collective discipline' and has always had a religious character (Durkheim 1963: 101). In the conjugal family he argues against Marianne Weber:

> family life is much more intense and more important than in previous types; the woman's role which is precisely to preside over life indoors, has also assumed more importance, and the moral scope of the wife and mother has increased . . . the more family matters intervene to occupy the man's mind, the more he falls out of the habit of regarding his wife as an inferior.
>
> (Durkheim 1980: 288)

Two elements thus stand out here: the significance of the sanctity of women which is decisively linked to the domestic rather than the sexual milieu, and the social distance between the sexes which should be minimized in the interest of the status of women in the minds of men.

The first of these issues relates to Durkheim's thesis that sexuality in modern society is essentially a site of moral ambiguity. On the one hand sexual relations are grossly immoral since by their very nature they violate the boundaries of the individual so carefully erected by society:

> in the sexual act this profanation reaches an exceptionally high level, since each of the two personalities in contact is engulfed by the other . . . this is what comprises the seed of basic immorality which is contained in this curiously complex act.
>
> (Durkheim 1979: 146)

> [Although it offends morality, through it are forged the closest of social bonds] there is no act which creates such strong bonds. . . . It has associative, and consequently moral power without compare . . . moral *conscience* . . . cannot advocate such an act, nor condemn it, nor can it praise it, stigmatise or above all declare it unimportant . . . [it] accepts the sexual act while at the same time requiring it to be veiled in darkness and mystery.
>
> (Ibid.: 142)

These arguments suggest the consequences Durkheim envisaged for the effects of the incest taboo. Having produced the separation of the two realms of sexual pleasure and domestic duty, modern domestic society finds itself at the centre of dilemmas that rival the problems of sacred blood in former times. Women now become polarized between the morally sanctified domestic milieu and the object of immoral sexual life outside the family. Official morality also finds itself paralysed in the fact of such a problem, and the only way they can be resolved is to explain sociologically the 'mutual opposition and correlation' of these two contradictory aspects (ibid.: 145). The moral superiority of the family is essential in modern society not only because it is the source of a unique moral complex of obligations and functional divisions, but also, as he had suggested in his earlier essay on the conjugal family (Durkheim (1892), 1978: 239), 'free union is a conjugal society in which . . . obligations do not exist. It is therefore an immoral society. And that is why children raised in such conditions present such great numbers of moral flaws. It is because they have not been raised in a moral environment'. This idea is complemented by his opposition to divorce since a shocking 'moral embarrassment' is felt when two people who have engaged in a sexual relationship 'treat each other like strangers whereas in fact, neither holds any mystery for the other'. The conditions of socialization are thus held to be essentially moral conditions and education primarily moral education.

Much of Durkheim's sociology is devoted to education, and the posts he held demanded he spend a considerable amount of his time teaching courses on education. His works in this sphere seem to represent a continuation of many of the themes elaborated in *The Division of Labour*, the moral authority of the social over the individual, the relation of the pre-social to the social, etc. The teacher's task as representative of social forces is primarily conceived of as being a morally formative one, making use of two natural 'predispositions': the child's propensity to form habits and his open suggestibility (Durkheim 1973: 134–43). The child is conceived as possessing a primitive mentality, and Durkheim even adopts the image of the kaleidoscope, taken up with such prominence by Lévi-Strauss. The child, like the primitive, is envisaged as emotionally unstable and given to wild outbursts of anger quickly oscillating between different states; but the elements necessary for moral education are general and limited: the teacher should take advantage of the hypnotic state induced by authority to suggest the habits of regular function that are the basis of the higher moral life of civilization. The acquisition of these complex forms is entirely cultural (Durkheim 1956: 125–6), and education is conceived as the action of an external social force which comes to the individual in a specific mode, a specific tone of authority. But in considering the relations of authority against the background of the history of educational practice Durkheim is led to an interesting development of his observations on violence. In the earlier forms of education appropriate to simple social forms, education is first linked to the initiation practices of the male religious life, and generally great gentleness and indulgence is shown towards children (Durkheim 1973: 184). With the development of civilization, however, the life of the child is darkened by an emergent violence located in the specialized organ, the school (ibid.: 189) which becomes so acute that it spills over into the domestic milieu (ibid.: 186–7). This violence arises from two forces: the separation of the school from the family and from public life, and the growth of a social and cultural distance between the life of the teachers and that of the pupils. Here Durkheim suggests a law, rarely noticed in commentaries on his work, that, under determinate conditions a group perceiving itself morally superior to another *normally* inflicts violence on the lower group. This view developed in his study of the history of education complements his development of his views on repressive law: the earlier societies do not exhibit overwhelming repressive sanctions, but violence and repression reflect centralization of power and absolute authority. In this perspective it is possible to see in Durkheim's sociology an emergent group of minor subjects who fall victim to this violence: the primitive to the civilized man, the younger children to the older ones, children to teachers, strangers to the established ethnic minorities, and of course women to men. This law is quite distinct from his disussions of the abnormal forms of control through violence in conditions where moral superiority has been lost.

Here violence is the normal outcome in certain conditions of moral superiority that is in no way threatened: violence in education is

> a special case of a law which might be stated this way: whenever two populations, two groups of people having unequal cultures, come into continuous contact with one another, certain feelings develop that prompt the more civilised group – or that which deems itself such – to do violence to the other.
>
> (Ibid.: 193)

The direct connection between social power, truth and violence is made by Durkheim in a review of Duprat's *Le Mensonge*:

> The lie – that is to say the intentional suggestion of error . . . has collective forms. It even possesses veritable social institutions which are its organs, such as the press, the sects, and the life of the salon with the polite customs which it implies. On the other hand there are social situations which foster the lie. . . . The conflict of civilisations of unequal worth very often obliges the representatives of the inferior culture to lie so that it can maintain itself; this is the case of the savage in the face of the European. It is also the condition of the woman; the education which she receives explains in part the aptitude for which she is often reproached. . . . It is above all the intrinsic power of resistance which makes the aptitude to lie more or less great.
>
> (Durkheim 1980: 131)

But different institutions are balanced internally in different ways, so the tendency is mitigated according to the action of counter forces. For example, the tendency for older children 'to treat the very young as inferior beings' is held in check by 'familial feelings' while in school this 'useful countercheck does not exist'. This tendency becomes increasingly influential in the development of the school *'so long as a contrary force does not intervene'* (Durkheim 1973: 195 [emphasis E.D.]). This force is public opinion and the state, which functions to moderate the actions of the social organs, while in the case of the family conjugal and familial sentiment arises to fulfil this role, thus children are protected from each other and from their parents, but also by extension, the woman from the man.

Durkheim's conception of the problems of the position of minor subjects was however incomplete, as can be glimpsed in his evident inability to provide answers to key problems in his remarks on sexual education and in *The Elementary Forms*. For example in the latter, certain discrepancies can be noted in the following comments that women are regarded as profane (Durkheim 1961: 342), but also 'woman is not absolutely profane' (ibid.: 161), indeed in one place the problem is put directly:

There is one interdiction of which we say nothing because it is very hard to determine its exact nature: this is sexual contact. There are religious periods when a man cannot have commerce with a woman. In this because the woman is profane or because the sexual act is dreaded. . . ? We set it aside with all that concerns conjugal and sexual rites.

(Ibid.: 342)

Again, in noting the importance of the ritual interdictions accompanying marriage, which reflect the 'grave change of conditions' implied in marriage, he says: 'the study of the system of juridico-religious rules which relates to the commerce of the sexes . . . will be possible only in conjunction with the other precepts of primitive conjugal morality' (ibid.: 351). This footnote seems to imply the beginnings of a recognition that such a morality exists in primitive society, and that Durkheim had some intention of considering this issue in order to resolve his area of doubt.

FEAR FOR WOMEN AND FEAR OF WOMEN

Durkheim's remarks on the inequality of the sexes should not then be seen as a passive acceptance of nineteenth century chauvinism. In the light of an examination of his general sociology it appears that he believed women were formed as a stratum among the first effects of the separation of the sacred from the profane, first to suffer the less propitious consequences of the creation of impure sacred phenomena. Stigmatized as feared beings, they became annexed to the evolving domestic milieu, but even here men elaborated complex ritual defences to enable them to meet them (even circumcision is seen as a mark made on the organ in order to 'put it into shape for resisting the . . . forces which it could not meet otherwise' (ibid.: 354). Eventually, in the atmosphere of the evolved conjugal family, women achieved a certain protection in the form of a determinate moral sanctity and developed familial sentiment, which also protected children. But the long exclusion from society had moulded them into creatures less able to accept culture; they had remained primitive in many respects, and a 'flagrant' inequality in mental and physical capacities had developed between the sexes.

This presented Durkheim with an acute dilemma: woman had become a different creature because of her exclusion from society, but her reintroduction into society, demanded by the egalitarian forces brought about by that very evolution itself, could not be admitted as 'legitimate' because of these very differences.[16] In this case, ironically, women's desire for equality could not be granted by the division of labour as it had not spontaneously furnished the means. The elements of this dilemma can now be specified. The problem centres on the difficulty of the question:

even if women possess different attributes why should not society freely allocate those attributes to functions itself? It can be seen that it is strictly compatible both with his discussion of society emergent beyond the instincts, and the evolutionary tendency towards the breakdown of all external inequalities, that such moral equality be facilitated. In fact, whenever Durkheim broached the subject of 'natural' requirements for the development or transmission of culture, the idea which dominates is always the idea that only modest and limited 'faculties' are required. This is especially so in respect of cerebral functions. It is society which, on the one hand, imposes its unequal demands on these resources in its formation of occupational strata. Although Durkheim talks of the natural endowments of women it is never directly related to the question of educability or occupational capacity (whereas for Schaeffle explicitly, it is politically determined that women should not be educated). In his discussions of these questions a curious avoidance of these issues occurs. It is certain, however, from remarks made across the span of his career that he thought woman a distinct being whose nature had perhaps even regressed with civilization.

Although he hesitated to use the term himself, women, then, seem to be regarded as an inferior caste outside the main forces of social development: he does not attempt to integrate the effects civilization has for women into his conception of evolution as a whole. Rather, women are seen to find a state of equilibrium dominated by the action of instinctual regulation, indeed protected against the vicissitudes of social currents. The transition from caste status to full membershp of society is regarded as a period of considerable danger for women. The mixture of proposals advocated by the left-wing position, from the simple political emancipation of women to the break-up of the bourgeois family, seemed to imply a conception of communism as a breakdown of obligations and a weakening of social bonds. Durkheim clearly saw these as utopian and 'anomic' in the sense that the predominant element is a negative, disillusioned rejection of current forms of solidarity combined with a rejection of the discipline of obligation. Such a conception of communism ran diametrically counter to his conception of the higher society, which could not be built on 'free love' or the pleasure principle. But, nonetheless, the claims for women's emancipation required a rational response: this question concerned the conditions and timing of such a re-introduction into society and the problems of readjustment inside the family.

It is interesting that such problems had already been considered by Durkheim's mentor in Germany, Schaeffle, in his critique of the Gotha Programme:

> every loosening of the bond [between husband and wife] would lead only to the emancipation of the man from the woman, to the loss for

the weaker sex of some of their strongest supports, to their abandonment by men, to a relapse into hetaerism in the highest degree deroga-
tory to feminine dignity.

(Schaeffle 1892: 133)

Schaeffle went on to emphasize the moral qualities of the family, its
training in 'self-conquest, in gentleness, in consideration for others, in
fairness', etc. (ibid.: 149) that would be lost should the family fall in
favour of 'fugitive unions'. Any change in the direction of 'free love'
would simply reduce man again to the animal, in the sense of the loss of
moral constraint, while creating a new aristocracy and a distribution of
women among men by a new criterion. An inevitable coarsening of
relations would result from the subsequent loss of 'those softening and
ennobling influences which is the case of the stable marriage-union' (ibid.:
157). Schaeffle also consistently opposed extending education and the
franchise to women as these measures would bring changes in the family
complementary to those of free love (even referring at one point to
'hetaerism in education') leading to a deterioration in the conditions of
all.

Durkheim seems to have adopted all these points: the civilizing effects
of marriage and the family, the exclusion of women from public life, but
added new elements of his own. Against the emphasis of Schaeffle,
Durkheim elaborated the idea that insofar as civilization was concerned
it was men who stood to lose most, for anomic currents affect them far
more than they do women. He also adds to Schaeffle's conception of the
degradation of female dignity, and the weakening of male protection of
women, the idea that without the shield of the family, women would
become objects of a normal violence inflicted by superior subjects. His
position therefore suggests that at the end of the nineteenth century
women had not reached the degree of development of the lower classes
of Rome or modern society, which, with their growth in intelligence and
aptitudes, had brought them into contact with higher classes, with a
resulting moral contagion. This had not led directly to new conditions
but a rearguard action by the ruling classes had imposed an abnormal
'forced' division of labour, falsely allocating ability to unnatural function,
while no external moral force had sufficient strength to intervene in the
process on behalf of the lower groups. He suggests, on the other hand,
a 'flagrant' discrepancy of intelligence and capacity between the sexes,
and it is therefore from that side of the question that the main danger
arises: the premature projection of such a caste into society, in the
absence of any strongly developed moderating force, would run the risk
of normal violence. Thus Durkheim's approach logically leads to the
maintenance of a certain fear of women (of course purified in the family)
and fear for women who are unfortunate enough to attract the normal

violence expected to issue from men in the period of transition (here a fertile field for a Durkheimian theory of violence against women) so long as no effective moral authority has been developed. His position can therefore be read as an attempt to reveal the complexity of the problem of the gulf between the sexes, the 'psychological' distance between them, and the possible consequences of bringing into direct contact creatures of such 'unequal cultures', one of which had limited powers of resistence as exemplified by her tendency to dissimulation. The logic of his position is thus to emphasize the need to bring the two natures more in line with one another as a preparation for social equality. But given Durkheim's analysis, in what possible way could this be achieved?

Right from the beginning of his work it is clear that Durkheim followed Schaeffle's line of maximal defence with its highly conservative implications and paternalistic stance. Instead of catching the major current, as Hertz was able to do, and before him Enfantin, Mill, Bebel and Engels, and developing the necessary connections which might attach all 'individuals' to society through education, and contributing to the formation and strengthening of a moral authority capable of sustaining the extension of citizenship, even of contributing to the demystification of the relations between the sexes, he took the opposite line, of rejecting such claims and measures even to the point of advocating indissoluble marriage, and a sexual education for adolescents which emphasized the necessarily mysterious nature of the sexual act and recommended consistently that it be 'grave and solemn'.

Chapter 2

Mary Wollstonecraft: woman as other

I shall not boggle about words, when their direct signification is insincerity and falsehood, but content myself with observing that if any class of mankind be so created that it must be educated by rules not strictly deducible from truth, virtue is an affair of convention.

(Wollstonecraft 1983: 182)

READING WOLLSTONECRAFT[1]

Very few readers, if any, have praised the writing in the *Vindication*.[2] If the work was well received when it first appeared (see Janes 1978), even someone as close to Wollstonecraft as William Godwin thought it a 'very unequal performance, and eminently deficient in method and arrangement' (1798). This may have been Wollstonecraft's own view: 'I am dissatisfied with myself for not having done justice to the subject – do not suspect me of false modesty – I mean to say that had I allowed myself more time I could have written a better book' (cited by Sunstein 1975: 214).[3] This view has remained more or less constant since. In 1913, H. N. Brailsford thought it had 'in abundance most of the faults that a book can have. . . . It is ill arranged, full of repetitions, full of digressions, and almost without a regular plan. Its style is unformed, sometimes rhetorical, sometimes familiar' (Brailsford 1913: 204). Madeline Linford (1924: 89) found it 'pompous and stilted and crowded with platitudes. The matter is pitchforked together with a hastiness that shows too plainly the short time that was devoted to it, and the main theme is constantly clogged with irrelevancy . . . it is almost entirely rhetorical'. Again, in 1932 H. R. James noted 'the want of a clear-cut plan and consecutive thought, a style not infrequently irritating, judgements hasty and one-sided' (James 1932: 66). The same judgement was given by George Preedy in 1937: the work was 'flung on paper in somewhat slovenly fashion . . . a work swollen with platitudes and padded with turgid rhetoric . . . [and] disfigured not only by the scolding tone that gave an unpleasant tinge to the whole composition, but by partiality, confusion of thought and prejudice' (Preedy 1937: 157–9).

This judgement is repeated in more recent criticism. Claire Tomalin (1974: 105) thought the book was 'without any logical structure: it is more in the nature of an extravaganza'. Or again: '*Vindication* is circular and often confused. It is exploratory, and often falls back on rhetorical repetition or sarcasm instead of argument' said Margaret Walters (1976: 316). Even in the introduction to the available paperback version, the judgement is that in this work 'one comes all too often, panting to the end of hopelessly long sentences, a little unsure of what the subject was' (Miriam Brody in Wollstonecraft 1983: 316).

There is a considerable amount of apologetics in the manner of Brailsford: *Vindication* 'is perhaps the most original book of its century, not because its daring ideas were altogether new but because in its pages for the first time a woman was attempting to use her own mind. . . . It has nothing of the learning, the formidable argumentative compulsion of Godwin's writing. But it is sold today in cheap editions, while Godwin survives only on the dustier shelves of old libraries. Its passion and sincerity have kept it alive' (1913: 199; 204). The idea is repeated in Claire Tomalin (1974: 104–5): 'She made no attempt to study the history of the subject or do any special reading or research. In fact she spent something like six weeks in all upon *A Vindication*. . . . There is no doubt that Condorcet's ten pages pack more logic than Mary's three hundred; but on the other hand she hit the exact tone of righteous indignation that is still effective – indeed it has become the staple tone of much successful journalism. Her book is still read, his essay has never been reprinted'. Some critics soften the tone: 'The *Vindication* has often been criticised for being rushed, hasty and repetitive. . . . But it is not just that the text itself sometimes appears rushed; it should, I think, be read as provisional' (Grimshaw 1989: 12).

In recent years, remarkably, there has been more than a softening of tone. Cora Kaplan suggests 'If we give ourselves up to *A Vindication*'s eloquent but somewhat rambling prose, we will also discover passim an unforgettable early account of the making of a lady, an acute, detailed analysis of the social construction of femininity. . . . Read *A Vindication* for its historical meanings and another text emerges' (Kaplan 1986: 34–5). And more radically, Mary Poovey suggests that the writing reveals the emergence of theoretical and political problems in her 'use of euphemisms and circuitous phrasing. Whenever Wollstonecraft approaches a subject that arouses her own volatile emotions, her language becomes both obscure and abstract; she shuns concrete nouns as if they were bodies she is trying to cover over. In fact she will fully indulge her feeling only when its object is physically absent or unidentified. Even then she uses artificial and abstract rhetoric to generalize the emotion and to idealize

the provocative situation' (Poovey 1984: 78). There is also a growing
acceptance that the work struggles with important dilemmas: 'the *Vindication* needs understanding . . . in the context of her other writings and
the ways in which these wrestled with the dilemmas thrown up by 18th
century politics, both radical and reactionary, and by contemporary views
on literature and philosophy on the nature of femininity. These dilemmas
were of course cast in an 18th century form, but then are ones which, in
altered shape, feminism still continues to encounter' (Grimshaw 1989:
12).

It is possible, then, to note a serious change of attitude in relation to
this text, from one where it is regarded in the most patronizing manner
as having irremediable faults which are explained by its rushed mode of
composition, to one where it is regarded as of the highest interest theoretically and politically and where its mode of composition has to be
explained symptomatically.

THE THEORY OF THE *VINDICATION*

There already exist a number of competent summaries of the argument
of the *Vindication* (e.g. Brody in Wollstonecraft 1983); consideration of
the theory is rare. It is not as if Wollstonecraft disguises her resources
or her theoretical terminology; the problem is more that the theory is
not directly recognizable to modern analysis in its eighteenth century
terminology.[4] Yet (against Reiss's reading that in the text woman 'is not
. . . some "Other" ' (Reiss 1989: 15)) it is surely one of the most important contributions to the problematic of social alienation ever written.
Indeed, Wollstonecraft's version, in substance, is surprisingly modern,
for it is a theory of repressive empowerment, and certainly bears comparison with all recent theories of repressive desublimation, repressive tolerance, repressive ambience, excremental culture. Indeed these more recent
developments can be seen to have important eighteenth-century roots in
the Enlightenment critiques of alienated social power when Wollstonecraft's theory itself becomes recognizable as the double action of alienation
and seduction.[5]

In some sense this contextualization is realized in modern interpretations and provides the content of much discussion of the dilemmas in
the exposition. But the fact that the theory is both a theory of oppression,
and a theory of the specific power (both terms used by Wollstonecraft)
both over and of women, is invariably interpreted as either Wollstonecraft's own argumentative dilemma, or her own personal dilemma. Thus
her theoretical position and her originality is obscured, since these terms
are not the site of a dilemma but a theoretical object.[6] She provides an
account of the 'making of a lady' but only as part of a theory of alienated
social stratification, seductive culture and their reproduction. Most prob-

lematically for modern feminism she develops an account of 'the false system of female manners' and how instinct is 'sublimated' into wit (Wollstonecraft 1983: 143), indeed into what she calls 'bodily wit' (ibid.: 236). She elaborates a theory of the effects of sexual power and privilege on the powerful themselves, taking as a crucial theoretical resource the analysis of Adam Smith on aristocratic corruption (ibid.: 148; see Kay 1986), and Rousseau who, she remarks, 'saw talents bent by power to sinister purposes' (Wollstonecraft 1983: 95; see Coole 1988: 103–32). Yet both Smith and Rousseau are turned into an unprecedented theory of women's oppression by putting Smith into Rousseau and adopting a new domain for the theory provided by Hume's comment 'this nation gravely exalts those, whom nature has subjected to them, and whose inferiority and infirmities are absolutely incurable. The women, though without virtue, are their masters and sovereigns' (cited in Wollstonecraft 1983: 124).

The primary fact is the separation and segregation of women in society and their almost total exclusion from civil rights and therefore duties. At the same time women come to enjoy 'the arbitrary power of beauty' (ibid.: 103), an 'undue power' (p. 123), through which 'they have more real powers than their masters' (p. 125). Indeed 'women, as well as despots, have now perhaps more power than they would have if the world . . . were governed by laws deduced from the exercise of reason' (p. 126). Yet the lure of this power is a trap: 'Taught from their infancy that beauty is women's sceptre, the mind shapes itself to the body, and roaming around its gilt cage, only seeks to adore its prison' (p. 131). The situation is paradoxical: 'Exalted by their inferiority (this sounds like a contradiction) they constantly demand homage as women' (p. 145).

The basic cause of this is men's sexual appetite: 'all the causes of female weakness . . . branch out from one great cause – want of chastity in men' (ibid.: 249). It produces a contradiction in male practice: 'Why do men halt between two opinions, and expect impossibilities? Why do they expect virtue from a slave, from a being whom the constitution of civil society has rendered weak, if not vicious?' (p. 134). This contradiction is even reproduced in what Wollstonecraft calls philosophical and poetic 'heterogeneous associations' of ideas – the 'fair defects', the 'amiable weaknesses' of women (p. 118); and women develop a pride in 'their weakness' (p. 262). The whole natural character of women, however, is alienated in the process: 'What can be a more melancholy sight to a thinking mind, than to look into the numerous carriages that drive helter-skelter about this metropolis in a morning of pale-faced creatures who are flying from themselves!' (p. 259).

FOUR RECENT READINGS

Before examining in more detail the remarkable argument of women's alienated empowerment through all its ramifications, some representative current readings can be examined to reveal the effects misrecognition of the theory has on modern interpretation. I will look at four representative recent essays, the analyses by Mary Poovey (1984), Cora Kaplan (1986), Timothy Reiss (1989) and Jane Spencer (1986). These readings either concentrate on the failure of the analysis or the costs in terms of repression that the work symptomatically displays.

A repressed feminism: Mary Poovey

Poovey located Wollstonecraft's position as an important but highly contradictory and passive (Poovey 1984: 79) variant of the Protestant ethic, a woman's version, with the radical possibilities this implies, and at the same time many of its repressive puritan implications: all the rewards in the system are deferred spiritual ones (ibid.: 65). It is essentially a philosophy in which all individuals 'are motivated primarily by an innate desire for love and respect' and a recognition of human weakness generates a philosophy of love and humanity (ibid.: 60). Wollstonecraft's fundamental critique of modern society suggests that it so establishes the predominance of statuses and property that there emerges a critical discrepancy between these and the true value of social contributions. Hers is a 'bourgeois assault . . . against aristocratic privilege' (ibid.: 62). The basic problem is that she spends far too much of her analysis pouring 'scorn' on those who submit to tyranny rather than 'systematically castigating tyrants' and simply ends up in an individualistic alliance with middle-class men (ibid.: 63).

The real breakthrough of the *Vindication* is that it realizes that the situation of women is produced by the practice of courtesy, institutionalized in language and reproduced through a specific mode of education (ibid.: 69). According to Poovey, Wollstonecraft's strategy 'is to emphasise the similarities between female behaviour and that of other groups: the wealthy soldiers, wits and dissenters. Arguing "from analogy", she then asserts that it is reasonable and morally requisite to teach women to recognise their essential affinities with men' (ibid.: 70). This strategy enables her to adopt a neutral voice and to speak with more assurance and security. For Wollstonecraft, she says, the crucial fact is that women are only, or 'essentially', stigmatized as sexual beings (ibid.: 71). Wollstonecraft 'simply' reverses this: for her it is more fundamental to argue that it is men who are dominated by sexual desires, appetites which are at 'the root' of injustice; thus, for example, Rousseau's theory of sexual difference is seen to represent his own 'repressed desire' (Poovey 1984: 71).

For Wollstonecraft, all the problems for women stem from this male interest: their exclusion, retardation, their cultivated innocence. Women become trapped in the sphere of sensual experience, and as a result women's thought is narrow, they become 'slaves to their own senses and thus hostage to every transient emotion' (ibid.: 73). The resort of women to cunning is a response of the powerlessness of women to their situation, as is the way they tyrannize their servants and children. But Wollstonecraft presses her argument too far, says Poovey:

> Repeatedly she implies that female sexuality is only a learned response to *male* sexuality. . . . Yet the closer we read Wollstonecraft's *Vindication*, the clearer it becomes that her defensive denial of female sexuality in herself and in women in general is just that . . . a *defence* against what she feared: desire doomed to repeated frustration. Contrary to her assertions, Wollstonecraft's deepest fear centres not on the voraciousness of male sexual desire but on what she fears is its brevity.
>
> (Poovey 1984: 74)

Poovey then seeks to invert Wollstonecraft's text to show that her actual position involves a necessary 'repression' since 'far from being the learned response she asserts it is (and wishes it were), female sexuality is actually as demanding as male sexuality' (ibid.: 75). Poovey finds two important passages which, when read symptomatically, prove the existence of this repression. 'Wollstonecraft actually aspires to *be* a man' (ibid.: 57) says Poovey, who cites Mary Jacobus: Wollstonecraft 'speaks not so much *for* women, or *as* a woman, but *against* them – over their dead bodies' (cited in Poovey 1984: 255).

The first is a passage which attacks the undignified overindulgence of appetites, both eating and sex (Wollstonecraft 1983: 247–8). Poovey says 'clearly her disgust embraces both sexes here, for she is indicting sexual desire itself' (Poovey 1984: 75; 1989: 207). The second concerns an indirect reference to Milton's *Paradise Lost*. Wollstonecraft (1989: 264) says 'What are the cold, or feverish caresses of appetite, but sin embracing death?' Poovey notes that Wollstonecraft 'unconsciously . . . betrays her fear that female desire might in fact court man's lascivious and degrading attentions, that the subordinate position women have been given might be deserved' (Poovey 1984: 76), since in Milton it is Death which is the active principle: Sin says

I fled, but he pursu'd. . . .
And in embraces forcible and foul

Ingend'ring with me, of that rape begot
These yelling Monsters
                    (Cited in Poovey 1984: 76)

Poovey has no problem with this inversion, it proves that in Wollstone-craft, it is woman, 'she is the aggressor' (ibid.: 76). Other passages are cited to confirm Wollstonecraft's exaggerated disgust with 'female bodies and female desires' (ibid.: 77).

However there are severe problems with Poovey's analysis, certainly when the full complexity of Wollstonecraft's theoretical position is given its due. Poovey's insistent desire to show Wollstonecraft's repressive puritanism leads to a damaging attack on women as such, a kind of virulent Victorian hypocrisy a century before its time (in fact there is an advanced critique of this in *Vindication* (ch. 8)) which goes unnoticed. In pushing this line of thought too strongly, Poovey produces her own repressions: this time on Wollstonecraft's own thought. In the first instance Wollstonecraft's appeal to the critical analysis of the aristocracy, army, dissenters, etc., is certainly not to reveal that women are simply human and can be brought into the sphere of moral and theological discourse. It is to reveal the effects of power and of corruption and at the same time alienation. Very rarely is Poovey able to acknowledge that Wollstonecraft argues that women have power, or rather some women have considerable power and that this power is disastrous for women as a whole. Nowhere does Wollstonecraft deny that women have sexual appetites, (but she is consistent in arguing that 'men are more under the influence of their appetites than women' (Wollstonecraft 1983: 247)); rather she notes 'I only exclaim against the sexual desire of conquest when the heart is out of the question' (ibid.: 146–7). This is not an isolated or aberrant comment (ibid.: 114). The problem is, however, that 'the moral character of the chaster part of the sex, is undermined' by 'a very considerable number who are . . . standing dishes to which every glutton may have access' (ibid.: 248). As Wollstonecraft's strategy is to fight for the dignity of women and men, she tries to justify as legitimate a sexuality that only occurs when 'the feelings of a parent mingl[e] with an instinct merely animal' (ibid.: 248, cited by Poovey 1984: 75). And she indeed forcefully criticizes Rousseau for practising sexual self-denial, for this desire was displaced and 'debauched his imagination' (ibid.: 183).

In the second instance that Wollstonecraft inverts the positions of Sin and Death in her allusion to Milton, this again is in fact entirely consistent with her theory of alienated empowerment of women. Poovey however translates this highly charged and active power in Wollstonecraft into the passive mood:

women are for the most part, satisfied with the sensual gratification of male attention. And, because they are they participate in men's

voluptuous designs. By internalizing 'false notions of beauty and delicacy', they cultivate that 'sexual character' of the mind that actually
strengthens their chains. Women embrace their inessentialness . . .
they seek out lovers whose ingratiating manners flatter their self-
images; they are content to derive their identities from their relationships to men.

(Poovey 1984: 73)

Poovey has altogether overlooked another vocabulary of the text: women
'become tyrants; for it is not rational freedom, but a lawless kind of power,
resembling the authority exercised by the favourites of absolute monarchs,
which they obtain by debasing means' (Wollstonecraft 1983: 270); or
'indirectly they obtain too much power and are debased by their exertions
to obtain illicit sway' (ibid.: 286). Women, says Wollstonecraft, will not
'willingly resign the privileges of rank and sex for the privileges of humanity'
(ibid.: 263). The discourse is coherent. For Poovey the discourse is deeply
divided as Wollstonecraft tries to speak both as a woman and in a neutral
voice: 'the frustrations behind the contradictions evident in . . . her strongest polemic would be dispelled only when she found a way to allow the
writer and the woman to speak with one voice' (Poovey 1984: 81).

A puritan feminism: Cora Kaplan

Like Poovey, Kaplan considers the text principally from the point of view
of its attitudes to sexuality and subsequently as an analysis of women as
'a *lumpen* group who must undergo strenuous re-education' (Kaplan 1986:
38). Compared with other radicals of the 1790s, she says, Wollstonecraft
presents the sober, repressed face of puritanism: 'Wollstonecraft sets up
heartbreaking conditions for women's liberation – a little death, the death
of desire, the death of female pleasure' (ibid.: 39).

The text presents the 'negative construction of the sexual' at a time
when revolutionaries were working to elaborate the positive vista of social
transformation. Even her language was explicitly conceived as plain and
direct, reflecting the fact that she explicitly aimed at the audience of plain
bourgeois men.

Kaplan contrasts Wollstonecraft with later writers who could conceive
women as vanguard protagonists in the class struggle because of their
unique experience of oppression. The overall impression of the text is a
negative one of and for women, though on closer reading the problems
are more complex:

In *A Vindication* women's excessive interest in themselves as objects
and subjects of desire is theorised as an effect of the ideological inscription of male desire on female subjects who, as a result, bear a double
libidinal burden. But the language of that sober analysis is more inno-

vatory, less secure, and less connotive than the metaphorical matrix used to point and illustrate it. As a consequence there is a constant slippage back into a more naturalised and reactionary view of women, and a collapse of the two parts of the metaphors into each other.

(Kaplan 1986: 43)

These metaphors link, for example, women to lap-dogs, 'but', says Kaplan, 'it is the metonymic association of . . . "women", "spaniel" that tends to linger, rather than the intended metaphoric distance' (ibid.: 43). Likewise, the image of mob violence and its similarity to 'women's uncontrolled sexual behaviour' (ibid.: 44) leads to a reinforcement of the stereotype, not its critique. Kaplan finds it understandable that the text has been read against itself as a dangerous celebration of subversive female sexuality.

The most important and innovatory component of the text is a new theory of the 'processes by which gender ideologies become internalised' (ibid.: 44) yet even here the account is an exaggerated one so that even if:

Woman's reason may be the psychic heroine of *A Vindication* . . . its gothic villain, a polymorphous perverse sexuality, creeping out of every paragraph and worming is way into every warm corner of the text, seems in the end to win out.

(Kaplan 1986: 44–5)

Thus Wollstonecraft has 'nothing complimentary to say about women as they are'. Thus the effect of the argumentative imbalance is that the possibility of 'masculine' women is given approval, but 'feminine' men are something that does not appear: the very 'definitions of the feminine ideal . . . are shot through with dehumanising and immoral sensuality' (ibid.: 46).

As a result of this asymmetry, Wollstonecraft's language could be appropriated by conservatives like Jane Austen. Kaplan gives an example: although it is Mary Wollstonecraft who says that 'while women live, as it were by their personal charms, how can we expect them to discharge those ennobling duties which equally require exertion and self-denial', Kaplan notes 'it might as easily be Austen on Mary Crawford. In the same sentence, and in much the same terms, Wollstonecraft denounces hereditary aristocracy' (Kaplan 1986: 47). Thus even Kaplan's acknowledgement of the combination of the critique of aristocracy with this denunciation does not rescue it, since for Kaplan the text should, but does not, mention 'sequential pregnancies, exhausting child care in the grimmest conditions, the double yoke of waged and unpaid domestic labour . . . as the cause of women's degradation' (ibid.: 48). Indeed the whole of Wollstonecraft's work is an attempt to invert or reverse already given binary categories of class sexuality 'doesn't work, but its a good try' (ibid.: 49). Kaplan then cites Foucault to the effect that there is no single uniform sexuality, but rather sexuality itself is divided by class.

Thus Kaplan's verdict is that the *Vindication* presents a programme of 'equal rights and self-abnegating sexuality' (ibid.: 50) a programme that was bound to be limited in its historical appeal. This was 'not because an immanent and irrepressible sexuality broke through levels of female self-denial, but rather because the anti-erotic ethic itself foregrounded and constructed a sexualized subject' (ibid.: 50).

What is noticeable in this account and critique is the recognition that Wollstonecraft does present a theory of women's repressive empowerment ('the anti-aristocratic critique is foregrounded . . .' (ibid.: 42)) but that the critique of women's alienation is too strong, or rather 'the amassing of these metaphors of debased and disgusting female sexuality, even when they are ostensibly directed at the behaviour of a discredited class has the effect of doubling the sexual reference . . . it became extremely difficult for Wollstonecraft to keep her use of such images tied to a social and environmental analysis' (ibid.: 43). The effect is that even Kaplan refuses to acknowledge that Wollstonecraft offers an alternative conception of sexuality which is based on classical mythology, radical eighteenth-century theology, Enlightenment moral philosophy and a puritan aesthetic. Kaplan overlooks the moments in the text where Wollstonecraft does appear to talk of a vanguard of women 'who will assemble the men of abilities around them' (Wollstonecraft 1989: 247). Again it is simply not true to say that no mention of the condition of poor women is made in the text ('with respect to virtue . . . I have seen most in low life' (Wollstonecraft 1983: 171). Nor is it true that there is no mention of 'feminine men' (ibid.: 103, 258), or no mention of sequential pregnancies (but see ibid.: 315). It is Kaplan herself who imposes the blanket uniformity of 'gothic' sexuality over the whole of Wollstonecraft's analsyis of the moral condition of the various ranks of eighteenth-century society, in order to suggest the severe costs involved in the denial of a legitimate non-repressive female sexuality.

A repressive authoritarian feminism: Reiss

Timothy Reiss's position is the most explicit denial of any theory of alienation in the *Vindication*:

> She did not see herself as a member of a totally deprived class seeking to be included in the fold (she is not *pace* de Beauvoir, some 'Other'). Rather she was trying to readjust the order of beneficiaries, so to speak, in the dominant order.
>
> (Reiss in Kauffman 1989: 15)

This comment indicates the general line of argument, that Wollstone-craft's analysis was neither materialist nor revolutionary and was caught within the narrow limits of bourgeois rationalism. Indeed, says Reiss, Wollstonecraft's position is even more narrow, since her formulations on citizenship restrict women's contribution to that of motherhood (ibid.: 23). In fact much of the reading of *Vindication*, says Reiss, has to try to understand how Wollstonecraft attempts to reconcile the general ambition of equality with men, and at the same time to acknowledge and legitimate the domestication of women. Reiss concludes that she was forced

> to make motherhood the primary function of woman as social being, as 'citizen', despite her own actual and stated experience of the subor-dinate status this *necessarily* imposed on women, not seldom taking the form of a moral and intellectual brutalizing of the mind. Situating the statement of individuality first, Wollstonecraft found the distin-guishing *human* characteristic to be the familiar one of reason, and the distinguishing *female* characteristic to be that of childbirth.
>
> (Ibid.: 25)

All Wollstonecraft could do was to claim that women's duties were at least human ones.

Reiss pursues this theme and ends with the conclusion that she reaches a reductive position where there is 'nothing social whatever about maternal sentiment, that it was completely natural and biological' (ibid.: 38). And when Wollstonecraft says that because a real difference in 'bodily strength' exists, women are naturally rendered 'in some degree dependent on men', Reiss again is quick to say 'And so we return to biological determinism' (ibid.: 42). Reiss argues that the problem lies in the fact that the terminology used by Wollstonecraft is itself repressive, and as such she is never able to escape its effects: 'relying on such concepts is the source of all Wollstonecraft's contradictions' (ibid.: 41). In most important respects these contradictions remain 'hidden'. If she wants to argue that women are indeed human, the appeal she makes to humanity represses the fact that not all men are admitted to the fold: yet she is forced to adopt an appeal to manly or masculine virtues. She is not interested in 'transforming society. She simply wanted to extend to the excluded half of the human race rights and benefits already enjoyed by men, and which they frequently use to oppress women' (ibid.: 43).

For Reiss, Wollstonecraft is never able to pass the limits of bourgeois formulas, where even on problems such as prostitution, it is easy to see 'her obvious confusion' (ibid.: 27). Was it men or the prostitutes them-selves that were to blame? He suggests a passage such as: prostitutes 'trample on virgin bashfulness with a sort of bravado, and glorifying in their shame, become more audaciously lewd than men, however depraved, to whom this sexual quality has not been gratuitously granted, ever appear to be' (cited in ibid.: 27; Wollstonecraft 1983: 228). He notes that 'she appeared to view women, unlike men, as having a sexual quality "gratuitously granted" thus echoing one of the eighteenth century's more unsavoury assertions about women. No longer did she hint at male responsibility' (ibid.: 27). And Reiss concludes that Wollstonecraft is so concerned with 'access to privileges enjoyed by [some] men' that she 'did not pursue the matter of prostitution into the thicket of social and political conditions, why she is unconcerned with matters of class' (ibid.: 30). All that Wollstonecraft is interested in, according to Reiss, is 'her right to the *same* place in the sun enoyed by men' (ibid.: 32), although this formula expressly contradicts his earlier judgement.

Finally, Reiss turns to the question of power. He notes that for Woll-stonecraft

> within society any power based wholly on command and subordination – from that of an absolute prince to that functioning within the army . . . – was a threat to a society founded on rational equality. . . . Such an argument may have appeared revolutionary to the eighteeth century, but it was a more logical application of the principles upon which the (imaginary) British constitution 'claimed' to rest.
>
> (Ibid.: 45)

Wollstonecraft is explicit in claiming that it is not power that is the aim, but equality. In order to achieve this men and women should be educated together on the basis of reason and virtue. For Reiss these ideas mean that the 'actual social order *did* actually correspond to' the principles of the British constitution (ibid.: 45). Indeed she was not 'able to see any order but that of possessive individualism and authoritarian liberalism' (ibid.: 47).

Again, as with Poovey and Kaplan, there are serious problems in this account (see the critique by Frances Ferguson in Kauffman 1989: 51–62). Reiss has to argue that the text had little impact since it was caught in the contradictions of rationalism, and lacked a materialist basis. His argument is contextualized by his comment that even the American and French Revolutions did not 'herald' a general social transformation. Prob-lematically, he does not investigate the way in which the reaction against the French Revolution in the 1790s closed around the radicals and radical analysis in Britain after an initial effervescence which included the recep-tion of *Vindication* (see Janes 1978). Part of his analysis ignores Wollstonecraft's actual argument. For example on the question of prosti-tution she not only wrote of the social and economic condition of prosti-tutes, but attached the eighteenth century solution – homes for reforming prostitutes as ineffective – since they did not remedy the cause of the problem (Reiss 1989: 140, 218; and see Spender 1982: 111). Again, his comment concerning the phrase 'women have a sexual quality gratuitously granted' is a serious misreading, since the phrase is used earlier in the text: 'women are born, I now speak of a state of civilization, with certain sexual privileges, and whilst they are gratuitously granted them, few will think of works of supererogation' (Reiss 1989: 126), thus Wollstonecraft certainly hints at male responsibility.

But the basic problem in Reiss's account is the confusion over whether women are an alienated group or not. Here he argues at one moment they are simply, for Wollstonecraft, insiders who want to enter the sphere of privilege, at another he argues that they are radically excluded and want to enter the sphere of humanity. This is compounded, as it is in other critiques I have examined, with a serious misreading of Wollstonecraft's analysis of power. To reduce Wollstonecraft's critique of parasitism and aristocracy to a simple celebration of the British constitution entirely misses her thesis that 'the whole system of British politics, if system it may courteously be called, consisting in multiplying dependents and contriving taxes which grind the poor to pamper the rich' (Wollstonecraft 1983: 256), she even criticizes 'the barbarous useless parade of having sentinels on horseback at Whitehall . . . mere gothic grandeur' (ibid.: 260). In effect her position supports the close union of social effort and social respect against parasitic elites, but also a genuine, not alienated empowerment of women. Her 'revolution in female manners' (ibid.: 317), is aimed not to give women power over men (as Reiss notes, p. 45) but, as Wollstonecraft says, to give women power over themselves. For Reiss this does not amount to more than reformist 'authoritarian individualism', missing entirely Wollstonecraft's characterization of the epoch as one in which 'combustible materials cannot long be pent up; and giving vent in foreign wars and intestine insurrections, the people acquire some power in the tumult, which obliges their rulers to gloss over their oppression with a show of right' (ibid.: 98).

A feminism against the ideology of femininity: Spencer

A potentially far more positive reading of Vindication is given by Jane Spencer (1986). Her reading requires comparing this text with Wollstonecraft's novel Maria, Or the Wrongs of Woman ([1798] 1989, vol. 1), for the Vindication is transitional. In Spencer's reading the Vindication is remarkable in its intransigent opposition to the leading tendency of eighteenth-century women's writing:

> By criticizing all these 'mistaken notions of female excellence' Wollstonecraft attacked the entire ideology of femininity that had been developed during the century, and on the basis of which women had been accorded acceptance and respectability. It is hardly surprising that A Vindication of the Rights of Woman found only limited favour

among other women writers of the time. Its arguments were calculated to undermine their hard-won position. . . . Her boldness swept male chivalry away and forced prejudice into the open.

(Spencer 1986: 100)

For Spencer, however, *Vindication* does not develop a positive acknowledgement of women's emotion or sensibility, indeed Wollstonecraft had 'suppressed sensibility and seen reason as the ideal, with the result that her vision of liberation did not include any liberation of sexuality . . . she deprecated all idea of sexual fulfilment' (ibid.: 133).

But during the years after 1792 Wollstonecraft's experience had a profound effect on her views, argues Spencer, and she was able to 'explore the problems of feminine sensibility in a way that the earlier female sentimentalists could not . . . she developed a revolutionary view of sexuality' (ibid.: 133; a parallel view can be found in K. Ellis (1989: 93), whereas Mary Poovey took the diametrically opposed view that 'every sexual relation she depicts is dehumanising and revolting' and that in many respects the later work is 'a retreat from' the *Vindication* (Poovey 1984: 109, 110)). The novel is built around the experiences of two women, Maria and Jemima, the first a respectable woman condemned to a madhouse by a rapacious husband, the latter coming from a background of poverty and prostitution. In the madhouse Maria falls in love with a wrongfully imprisoned young man, and with assistance from Jemima, they escape. However, Maria's husband sues the young man for seduction and claims damages. Maria argues in court that this claim annihilates her as a woman since it suppresses the fact that she acted out of her own will. In the case of Jemima, it is clear on the other hand that since she was only ever forced into sexual submission, she too is also annihilated as woman. Spencer quotes Maria 'When novelists or moralists praise as a virtue, a woman's coldness of constitution, and want of passion. . . . I am disgusted . . . we cannot, without depraving our minds, endeavour to please a lover or husband, but in proportion as he pleases us. Men, more effectually to enslave us, may inculcate this partial morality' (cited in Spencer 1986: 134). Against this the judge in the case notes strictly that 'if women were allowed to plead their feelings, as an excuse or palliation of infidelity, it was opening a flood-gate for immorality' (ibid.: 134–5). For Spencer, Wollstonecraft's position moves therefore to one which recognizes not just the right to sexual feeling but also 'feeling as a necessary instrument of female liberation', since it was the basis from which artificial notions of female sensibility could be attacked as an 'oppressive social construct' (ibid.: 135). The process is reflected in the experience of Jemima, who is described in the novel as having her humanity numbed by her tribulations, but on hearing that 'Maria's child was torn from her breast that "the women awoke in a bosom long estranged from feminine emotions" and she is redeemed through feeling'. Spencer concludes that the novel 'turns all the assumptions of the seduction tale upside-down, and within its keen analysis of women's imprisonment within patriarchy is an optimistic vision of liberation through the feeling that in most seduction leads to ruin' (ibid.: 136).

The problem with this analysis does not lie with the interpretation of the novel, but rather with that of the *Vindication*. Clearly Wollstonecraft attacks the notion of seduction in exactly the same way, but adds that the law should remain in force as long as women 'depend on man for subsistance' (Wollstonecraft 1983: 164). But it is necessary to look in detail at Spencer's argument. The passage which is used as the key in Spencer's analysis is Wollstonecraft's notorious suggestion that 'In order to fulfil the duties of life . . . a master and a mistress of a family ought not to continue to love each other with passion. . . . I will go still further, and advance . . . that an unhappy marriage is often very advantageous to a family, and that the neglected wife is, in general, the best mother' (cited in Spencer 1986: 133). This is an astonishing passage, and sufficiently complex to lead many interpretations immediately to the conclusion that Wollstonecraft simply calls for a repressive regime which will add to the miseries of women. Spencer argues just that.

However, on closer analysis, it is clear that Wollstonecraft sanctions a period of 'love with passion' as well as one of 'tenderness' after passion; also that the unhappy marriage is not always, her word is 'often', advantageous; and third, the best mothers are 'in general' neglected wives. The rationale for these views lies in Wollstonecraft's notion of the dangers for women and children: if the mother is 'lost in the coquette, and, instead of making friends of her daughters, view them with eyes askance, for they are rivals – rivals more cruel than any other' (Wollstonecraft 1983: 137). Indeed as her doctrine predicts the inevitable decline of love, it is important that the wife establishes 'her husband's respect before it is necessary to exert mean arts to please him and feed a dying flame, which nature doomed to expire when the object became familiar . . . this is the natural death of love'. Wollstonecraft also adds that if the woman be widowed she should remain simply devoted to her children, she ideally 'represses the first faint dawning of a natural inclination, before it ripens into love . . . forgets the pleasure of an awakening passion . . . her children have her love' (ibid.: 138–9). Essentially power over emotion must develop (ibid.: 161) accompanied by affection, friendship, respect; what she calls elsewhere 'chaste love', and she mocks those husbands who 'seduce their wives' (ibid.: 167). 'Love and friendship cannot subsist in the same bosom . . . and for the same object can only be felt in succession' (ibid.: 167). And 'why must the female mind be tainted by coquettish arts to gratify the sensualist, and prevent love from subsiding into friendship, or compassionate tenderness?' (ibid.: 115).

But there is another reason why love should die in marriage, or rather as she insists love 'considered as an animal appetite', at least when there are children. First, women who are 'rendered licentious' neglect their children (ibid.: 167). (Later in the text she argues that 'the tenderness which a man will feel for the mother of his children is an excellent substitute for the ardour of unsatisfied passions, but to prolong that ardour is indelicate, not to say immodest for women to feign an unnatural coldness of constitution' (ibid.: 238); cf. 'the cold caresses of appetite' (ibid.: 316).) Second, 'there are many husbands so devoid of sense and parental affection that, during the first effervescence of voluptuous fondness, they refuse to let their wives suckle their children' (ibid.: 167, 254). Furthermore, if 'women suckle their children, they would preserve their own health' and she notes if things were wisely ordered 'there would be such an interval between the birth of each child, that we should seldom see a houseful of babes' (ibid.: 315). On the other hand, the situation of infidelity in marriage by women calls forth her most violent denunciations: a woman in this situation breaks 'a sacred engagement and becomes a cruel mother when she is a false and faithless wife. If her husband have still an affection for her, the arts which she must practise to deceive him, will render her the most contemptible of human beings' (ibid.: 241). Thus the 'neglected' wife should not be thought the deceived wife, and if the wife does not love the husband this in itself is not a sufficient condition for virtue, since some women in this condition often 'give themselves entirely up to vanity and dissipation, neglecting every domestic duty' (ibid.: 242).

But Wollstonecraft does not hold conventional ideas about marriage[8] or parenthood[9] in any case. She admits she 'respects' marriage, and finds it 'the foundation of almost every social virtue' (ibid.: 165), she opposes polygamy, and refuses the title wife to mistresses who bear children to men otherwise married, yet she insists they should not be treated as prostitutes but with respect. Essentially, most of the trappings of marriage, for Wollstonecraft, are purely formal, like the concern for a reputation 'independent of its being one of the natural rewards of virtue'. True religion and virtue lie elsewhere, and 'when they reside in the heart' do not 'require such a puerile attention to mere ceremonies' (ibid.: 243). Her attitude to parents is at least as radical as her attitude to women, for she also applies, with qualifications, the whole critique of aristocracy to this group as well (ibid.: 268).

In the end, however, Spencer notes that the outcome of the novel *Maria* actually runs as would be expected from the *Vindication*. Maria's lover 'proved unfaithful, but [this] is implicit in the lovers's relationship from the outset . . . the heroine's tendency to fall into romantic idealization is linked to women's general condition, as *The Rights of Woman* had argued' (Spencer 1986: 135).

COMPONENTS OF WOLLSTONECRAFT'S THEORY

It could certainly be argued, and indeed has (see Guralnick 1977), that the *Vindication* is above all a radical political intervention even before it is a feminist statement. Its first chapter scarcely mentions women and stakes its claims in a range of contested terrains: philosophy, politics, theology, history, sociology, literature. For a woman to think for herself, she says later (Wollstonecraft 1983: 257), 'is an Herculean task . . . she has difficulties peculiar to her sex to overcome'. In the first chapter she rapidly sets out a set of claims worked out primarily in relation to an appropriation and critique of radical Enlightenment theory. The framework constructed is of a transformed Rousseauism: a corrupt society can be revolutionized by an oppressed people and humanity perfected if it recognizes the force of reason and virtue in all its citizens by rigorously opposing all forms of tyranny. The crucial thesis is one which identifies the true source of modern corruption, the couple: pleasure and power. Where commentators like Poovey have seen only a list of institutions that can form the basis of reasoning by analogy, Wollstonecraft in fact presents a thesis: 'every profession in which great subordination of rank constitutes its power, is highly injurious to morality' (ibid.: 96). Conversely 'the more equality there is established . . . the more virtue and happiness will reign' (ibid.: 96). The basic and crucial dynamics here are suggested as articulated around the fact that where power differentials exist 'all feelings . . . are stifled by flattery, and reflection shut out by pleasure' (ibid.: 96). Thus she has no hesitation in describing 'the great' as weak, 'artificial beings' (ibid.: 81), the 'insignificancy of character which renders the society of the *great* so insipid' (ibid.: 140). Logically this should mean that the great are themselves caught, and are oppressed. In fact, consistently, she does call for the time when 'kings and nobles, enlightened by reason, throw off their gaudy hereditary trappings' (ibid.: 103) as if they were the chains of enslavement. Even more surprising is her view that 'the present system of war has little connection with virtue of any denomination, being rather the school of *finesse* and effeminacy than of fortitude' (ibid.: 258). Indeed 'the days of heroism are over' (ibid.: 255).

The second and third chapters examine closely representative opinions on sexual differentiated culture. They provide critiques of Milton, Gregory and Rousseau on a wide front. But it is towards the end of the third chapter that Wollstonecraft's central argument is presented in quasi-theological terms:

> if the existence of an evil being were allowed who . . . went about seeking whom he should devour, he could not more effectually degrade the human character, than by giving man absolute power. The argument branches into various ramifications . . . every extrinsic advantage

that exalt a man above his fellows, without any mental exertion, sink him in reality below them. . . . Women . . . obtaining power by unjust means, by practising or fostering vice, evidently lose the rank which reason would assign them, and they become either abject slaves or capricious tyrants. They lose all simplicity, all dignity of mind, in acquiring power.

(Ibid.: 131–2)

There follow four paragraphs of intense, anxious theological reflection.[10] But the specific features of Wollstonecraft's argument become clear. In the case of women we find not only the corrupting existence of power but also that this power is unjust, resulting from 'sensual homage paid to beauty: – to beauty of features' (ibid.: 134). However it is only in the fourth chapter that Wollstonecraft presents Adam Smith's long description of the corruption of the aristocracy which she then applies directly to women who are, from that moment, treated directly as a sexual aristocracy. Wollstonecraft turns on this aristocracy the full venom of the Enlightenment critique of parasitic elites, with the further specification that this particular aristocracy is not like any other, for it is the most oppressed, and she notes that 'the gangrene which the vices engendered by oppression have produced, is not confined to the morbid part, but pervades society at large' (ibid.: 299).

In order to highlight the specific features of Wollstonecraft's theory of alienation, it is necessary to sketch very briefly her notion of non-alienated sexuality.[11] What she terms natural human sexuality necessarily combines mind and body: it therefore transcends pure sensual appetite, but is driven by it. The appetite and passion that bring man and woman together, she says, must be given human dignity through their relation to the purpose of conception. The act is then not merely a physical indulgence, a pure pleasure; it is rather, in this perspective, both meaningful and useful. This natural creativity should not be interrupted after conception (with abortion) or after birth of the child (abandonment). In a marriage, the initial passions should be transformed into the sublime emotion of friendship based on respect (ibid.: 167). To enable this necessary transition to occur in society implied, she thought, the overturning of the current order of values.

Thus the sexual revolution in the 1790s was constructed as a struggle against the submission to pure desire (passion), pure physical pleasure (appetite), phenomena associated in theory with aristocracy, wealth, corrupt power. In the sphere of sexuality, it was clear to Wollstonecraft that the driving force of the 'false system' was male appetite (and its mode: gallantry) with the corresponding formation and seduction of a parasitic sexual aristocracy (women). Wollstonecraft gave a full account and critique of the system of education which reproduced mentally and physically purely 'feminine' women. It was a system which segregated females from males, and systematically enfeebled them: the ideologies supporting this system were irrational and closely driven by male sexual interests, but male attention was not a genuine homage but an insincere servility.

The resulting feminine domination was not simple, however. There is a double enslavement: the libertines to women (women become a 'pampered' aristocracy); but women become trapped in their own egotistical and artificial pleasure–power prison, with disastrous consequences for the social and political position of women as a whole. The entire superstructure of sexual behaviour, based on the ennoblement of women through courtesy and ritual, creates the 'fair sex'; with no means to attain virtue, it deludes itself that it can retain social respect, for at base men despise women after they have used them precisely because they have barred them from reason and, therefore, active, positive virtue: 'men of fancy . . . outwardly respect and inwardly despise the weak creatures they . . . sport with' (Wollstonecraft 1983: 196). Thus 'the libertinism, and even the virtues of superior men, will always give women, of some description, great power over them; and these weak women, under the influence of childish passions and selfish vanity, will throw a false light over the objects which the very men view with their eyes, who ought to enlighten their judgement' (ibid.: 294).

On the other hand 'in proportion as men acquire virtue and delicacy, by the exertion of reason, they will look for both in women' (ibid.: 295). Virtue is the pivotal term around which the theory turns: it is a quality which must be earned, the product of moral labour, yet appears in two different forms. As society is constituted, says Wollstonecraft, it is men who have access to the positive, active vritues, while women insofar as they are virtuous claim merely the negative ones (patience, chastity, docility, good humour, flexibility, etc. (ibid.: 148)). Enlightenment philosophers generally held the view that 'passions were conquerable, not merely by theoretical reason, but by the actual practice of virtue, politeness, or religion', notes Mullan (1988: 24). Clearly one of the great exceptions, apart from Mandeville and Hume, was Wollstonecraft, for whom the virtues of women, this 'stupendous fabric' were nothing but a result of the 'wayward fluctuating feelings of men . . . virtue, as well as religion has been subjected to the decisions of taste' (Wollstonecraft 1983: 116); indeed a basic thesis is that 'the grand source of female depravity, [is] the impossibility of regaining respectability by a return to virtue, though men preserve theirs during the indulgence of vice' (ibid.: 242), dependent on the conclusion that 'the sexual distinction which men have so warmly insisted upon is arbitrary' (ibid.: 318).

Thus the conception of the position of women in society begins and ends with the claim that what is essential to humanity is the potential of each person to achieve vritue through the action of reason, that is, in the active useful work which results in positive moral progress. Some men have access to this sphere; women, who nevertheless have all the apparent attributes of human creatures, are barred from it by a whole social system: thus the most oppressed among women are those women who actively develop their talents, inwardly attain virtue, but are then denied any social recognition (ibid.: 262). Current society is characterized by severe discrepancies between virtues and reward, and is dominated by a number of specific 'false systems' which act to appropriate just approbation at the formal level.

Despite Wollstonecraft's critical distance from materialism,[12] her analysis considers both the physical and the intellectual effects of these false systems on women. Women are physically weakened, and there is a serious regression in the aesthetic ideal in Western civilization compared with antiquity. Conventions exclude women from physical effort, and the ideal is a perverted, unnatural one of 'listless inactivity'. Because intellect is not developed, women are dominated by the senses, and are 'localized' both socially and intellectually. 'Slaves to their senses' as a way to achieve power, but through this power they are multiply trapped and oppressed. They lose contact with their own nature, their individual potential human capacity to create virtue; they become the despised and pitied half of humankind, formed and colluding in a system that reproduces their position as paradoxically dependent and corrupt. What is striking in Wollstonecraft's account is that although women are the oppressed sex, this is not merely a passive process whereby women are simply dominated by a superior force: they are challenged to enter (ibid.: 231), after having been suitably formed subjectively, into a sport.[13] Behind this sport is the formation of women's dependence and the 'insolent condescension of protectorship' (ibid.: 232). But the play is between 'gallantry and coquetry' (ibid.: 288) which mirror each other in their structure. Gallantry based on 'libidinous mockery' (ibid.: 232), and coquetry on 'metricious airs and a whole science of wantonness' (ibid.: 165). This leads to a vanity evident in ornamentation, in fashion, even in writing: this is why the *Vindication* begins with the ambition and intention of being useful and, in not 'fabricating the turgid bombast of artificial feelings' it will be 'employed about things, not words' (ibid.: 82). The challenge of the *Vindication* is that it is in its own terms an intellectual effort of reason: this alone makes it a claim on virtue, but it is also a practice of creating positive virtue and the specific refusal of the 'impudent dross' of seduction (ibid.: 231).

The fundamental contrast in the *Vindication* is that between authority based on reason and beauty of mind ('male beauty' (ibid.: 162)), and that based, in relation to women, on physical beauty. It produces in men a dual standard, a radical inconsistency: 'why do they expect virtue from a slave, from a being whom the constitution of civil society has rendered weak, if not vicious?' (ibid.: 134). But if men pay 'sensual homage' to beauty (ibid.: 134) and 'women . . . cunningly obtain . . . power by playing on the *weakness* of men' (ibid.: 125), this notion of beauty is 'artificial' and 'genteel women are, literally speaking, slaves to their bodies, and glory in their subjection' (ibid.: 130). Yet at the same time 'They want a lover, and protector; and behold him kneeling before them – bravery prostrate to beauty!' (ibid.: 225). But Wollstonecraft displays her own hand: in love, the revolution means that one must submit not to physical charm or beauty but to reason: 'I love man as my fellow; but his sceptre, real or usurped, extends not to me, unless the reason of an individual demands my homage; and even then the submission is to reason, and not to man' (ibid.: 121).

The fact that women's power rests on an 'extrinsic' fact, that

> females have been insulated as it were; and while they have been stripped of the virtues that should clothe humanity, they have been decked with artificial graces that enable them to exercise a short-lived tyranny. Love in their bosoms, taking place of every nobler passion, their sole ambition is to be fair, to raise emotion instead of inspiring respect; and this ignoble desire, like the servility in absolute monarchies, destroys all strength of character. Liberty is the mother of virtue, and if women be, by their very constitution, slaves . . . they must ever languish like exotics, and be reckoned beautiful flaws in nature.
>
> (Ibid.: 121–2)

Towards an alliance with men

Thus Cora Kaplan is perhaps wrong to think that the gothic villain is raw sexuality itself, for sexual appetites are only one among many that have to be subordinated in order to humanize and politicize them. Wollstonecraft's gothic feminism is more direct, and unveils a portrait of a seduced, alienated, tyrannical woman as a crucial enemy of the women's cause, a woman who claimed a 'distinguishing taste and puny appetite', yet who can insult a 'worthy old gentlewoman, whom unexpected misfortunes . . . made dependent on her ostentatious bounty'. This woman, says Wollstonecraft is 'not a more irrational monster than some of the Roman emperors who were depraved by lawless power' (ibid.: 130). Such women are alienated from their body, their mind, their family, the community, their emotions, and from themselves. Wollstonecraft had little hesitation in endeavouring to persuade women, these 'monsters who scarcely have shewn any discernment of human excellence' (ibid.: 122) to become 'more masculine' (ibid.: 83) in order to realize their true nature.

The positive value and the emphasis given to the 'masculine' in

Wollstonecraft, has almost invariably been read as a simple but deep capitulation and acceptance of male hegemony, even a desire to be a man. Some have recognized, like Caplan and Spencer, that there is another more complex aspect to this, but her vocabulary is 'innovatory' and 'uncertain'. There are exceptions to this general view. Easlea (1981) ends his examination of science and gender oppression with a strong appeal to the validity of Wollstonecraft's ethic of compassion and communication, against the desires of masculine power and grandeur – which call, he says, for a gentler world ('the welfare of society is not built on extraordinary exertions' (Wollstonecraft cited in Easlea 1981: 281)). Veeder has also noted that she calls for a 'redefinition of masculinity' in a perspective that has a complex view of men: power makes men 'effeminate' but 'virtue knows no gender' (Veeder 1986: 28). Indeed, says Veeder, Wollstonecraft tries to outline a series of virtues to which men, like women, must submit.

These analyses point to a new and important direction in the debate on Wollstonecraft, but take only the first steps. Clearly reason, like virtue, is not gendered in itself for Wollstonecraft, since she appeals to it herself and insists that it must be open to all. Other terms like modesty and chastity, have positive value and are already shared to some extent between the sexes (modesty is not the monopoly of women 'for the world contains many modest men' (Wollstonecraft 1983: 230)). Yet 'as a sex women are more chaste than men' and as modesty is associated with chastity this is an important way in which a virtue is achieved. But here, Wollstonecraft insists, this achievement is not the result of activity (the 'virtue is ascribed' (ibid.: 231), whereas men 'produce' modesty through the action of reason.[14]

Wollstonecraft's reflections do not stop here. She suggests that 'a man of delicacy carries his notion of modesty still further, for neither weakness nor sensibility will gratify him – he looks for affection' (ibid.: 233). These terms are highly significant and begin to make up an inventory of the feminine virtues and graces, even if they are immediately applied both to women and men. In fact she makes her own fundamental challenge to men in these very terms: sexual conquest can be envisaged in two forms she says – either where a 'sensibility is surprised', a triumph over a personal weakness, or a 'real conquest . . . that over affection not taken by surprise . . . where a woman gives up all the world deliberately for love' (ibid.: 233). All the 'advantage' on this side of the equation is with women, especially in relation to 'propriety of behaviour'; it is from this point of view that 'men must become more chaste' if women's position is to be radically transformed.

At this juncture, however, to point up the political orientation of these observations, it is necessary to return to the short introduction to the text where Wollstonecraft insists on 'dismissing . . . those pretty feminine phrases, which the men condescendingly use to soften our slavish dependence'. Here, 'soft phrases' about '*fascinating* graces', 'susceptibility of the heart', 'delicacy of sentiment', 'refinment of taste', 'elegancy of mind', 'sweet docility of manners', are said to be 'almost synonymous with epithets of weakness', which 'characterise the weaker vessel'. Such terminology is stigmatized as part of the weaponry of male supremacy and manipulation (ibid.: 81–2).

Wollstonecraft applies to this region of social struggle exactly the same logic as to all others and immediately conjures up the possibility of 'false delicacy', or 'squeamish delicacy' and prudishness. She stresses consistently the necessity for an openness of language on the question of sexuality especially in education.[15] If delicacy is a term closely embedded in her vocabulary relating to the body and sexuality, indelicacy is associated with indecency and disgust (ibid.: 235, 316): purely physical bodily processes without human compassion or meaning immediately produce revulsion and nausea. 'Squeamish delicacy' can produce an inability to help a sick person or to help a sick person with dignity; more generally, in contrast to male society, 'women are too familiar with each other' (ibid.: 234–5, a widely held view in this period, see Tomalin 1974: 18; and Auerbach 1978: 14–15).

This logic leads Wollstonecraft to her asceticized concept of human 'graces' which are developed specifically, but from a completely altered point of view, to women: cleanliness, neatness, personal reserve. She stresses now, however, that these are to be equally applied to both sexes as a pillar of 'domestic affection'. Elsewhere she had prepared the ground by insisting on the necessary discipline and severity of attitude that the self must be subjected to (Wollstonecraft 1983: 160), yet at the same time the attitude to the body which is at the foundation of this must be resacralized (ibid.: 230, 238). Although she associates a number of male figures with modesty (ibid.: 227–8) she invokes the beauty of the image of the Goddess of chastity, Diana, her 'conscious dignity', her 'placid fervour', her 'mild reflection' and the quality of the virtue of modesty that chastity, under the impress of understanding and humanity, achieves. And the importance of modesty, says Wollstonecraft is that it mellows 'each harsh feature of a character . . . and softens the tone of the sublimest virtues till they all melt into humanity' (ibid.: 227).[16] This reversal is one of the most striking strategic components of the text as it becomes clear that, although the virtues cannot be reduced to sexual difference, they nevertheless are gendered and constitute the site of an intense struggle. But social progress is not easy here; for, instead of demanding an inner chastity, the current social order induces women to establish a 'good reputation'. But no basic improvement in women's condition can be achieved on the basis of an imposition of 'rules of behaviour' (ibid.: 247), since they only produce 'insipid decency' (ibid.: 242). In fact 'in proportion as this regard for the reputation of chastity is prized by women, it is despised by men: and the two extremes are equally destructive to morality' (ibid.: 247). There is a gross hypocrisy in 'the woman of reputation' who is 'white as the driven snow [yet] who smiles on the libertine whilst she spurns the victims of his lawless appetites and their own folly' (ibid.: 250), and her contribution to the cause of women is rendered nugatory.

Wollstonecraft's revolution begins as an inner one and cannot be accomplished through the simple alteration of forms, ceremonies and rules of behaviour, though these rituals are productive of false systems. But on the basis of hard-won inner strengths and a revolution in manners, Wollstonecraft attempts to construct an alliance with men (especially 'men who are not always men in the company of women' (ibid.: 230)[17] to specify the conditions for the formation of this consciousness and to break up the univocal correspondences between sex and gender. Although read as an appeal to women to become masculine, *Vindication* more dangerously appeals to a purer political, egalitarian, more complex humanist practice of modesty and compassion in the completion of the bourgeois revolution, and in so doing, intervenes in the process of the highly political formation of both femininity and masculinity.

Chapter 3

Karl Marx: woman as black Madonna

Who of my many slanderers and snake-tongued enemies had ever reproached me that I am destined to play the role of chief lover in a second-class theatre? Yet it is true.

(Marx in Padover 1979: 103)

Marx himself wrote sparsely on gender issues, almost nothing on sexuality and very little on the 'woman question'. Recent examinations, such as Christine Di Stephano's essay ('Masculine Marx' in Shanley and Pateman 1991), spend little effort in textual analysis, and symptomatically, Di Stephano devotes only eight pages of her thirteen-page essay to a discussion of Marx himself, and all she wants to argue is that Marx 'evinces a combative, heroic, and hence masculine style'. Her starting point is the conceptualization of society as given in works such as *The German Ideology* which, in her view, suppresses the whole fact of human physical reproduction so that the appearance of man is a magical creation *ex nihilo*: men appear 'already born and nurtured'. Thus the whole account of gender in Marx is deeply 'complicitous with patriarchal history and ideology' (ibid.: 153). Marx's conceptualization of communism, she says, in which individuals are alone responsible for their own creation of reality exists in a form of 'post-embeddedness' which is a 'dangerous and arrogant fiction'. Even if there is, in the young Marx, a 'yearning for a genuine, mutually reciprocal relation . . . between men and women' there is, in general, in his mature writings a systematic repression of the importance of the mother. His theory represents in this form a 'clean and ultimate release from the (m)other' (ibid.: : 153–9).[1]

In fact, this account, which is not altogether untypical, seems to avoid a direct examination of Marx's thought on gender, or on women, or on issues directly related to the status of women. It does not try to account, either, for the fact that there is so little discussion of women in Marx, nor pose the more interesting question as to why there is no original contribution to the question of gender oppression from such an original and daring, and one must insist, dangerous thinker. In this chapter I want to pursue this, but in order to do so it is necessary to chart briefly some elements of the background to Marx's own personal development and involvement. Marx's theoretically formative years, especially those between 1836 and 1848 (from his eighteenth to thirtieth years) have been the subject of intense scrutiny, and now there are a number of excellent attempts to identify the precise phases of his intellectual evolution. These attempts either begin with the crucial facts of the biography, or the specific stages of his thought. If there is an attempt to link the two together, the biographical and the analytical-theoretical, it is primarily at the point at which the political experiences interconnect with the problems encountered in theoretical development. It is my contention that this line of enquiry must be broadened considerably if we are to pose questions fruitfully here about gender in relation to Marx – about Marx's own attitudes to gender, to masculinity – and ultimately why, in the formation of the objects of his theoretical work, gender was fundamentally excluded.

Firstly then, the discussion requires a good deal of contextualization. Marx was born in 1818 in the period that was in the immediate aftermath of the French Revolution and the wars which followed it. In Germany there had been widespread support for the Enlightenment criticism of traditional authority, as witness the celebration of reason in Kant and Hegel. In Marx's youth, Hegel was the dominant force in German philosophy and was generally supported by the liberal state up until 1840 and the death of Wilhelm III. In fact, Hegel's philosophy was interpreted in many different ways: there was liberal-state Hegelianism, and there were right-wing and left-wing Hegelian philosophical schools. The influence of Saint-Simonian ideas also spread rapidly to Germany through intellectuals such as Heine. In this situation there were also strong bases for conservative and reactionary counter-currents in various spheres; in art, in theology, and in the state itself. In the 1840s there was intensified polarization and division amongst the various social and intellectual forces, which was to culminate in the revolutions which spread across Europe in 1848. After the revolutionary waves subsided, there were trials of the leading communists, and the revolutionary organizations themselves were disbanded.

Some of the spheres of increasing debate and antagonism must be examined in more detail.

The Church

The most notable feature of the religious background was the Protestant Pietist awakening – the 'Erweckungsbewegung' – which began in the 1820s. It was a movement of intellectuals and officials, a 'major reaction against eighteeth-century rationalism' (Crouter 1988: 69), not a genuine social movement from the community. Its main aim was 'the control and discipline of subjective religious experience by orthodox dogma, and the total subjection of the individual to divinely constituted authority' (Toews 1980: 245). Initially an alliance between the followers of the theologian Schleiermacher at Berlin University, and a group of Prussian aristocratic 'patriarchs', united by friendships and intermarriage, it developed into a Hegelian conservatism linked also in alliance with Catholics (e.g. F. K. von Savigny). The institutional forum was the Evangelische Kirchenzeitung, of 1827, but by 1830 this had split into an ultraconservative wing around the writings of Hengstenberg (1802–69) on the one hand, and Schleiermacher (now sometimes called the 'father of Protestant liberal theology' (Foreman, J. 1977: ix)) on the other. In the version developed by Hengstenberg, the only way to salvation was the acknowledgement of human depravity and utter self-surrender to God. Salvation required faith, not reason; and therefore the approach to the Bible was literalist. This movement was also strictly opposed to social revolution, as this violated divine law embodied in social relations. Liberal theologians, such as Strauss, were dismissed by universities under the influence of this movement which gradually extended its control. The leading hope of the movement was the young Crown Prince, Wilhelm, who came to power in 1840. The essential aspect of Wilhelm's reign was an 'attempt to replace the rational absolutism of the bureaucratic state with a political community in which the king ruled by divine right' (Toews 1980: 253). The new reign systematically replaced Hegelians as well as liberals throughout the educational institutions, and Schelling was tempted back to Berlin in an attempt to counter the subversive tendencies of Hegelian rationalism.

Romanticism and art

German Romanticism was born at the end of the eighteenth century with a wave of philosophers and poets (including Fichte, Schiller, Novalis, Schlegel, Hölderlin, Kleist and many others). This was a vast movement of protest against a simple killing off of the gods in a new technical quantitative universe, it is the 'first self-critique of modernity', for 'the romantic generation suffers from the increasing profanation of the world, from its mere mechanistic interpretations, from the disappearance of the poetry of life' (Henkel, cited in Wessell 1979: 16). Hegel wrote a critique of the movement in his *Aesthetics* where he defined the romantic as facing a profound bifurcation in the world: the purely spiritual world and the external empirical and real world. Romanticism is characterized by renewed valorization of love and honour. In religion it is love which comes to dominate all attitudes. Love is, then, lived in its vicissitudes, its collisions with legal and family realities, collisions with misfortunes stemming from reality, confrontations with contingencies of all kinds.

And, says Hegel, 'since it makes itself alone into the essential and even the sole or supreme business of life, not merely can it decide to sacrifice everything else and fly with the beloved into a desert, but in its extreme, where indeed it is unbeautiful, it proceeds to the unfree, slavish, and shameless sacrifice of the dignity of man' as in von Kleist (Hegel 1975, vol. I: 565).

But against the whole tendency of romantic art, there was an attempt on the part of the reaction to Enlightenment extremes; a group of artists, the Nazarenes, tried to resurrect gothic forms. These artists, wearing long hair after the style of Dührer, went to live as chaste artist-monks in a monastery near Rome where they became a centre of specifically neo-Catholic opposition to the Enlightenment. The Prussian feudalist aristocracy became major patrons of this movement, symbolized by the painting of the Madonna by Peter Cornelius. For radical Saint-Simonian influenced critics like Heine, this movement produced mournful spiritualized paintings of a 'sadness unto death'. For Heine, the Nazarenes were strictly a reactionary tendency which opposed the light and ideals of the Greeks. Heine proposed a Saint-Simonian reading of Hegel's aesthetics which stressed the radical, avant-garde role of the artist as the poetic innovator of the new society, even though Hegel had criticized the Greek's enslavement to the senses. This radicalization of Hegel was taken further by Bruno Bauer, who even talked of Hegel's Hellenic Jacobinism. This interpretation of art was highly critical of apolitical, or reactionary forms, and wanted a practical, partisan political art. Feuerbach also criticized the 'false consciousness' of these paintings: the church Madonna remains lifeless in the church, a suitable art for Prussians who were alienated from their own senses. In a typically acidic analysis he said 'the more meaning they placed on the negation of sensuality, the greater . . . the meaning of the virgin Mary . . . the more the sensual is denied, the more sensual is the God, to whom the sensual is sacrificed' (cited in M. Rose 1984: 29). This neo-gothic art was, for Feuerbach, an ally for the Pietists in which sublimated sensuality only gave issue to pallid fetish.

Philosophy

Hegel's work, as we have seen, appeared essentially ambiguous and wide open to interpretation. In the period 1797–8 he wrote a highly romantic fragment on the theme of love, where two lovers formed a living whole, in which property could come to separate them 'by making them aware of their individuality as well as destroying their reciprocity': 'genuine love excludes all oppositions' he pronounced (cited by Benhabib in Shanley and Pateman 1991: 137). But Hegel did not develop a radical or revolutionary analysis out of this, indeed he ended by defining the specific sphere of the woman's realm as the family and motherhood. This was strictly conceived as a modern egalitarian form where monogamy was appropriate to the highest ideals of reciprocity and complementarity. His venom was aimed mainly at the revolutionary excesses of Romanticism, in this case Schlegel rather than Kleist: free sexuality simply translates into a new exploitation of women under the guise of a new freedom. Where the revolutionaries attack marriage, this is done, he said, in complete surrender to the principles of inner subjective freedom and in total abandonment of objective principles of law. Schlegel's *Lucinde* was based on the real character Caroline Michaelis, who, as an 'intellectual companion, a revolutionary, a mother, and a lover', lived in the same house as Hegel 1801–3 (Benhabib 1991: 140). Hegel was appalled: 'the Devil has fetched her' he is reported to have said. Hegel attacked Schlegel for indulgence in allowing the free reign of love and sexual passion over objective relations. Schlegel argued that Greek art culminated in periods in which women had equal attributes and status, and that the division between the sexes was a tragedy which deprived men of essential qualities. His interpretation of *Antigone* represents Antigone as an androgynous ideal; Hegel's interpretation, as Benhabib points out, donates to Cleon the powers of this world, and the decline of the significance of family and of women is precisely what makes possible the rise of the Enlightenment. Women came to represent for Hegel 'the everlasting irony [in the life] of the community' – who change 'by intrigue the universal end of government into a private end' (see Benhabib 1991: 142).

There was a striking internal differentiation of position among the left Hegelians, the leaders of whom were Strauss, Bauer, Ruge, Stirner and Feuerbach (see Toews 1980: 235ff.). It was probably the latter who symbolized the whole trend in the development of a 'new philosophy' that was at once more in touch with 'reality' and for whom 'only in feeling and in love does "this" as in "this" person . . . have absolute value' (Feuerbach 1966: 52). The movement against Hegelian and Nazarene abstraction is clear: 'God, the One . . . is known by contact and direct presence; (ibid.: 46). Nazarene monks and their new forms of mortification, not rehabilitation, of the flesh, 'could more easily dispense with real woman in proportion as an ideal woman was an object of love . . . the greater the importance they attached to the denial of sensuality, the greater the importance of the heavenly virgin' (Feuerbach 1957: 27). Feuerbach's notion of alienation and his critique of Hegel are implicit in these formulations which stress that 'whatever religion consciously denies it unconsciously restores in God' (ibid.: 27). Feuerbach's philosophy restores the value of the sensuous, a 'love which is flesh and blood' (Feuerbach 1957: 48). Curiously, however, much as Feuerbach stresses the alienated spirit of Christianity, his reading also points to the feminine character of the son of God, and the fact that the 'highest and deepest love is the mother's love. The father consoles himself . . . he has a stoical

principle within him. The mother on the contrary, is inconsolable. . . .
Love is in and by itself essentially feminine in its nature' (ibid.: 72). It
is Protestantism which has waged war on this principle, he argues, and
by definition represents the masculine. Finally it is not faith which is the
root of love, faith can only produce hatred and hell. There is no contradiction between reason and love, for God is love, and love is founded on
reason (ibid.: 263–6). Marriage is, in its essence, a 'free bond of love'
that is willed and spontaneous (ibid.: 271).

From the Hegelian perspective, Feuerbach is a romantic, and gives
free reign to the leading role of the secular principle of love. But against
this Feuerbach clearly developed a passionate response to Hegelian
reason and logical dialectic, which he stigmatized as repressive. Feuerbach
was capable of producing a critique of the Nazarenes, and the Prussian
state from the simple principles of his philosophy. There is also clearly
a rejection of the whole tendency of Pietist theology. And he made his
own appeal to the new woman in his 'Epigrams' an appeal to the 'fair
sex': 'Dear Maidens and Women! Take the noble ancients as your
example / And once again drive away theology' (Feuerbach 1980: 251).

Communist organization: toward 1848

There were expulsions of political activists throughout the 1830s, and in
1834 the Outlaw's League was established in Paris from German exiles
living there. A dissatisfied section broke away to form the League of the
Just in 1836 as a secret organization of revolutionaries: and it was this
organization which was involved in the abortive May uprising in Paris in
1839. After this the German leaders (Schapper and Heinrich Bauer) went
into exile in London, where from 1840 the League functioned as the
German Workers' Educational Association, which then in turn spread
branches to the continent. The League had as its principle ideology the
primitive utopian Christian communism of Wilhelm Weitling; the principal character of the League was its support of artisanal socialism. Engels
was invited to join in 1843 but refused. During this period there was
increasing criticism of Weitling's argument, and Engels and Marx were
invited to address the League in debate in 1847. There were two con-
gresses, at which all the major differences between the internal factions
were debated. After the debates, Engels and Marx were invited to draw
up a manifesto based on their ideas. Clearly this manifesto, mainly drafted
by Engels, was constructed on a conception of 'scientific' communism
which was quite different from the romantic utopianism of Weitling, and
was aimed at the interpellation of a different social class. Engels later
reflected 'while I was in Manchester it was tangibly brought home to me
that . . . thanks to large-scale industry . . . especially in England' a
new industrial working-class, and therefore a different communism, was

beginning to emerge (Marx and Engels 1968: 442). The League drew up special demands for Germany, and these included a wide programme of nationalization, the abolition of feudal estates, limitation on the rights of inheritance, and so forth. But there were soon many disappointments as the revolutions of 1848 and 1849 in Germany were defeated. First the League was reformed, and then, after further splits as large numbers of exiles came to London, and the trials of insurrectionists began in Germany, the League was dissolved in 1852 as the revolutionary tide receded.

In 1864 Marx became involved in the detail of the formation of the First International, The International Workingmen's Association, which was, like the earlier organizations, deeply divided through internal ideological dissension. The later collapse of this organization was connected with the defeat of the Paris Commune of 1871, which Marx hailed as the first experiment in communism and which revealed the true nature of the proletarian dictatorship.

MARX'S INTELLECTUAL DEVELOPMENT

It is now possible to examine Marx's own evolution in the context of these developments (without looking specifically at the issue of gender).

Marx's Pietistic phase: a first fetishism

Karl Marx's family had deep rabbinical roots, but the family's religion in Karl's youth was Evangelical. It was Marx's remarkable father who, after a Jewish marriage, had broken with the Jewish religion and converted to Christianity, though the family was never whole-heartedly accepted. One of the earliest surviving documents of Karl's writing from September 1835, is an essay entitled 'On the union of the faithful with Christ according to John xv, 1–14, described in its ground and necessity, in its unconditional necessity and in its effects' (in Payne 1973: 39–43).

Little background is known for the document, but it seems clear that it is a devout Pietist text. Marx says 'in our union with Christ, we turn a loving eye to God and we feel a most ardent gratitude toward Him, and joyfully fall on our knees before him' (ibid.: 43). Marx argues in this essay that union with Christ is an important route to the achievement of a balanced tolerance of the world, and 'virtue is no longer a gloomy caricature, as it is in Stoic philosophy . . . what it accomplishes is accomplished out of love for such a pure source, then it appears free of all earthly attachments, and is truly divine'. At this stage Marx sought a theology of love and purity. The 'union with Christ contribute to an inner uplifting, and a heart that is open to love for mankind and for all noble and great men, not out of ambition or love of fame, but through Christ: this union with Christ produces a joyfulness which the Epicureans sought in vain in their frivolous philosophy, their deepest thinkers striving to acquire it in the most hidden depths of knowledge' (ibid.: 43). In this short essay, Marx has expressed the notion of the serious yet joyful synthesis that Christianity provides, through Christ, a love of humility and humanity. Judaism, for him, was an inferior religion, best thought of as an aspect of Christianity.

Marx's romantic phase: a second fetishism

Marx's writing in the next year up to the summer of 1837, was dominated by romantic themes, as Marx intended to become a romantic poet. To his father's great regret Karl began to dabble in the problematic of evil, and to poke fun at Christian notions of heaven, or to make the ascent to heaven ridiculously sensual. As Wessell has pointed out, there are poems of Oneness with the cosmos, of alienation of the self, and of incipient pain, hatred and revolt against the world. Heinrich Marx asked 'that [heart of yours] is apparently animated and ruled by a demon not granted to all men, is this demon of heavenly or Faustian nature?' (cited in Wessell 1979: 10). One important poem indicates the way that the Faustian thematic seems destined to work to self-destruction. The poem exists in different translations ('The Fiddler' in *Collected Works*: vol. I, 22–3); 'The Player' in Payne 1973: 59 and in Wessell 1979: 239; and 'The Minstrel' in Johnston 1967: 226–7). The Prince of Darkness makes his appearance.

> 'Fiddler, with scorn you rend your heart,
> A radiant God lent you your art,
> To dazzle with waves of melody,
> To soar to the star-dance in the sky'

> 'How so! I plunge, plunge without fail
> My blood-black sabre into your soul,
> That art God neither wants nor wists,
> It leaps to the brain from Hell's black mists.'

> 'Till heart's bewitched, till senses reel:
> With Satan I have struck my deal.
> He chalks the signs, beats time for me,
> I play the death march fast and free.'

> 'I must play dark, I must play light,
> Till bowstrings break my heart outright'
> (Marx and Engels 1975a: 22–3)

The poem could be read as depicting 'the poet as a kind of sacrificial victim to the powers of darkness', perhaps the poet sacrifices himself so that others will not have to face 'similar dark forces within themselves' (Johnston 1967: 267). There is another poem entitled 'Invocation of One in Despair' which begins in an angry phrase

So a God has snatched from me my all
In the curse and rack of Destiny.
All his worlds are gone beyond recall!
Nothing but revenge is left to me!

On myself revenge I'll proudly wreak . . .

I shall build my throne high overhead,
Cold, tremendous shall its summit be . . .
            (Marx and Engels 1975a: 563–4)

Epicurean phase: Greek Enlightenment and Hegel

Marx criticized this early period of poetic writing in 1837, and the next phase was closer to Hegel and an approchement with the Epicurean philosophy which culminated in the position adopted in his doctoral thesis of 1840. In this thesis, dominated by Hegelian concern with contradictions, his position moves consistently towards Epicurus. It is a study which moves to a consideration of Epicurus on atoms and meteors, not as a simple study of the universe, but because the representations of the universe for the Greeks represented 'the solar system of the mind' of men (Marx and Engels 1975a: 66). Marx's thesis is a brilliant, virtuoso juggling of Hegelian dialectics, in which he concludes with the paradox that in opposing the whole outlook of Greek thought by stressing multi- or complex causality of the individual, Epicurus can only say that where his principle 'becomes reality it will cease to have reality for him', that 'abstract-universal self-consciousness has, indeed, the intrinsic urge to affirm itself in the things themselves in which it can only affirm itself by negating them'. Epicurus finds 'his previous categories break down. . . . And the profoundest knowledge achieved by his system, its most thorough consistency, is that he is aware of this and expresses it consciously' (ibid.: 66–73). This doctoral thesis was dedicated to Jenny's father, Baron von Westphalen.

The critique of Hegel: radicalization

In the early 1840s, after Marx had achieved his doctorate but found it impossible to find a university position as the increasingly anti-Enlightenment trends began to assume hegemony Marx's writings became increasingly critical of Hegel. Here Marx found Feuerbach's emphasis on the theme of the sensuous materialist base of experience essential in criticizing the inner mysticism of the Hegelian system. Fundamentally, as Althusser has pointed out, Feuerbach presented Marx with a subtle philosophical humanism (see Althusser 1982: 176–86). But by explosively reintroducing a complex dialectic into Feuerbach's humanism, by linking this to a social science as the theory of the revolution by the new industrial proletariat as the negative principle of the social system, and by seeing armed revolution and its triumph as necessarily leading to a scientifically justified social dictatorship of the proletariat, Marx certainly broke with all theoretical and political humanism, in driving to a ruthless critique of philosophical and political sentimentality. It has been said that for Marx at this moment the proletariat had become the 'irony' of the community (Wessell 1979); but it seems that Marx here had outstripped Hegelian irony, and the only surviving Hegelian element is a completely radicalized notion of the labour of the negation seen here in irreconcilable class struggle.

The project of the pure science for the proletariat: *Capital* (1850–67)

After the dissolution of the Communist League and the fading of the revolutionary tide of 1848, Marx concentrated almost entirely on journalism and the project of writing *Capital*; writing his critique of the fetishism of commodities, he reflected that this could only have been done in London with 'the enormous amount of material . . . in the British Museum, the fact that London is a convenient vantage point for the observation of bourgeois society, and finally the new stage of development which this society seemed to have entered . . . induced me to start again from the very beginning'. (Marx [1859] 1971: 22—3). Marx laboured on this project, seeing only the first volume published in 1867. To Paul Lafargue who was intent on marrying Laura, Marx's daughter, Marx wrote: 'you know I have sacrificed my whole fortune to the revolutionary struggle. I do not regret it. . . . But I would not marry. Insofar as it is in my power, I want to protect my daughter from the kind of rocks on which her mother's life has been wrecked' (in Padover 1979: 216).

MARX AND GENDER

Having presented the essential context, and sketched the main outlines of Marx's intellectual biography, it is now possible to begin to elaborate the interconnections of these developments with Marx's conception of gender and the way in which these intersected with his own practice.

Jenny von Westphalen

The writings which follow Marx's early essay are dominated by literary efforts, poems and plays, and by letters to his father, as by this time he had left home for Bonn, and then Berlin University. He had also fallen in love with Jenny von Westphalen, four years older than he was, and quickly became secretly engaged in August 1836. His father became aware of this but Jenny's parents did not know for some time. The situation was dramatic and tense, as Jenny was not only considered beautiful and well educated, but she came from an aristocratic background, and as Marx's father pointed out was making a considerable sacrifice in waiting for a seventeen- or eighteen-year-old undergraduate, however brilliant. As Eleanor Marx was to claim many years later, Marx was 'an unrivalled story-teller' from an early age, and at this stage in his life wanted to become a poet and dramatist, and did have poems published (Prawer 1976: 1). This second period lasted until the summer of 1837, and was dominated by the struggle between romantic egoistic individualism and the constraint of community (see Lifshitz [1933] 1973: 13). At this time Marx's attitude to Hegel was a negative one, with Hegel's influence seen as a failure to struggle against reality. It is also deeply influenced by Goethe's theme of Mephistopheles; clearly a theme of sexual guilt is developed within the framework of the problem of the role of the artist.

Clearly Marx now faces not just a God but a Goddess:

Jenny! Teasingly you may inquire
Why my songs 'To Jenny' I address,
When for you alone my pulse beats higher,
When my songs for you alone despair,
When you only can their heart inspire,
When your name each syllable must confess,
When you lend each note melodiousness,
When no breath would stray from the Goddess?
'Tis because so sweet the dear name sounds . . .
(Marx and Engels 1975a: 521–2)

In a poem called 'The Awakening' there is an account of a soul rising from the daemonic abyss:

. . . and endless rising
Your endless rising
Is with trembling lips –
The Aether-reddened,
Flaming, eternal
Lovekiss of the Godhead
(Ibid.: 563)

This is unashamedly sensual, part of a sequence of poems which are passionate and invoke despair, elation, overcoming and humour (the poem 'The Last Judgement' where he gets thrown out of the courtroom of the last judgement as a 'noisy lout', and notes

> There can only be one Heaven,
> That one's fully occupied,
> We must share it with old women
> Whom the teeth of Time have gnawed.
>
> While their flesh lies underground
> With decay and stones o'ershovelled,
> Brightly hued, their souls hop round
> In spier-dance enravelled.
>
> All so skinny, all so thin,
> So aethereal, so chaste,
> Never were their forms so lean,
> Even when most tightly chaste.
>
> (Ibid.: 573)

There is also a 'freely rendered' Elegy, from Ovid's *Tristia* which says, and Marx will come back to this many years later:

> Only my pain shall mate with you,
> Only my sorrow's darkest night.
>
> Shaggy and rough you may appear,
> Like one whose hair unkempt hangs down,
> Not rendered wondrous soft and fair
> By smoothing block of pumice-stone.
>
> If darker is your pallid face,
> It is because by me 'twas stained,
> Oh, how my tears have flown apace
> And hotly down on you have rained.
>
> (Ibid.: 549)

Marx also wrote a melodrama, in which the struggle of light and dark is fought out with more deadly weapons. The tragedy is called *Oulanum* and the story involves Oulanum (=Immanuel?), and his companion Lucindo (lux/light?), who find as their adversary Pertini and his aid Alwander. In a mountain village, Pertini offers Oulanum and Lucindo hospitality since the village is full of strangers, recognizes the power of Oulanum and begins to plot. Pertini and Lucindo argue, and Pertini says 'You think of Faust and Mephistopheles. You've brooded on them deeply, I dare say'. Lucindo replies 'The abyss yawns gaping night to both of us, If you sink down, smiling, I'll follow you, And whisper to you, "Down! Come with me! Comrade!" '.

Pertini replies 'It seems you're gifted with imagination. You have dreamed much already in your life?' And then, 'Am I to be the brush that lends you tone? . . . . I know what I am. Tell me, what are you? . . . . You are still nothing'. But Lucindo admits this: 'I call myself Lucindo. . . . That is my name. . . . What men call being, I do not possess'. And Pertini mocks the poet who 'would most gladly Himself be author of the poem of Life'. Pertini challenges him to a duel and is refused. The challenge is altered: 'Do you believe in God?' To which Lucindo replies 'I don't believe with what is called belief, And yet I know Him as I know myself'. Pertini plays with him on his refusal to say he believes, and challenges him to swear he will cherish friendship for himself. Pertini offers to show him a mysterious place, and Lucindo follows. There follows a soliloquy by Oulanum, a pure, passionate statement of hatred of the world which ends 'Destroy what only poetry's lie contrived. A curse shall finish what a curse conceived'.

What follows is the working of Pertini's plotting. Lucindo is manipulated to meet Beatrice. He is immediately seduced by her. Commentators have identified Beatrice as Jenny von Westphalen (Payne 1973: 63). If so, the play has a complex message, for to Lucindo's poetic flattery she replies 'reproof I cannot find within my heart, You dress the poison, sir, with such sweet art'. She confides that her father wants her to marry a man she loathes, and Lucindo declares that he 'must act quickly. . . . Death is in every minute. . . . It is as if the music I heard sound Within my own heart, living form had found.' But Beatrice is uncertain:

Yet my breast tightens under fearful strain
As if delight were mixed with searing pain,
As if between our union there came floating
A hissing sound mixed in by devils gloating
   (Marx and Engels 1975a: 588–607)

As they embrace Wierin bursts in, and accuses Lucindo. The play ends unfinished with the prospect of a duel, and Beatrice says 'I'm full of fear' (ibid.).

Many of these literary pieces were gathered together and offered to Marx's father in 1837. Heinrich Marx's letters to his son at this time are full of further information as to the reactions of the family and Jenny to these literary pieces. Marx's father offers detailed advice on a wide range of matters, and in some respects not only acted as a go-between for Karl and Jenny, but actually offered advice to Karl on how to conduct his relations with Jenny. He advocated 'exemplary behaviour, by manly, firm efforts [to] win people's goodwill and favour'. But he had grave doubts about the affair: 'If I were powerful enough to protect and soothe this noble being in some respect by vigorous intervention, no sacrifice would be too great for me. Unfortunately, however, I am weak in every respect. She is making a priceless sacrifice for you. . . . Woe to you if ever in your life you could forget this!' (ibid.: 664–5). Heinrich Marx foresaw great difficulties for the couple to overcome, as Marx was so young, but he tried to present the problem: 'how old must you be to hold an academic post?' he asked (December 1836). Karl's sister Sophie wrote to say that 'Jenny . . . wept tears of delight and pain on viewing your poems' (ibid.: 666–7).

In February 1837, Marx's father wrote of Jenny 'It weighs on her mind that her parents do not know or, as I believe, do not want to know' (ibid.: 668). His advice to his son was to write a sealed letter to her 'of devoted feeling and pure love . . . and resolutely demand, with manly audacity in the face of which [tell] the poor child . . . that she must not waver' (ibid.: 668–9). But by September 1837 the situation had not improved: 'that [Jenny] does not write to you [is] – I cannot call it anything else – childish, headstrong. For there can be no doubt at all that her attitude to you is one of the most self-sacrificing love, and she was not far from proving it by her death' (ibid.: 681). But of Marx's poetry he was bitter and angry, and would not 'accept, a crazy botch-work which merely testifies how you squander your talents and spend your nights giving birth to monsters; that you follow the footsteps of the new immoralists who twist their words until they themselves do not hear them' (689). His letters are full of foreboding that his son had a fatal flaw in his personality.

Jenny herself wrote a long letter to Karl in Berlin (1838/40?), which is remarkable in its daring: 'how little you know me, how little you appreciate my position. . . . A girl's love is different from that of a man, it cannot be but different. A girl, of course, cannot give a man anything but love and herself and her person, just as she is, quite undivided and forever. What makes me miserable is that which would fill any other girl with inexpressible delight – your beautiful, touching, passionate love, the indescribably beautiful things you say about it . . . all this only causes me anxiety and often reduces me to despair. The more I were to surrender myself . . . the more frightful would be my life . . . if you became cold and withdrawn. Since your last letter I have tortured myself with the fear that for my sake you could become embroiled in a . . . duel. Day and night I saw you wounded, bleeding . . . and Karl to tell the truth, I was not altogether unhappy in this thought: for I vividly imagined you had lost your right hand, and Karl I was in a state of rapture, of bliss because of that. . . . I thought that then I could write down all your dear, heavenly ideas and be really useful to you' (ibid.: 696–7). Her letter remarkably describes a meeting of the couple that could also have been a moment in Oulanum: 'how you looked at me the first time . . . and then quickly looked away, and then looked at me again, and I did the same, until at last we looked at each other for quite a long time and very deeply, and could no longer look away' (ibid.: 698).

The sensuous Madonna

I have discussed the antagonism between the left Hegelians and the Nazarenes, who sought to resurrect pallid versions of the Madonna and began to attract patronage from the Prussian conservatives. Marx was also tempted to join in this critique and agreed to write on this for Ruge's *Rheinische Zeitung* in 1842. In fact only one of four pieces was written, and Marx's position, come to be known as the 'lost aesthetic', has to be reconstructed from scattered comments and notes. The books Marx read in preparation are known, and passages which Marx thought relevant were quoted at the time in other contexts. In one article, of May 1842, he cites Goethe as saying that 'the painter succeeds only with a type of feminine beauty which he has loved in at least one living being' (Marx and Engels 1975a: 137). Rose says this is 'related to Marx's interest in the sensuous and material bases of the painting of female beauty by the madonna painters of both the Middle Ages and of his own time'. And she draws attention to a similar remark in a subsequent article, which suggests the arguments over the freedom of the press should be expressed in the language of experience, just as 'Rembrandt painted the Madonna as Dutch peasant woman' (ibid.: 171–2). Rose notes that Goethe had also drawn attention to that work in 1776, comparing that representation to one by Raphael.

> Where Hegel was later to praise Raphael because he was able to depict a 'transcendental' type of love with his madonnas . . . Goethe had praised both Raphael and Rembrandt on account of thier ability to represent natural motherly love. This was much closer to Marx's interest in uncovering the sensuous, materialist basis to the painting of the Madonna in Western art than Hegel's, and Marx's reference to it is an indication of his interest, at that time, in developing a critique of religious painting which would serve to uncover a more 'Hellenistic' side to the arguments put forward by Hegel. . . . Goethe's argument that the paintings of the Madonna (by either Rembrandt or Raphael) could be seen to be based on the artist's experience of sensual love may also . . . have suggested to Marx a way of interpreting the 'ortho- dox' Hegel's less materialistic analysis of Raphael's madonna pictures in a more materialistic manner, in the way suggested by Bauer in his 'esoteric' interpretations of the orthodox Hegel as a concealed but radical Hellene.

(Rose 1984: 63)

Rose's close analysis of the excerpts and notes taken by Marx from books read for his essay on art reveals certain strands of interest, and suggest that Marx was interested in the continuity of fetishism in pagan and Christian art. Following Lifshitz, Rose argues that it could well be that Marx wanted to 'apply the Christian criticism of fetishism in Greek art to Christian art itself' (ibid.: 65). Lifshitz argues that Marx's position could be interpreted as suggesting that

> on the one hand, the realism of ancient art [was] based upon the democracy of the Greek republics; on the other hand, the Oriental religious outlook [was] based upon oppression and submission. Christian art of the post-classical period reproduced on a new level the aesthetics of Asiatic barbarism.
>
> (Lifshitz 1973: 37)

In his notes Marx shows little interest in praise for Raphael, and considerable interest in the notes on similarities between Greek pagan art and Christian madonna painting, particularly on questions of clothing. Rose goes so far as to speculate that Marx may well have envisaged also a radicalization of Hegel's admiration for Christian madonnas, given Hegel's comparision of examples of these to Egyptian and Greek works (Rose 1984: 66). Thus a number of possibilities of interpretation exist but a framework of analysis is established in which the work of the Nazarenes could be attacked from the radical position of the Hellenes, or the subversive position of Hegel which could reveal a continuity in the sensuous fetishism of Greek art into the Renaissance. (Heine had prefigured these remarks in 1830 by arguing that Nazarene art was a pale reflection of the Renaissance model, but had criticized the latter itself as an alienated fetishistic projection (Rose 1984: 29)).

Marriage

At this time, when the tendencies of arch-conservativism were beginning to become manifest, there were also new divorce laws being discussed in 1842 in secret. Marx's paper, the *Rheinische Zeitung*, published the draft bill, having received the leaked document. Its refusal to name the source of the leak, and the fact that it published the document at all were the grounds used to close the journal. Marx wrote two articles on these proposals, and these reveal the basis of his critique of Prussian law, as well as his opposition to radical demands for free love.

The critique of the theological manipulation of marriage law he said began with a consideration 'that the essence of marriage is not human morality, but spiritual sanctity, and therefore puts determination from above in the place of self-determination, a supernatural sanction in the place of inner natural consecration' (Marx and Engels 1975a: 274). Prussian law constructs this apparent contradiction and then bases itself

> on an intellectual abstraction which being in itself devoid of content, conceived the natural, legal, moral content as an external matter which in itself knows no laws and then tried to model, organise and arrange this spiritless and lawless matter in accordance with an external aim.
>
> (Ibid.: 275)

Thus, as with art, a bifurcation and an abstraction is posed against a living reality, the classic pattern of alienated power.

But Marx begins to draw the line, in exactly the Hegelian manner, against the radicals: he can 'by no means approve of their unconditional apologia' for a truly liberal free system. Those liberals

> always speak to us about the unfortunate position of the husband and wife tied together against their will . . . they think only of the two individuals and forget about the *family*. They forget . . . that even from the juridical standpoint the children and their property cannot be made to depend on arbitrary will and its whims . . . [they] pay no attention to the *will of marriage*, the moral substance of this relationship.
>
> (Ibid.: 308)

Marx insists on this argument and begins a critical attack on ideas dependent on the sovereignty of 'arbitrary desire', and in marked contrast to his conclusions as to the compulsions of wage slavery he insists that 'no one is forced to contract marriage'. His conception is that there is, in this sphere, complete equality of entry into marriage and that this contract must at all costs be defended in the interests of all those affected by its consequences. Clearly the progressive view is, he maintains, that 'arbitrary wishes must be subordinated to marriage' (ibid.: 308).

Marx's whole argument leads to a reconsideration of what the moral content of the marriage actually is. He defines it in a secular fashion, against Hegel who, he argues, says 'nothing specific about marriage' other than indicating its conceptual form, 'but no . . . marriage corresponds exactly to its concept' says Marx. The crucial question is the life of the relationship itself and this is determinant:

> neither the arbitrary decision of the legislator, nor the arbitrary desire of private persons, but only *the essence of the matter* can decide whether a marriage is dead or not, for it is well known that the statement that death has occurred depends on the facts . . . is it not clear that the legislator should be allowed the fact of a moral death only on the basis of the most indubitable symptoms, since preserving the life of moral relationships is . . . his duty.
>
> (Ibid.: 309)

Again to emphasize the fact that there is a moral duty on the shoulders of the state, and that the life of a family is a distinct moral reality independent of the individuals involved in it, he says 'indulgence of the wishes of individuals would turn into harshness towards the essence of the individuals, towards their moral reason, which is embodied in moral relationships' (ibid.: 310). Thus Marx is prepared to adopt an extremely conservative defence of marriage as providing the married individuals with a social essence which the state must defend, even against the individuals own 'whims' and 'desires' if they are shown to be in opposition to their own 'reason'.

From la bohème to bourgeois respectability

It is clear that the section on women and the family in the *Communist Manifesto* which indicates that communists want to abolish the family, is in considerable contrast to Marx's former statements and indeed his practice. In this work of 1848, drafted by Engels, the inner life of the family, now defined as a bourgeois form, is immediately reduced to property ownership. Indeed it suggests that the family as such is virtually unknown amongst the proletarians, a position Engels had begun to elaborate after his experience in Manchester. It is unlikely that Marx ever had any real sympathy for this view, or if he did it was outweighed by other considerations. Jenny Marx herself violently disagreed with it and would not meet the exemplar of the new proletarian independent woman, Engels's partner Mary Burns, or receive her in her house. Marx wrote virtually nothing on the subject of the new woman.

Yet it is evident that Jenny Marx had her own clear position, which was elaborated in letters and indeed in her own autobiographical statement. 'A short sketch of an eventful life' though this exists only in a mutilated version (in Payne 1973: 119–39). This document charts the inner life of the Marx family as it is punctuated by its relations with political events. Although some have suggested that Jenny Marx was no Marxist (Payne himself in his introduction), it is clear that Jenny was certainly a convert to Marx's communism as a social form, and she was indeed the only woman signatory to the declaration of the Communist League. She was a close follower of all of Marx's theoretical and political work, and in her letters she supported Marx's attack on the utopian communism of Weitling. She knew that Marx 'willingly' gave the revolutionary workers money to buy arms 'for he had just come into an inheritance' (in Payne 1973: 121). She too, like Marx himself, was imprisoned in a place 'where they brought beggars who could find no shelter, homeless wanderers and wretched fallen women' (ibid.: 121). But she resisted a number of developments in the communist milieu consistently: one was any move towards Saint-Simonian communalist experimentation in sexual life. In the autobiography Jenny refers to August Willich who made an appearance in her bedroom 'early one morning . . . roaring with Prussian horse-laughs, perfectly willing to begin . . . a debate on "natural" communism. Karl put a quick end to these attempts' (ibid.: 124). Another was any acceptance of common-law marriage which she found an offence to social honour. Third, she refused to accept Engels's model of the new proletarian woman as a higher form, indeed the whole breakthrough claimed by Engels as a specific form of emancipation for women which made possible genuine 'sex-love'.

The years in London were years of poverty for the Marx family, and in 1850 they were evicted, and were saved from the 'bitterest of privations' only by gifts from Jenny's mother. When the revolutionary movement subsided, Marx 'withdrew into private life' (ibid.: 125), and Engels went back to his position in Manchester. In 1851 the birth of Karl's and Helene Demuth's son was described by Jenny Marx simply as 'an event' which brought, she says, 'a great increase in our private and public sorrows' (ibid.: 126). After 1852 Jenny became Marx's secretary, and she described those days as 'the happiest of my life', but they were still days of great poverty. In 1856 they received a small inheritance and this, she said, 'gave us our freedom'; within a short time they were on 'the road to "respectability" . . . with our ownership of a house, *la vie de bohème* came to an end, and where previously we had fought the battle of poverty in exile freely and openly, now we had the *appearance* of respectability, and held up our heads again . . . but the humour had gone. I first came to know the real oppression of exile during this first phase of our truly bourgeois life as Philistines' (ibid.: 130).

Within the family Marx was romantically attached to his wife, as Eleanor was proud to say many years later: 'His whole life long Marx not only loved his wife, he was in love with her. . . . Called to Trier by the death of his mother in 1863, he wrote . . . saying he had made "daily pilgrimages to the old house of the Westphalens. . . . I am asked daily on all sides about the former 'most beautiful girl in Trier' and the 'Queen of the Ball'. It is damned pleasing for a man to find his wife lives on in the imagination of a whole city as a delightful princess" ' (in Kapp 1976: 738).

But the most remarkable document in Marx's love letter to Jenny Marx of 21 June 1856, written from Manchester, which is rarely quoted in full as it needs to be, for perhaps we are now in a better position to understand how consistent Marx's position is:

My heart's beloved,
I am writing you again, because I am alone and because it troubles me always to have a dialogue with you in my head, without your knowing anything about it or being able to answer. Poor as your

photograph is, it does perform a service for me, and I now understand how even the 'Black Madonna,' the most disgraceful portrait of the Mother of God, could find indestructible admirers, indeed even more admirers than the good portraits. In any case, the Black Madonna pictures have never been more kissed, looked at, and adored than your photograph, which, although not black is morose, and absolutely does not reflect your darling, sweet, kissable *dolce* face. But I improve upon the sun's rays, which have painted falsely, and find that my eyes, so spoiled by lamplight and tobacco, can still paint, not only in dream but also while awake. I have you vivaciously before me, and I carry you on my hands, and I kiss you from head to foot, and I fall on my knees before you, and I groan: 'Madame, I love you.' And I truly love you, more than the Moor of Venice ever loved. The false and worthless world views virtually all characters falsely and worthlessly. Who of my many slanderers and snake-tongued enemies had ever reproached me that I am destined to play the role of chief lover in a second-class theatre? And yet it is true. If the scoundrels had had any wit, they would have painted 'the production and direction' on one side, and me lying at your feet on the other. *Look to this picture and that* – they would have written underneath. But dumb scoundrels they are and dumb they will remain, in *seculum seculorum*.

Momentary absence is good, for in constant presence things seem too much alike to be differentiated. Proximity dwarfs even towers, while the petty and commonplace, at close view, grow too big. Small habits, which may physically irritate and take on emotional form, disappear when the immediate object is removed from the eye. Great passions, which through proximity assume the form of petty routine, grow and again take on their natural dimension on account of the magic of distance. So it is with my love. You have only to be snatched away from me even in a mere dream, and I know immediately that the time has only served, as do sun and rain for plants, for growth. The moment you are absent, my love for you shows itself to be what it is, a giant, in which are crowded together all the energy of my spirit and all the character of my heart. It makes me feel like a man again, because I feel a great passion; and the multifariousness, in which study and modern education entangle us, and the scepticism which necessarily makes us find fault with all subjective and objective impressions, all of these are entirely designed to make us all small and weak and whining. But love – not love for the Feuerbach-type of man, not for the metabolism, not for the proletariat – but the love for the beloved and particularly you, makes a man a man.

You will smile, my sweet heart, and ask, how did I come to all this rhetoric? If I could press your sweet, white heart to my heart, I would keep silent and not say a word. Since I cannot kiss with my lips, I must kiss with language and make words. I could really even make verses and rhymes like Ovid's *Libri Tristium*, which in German means *Bücher des Jammers*. But I am exiled from you, which is something Ovid did not conceive.

There are actually many females in the world, and some among them are beautiful. But where could I find again a face, whose every feature, even every wrinkle, is a reminder of the greatest and sweetest memories of my life? Even my endless pains, my irreplaceable losses I read in your sweet countenance, and I kiss away the pain when I kiss your sweet face. 'Buried in her arms, awakened by her kisses' – namely, in your arms and by your kisses, and I grant the Brahmins and Pythagoras their doctrine of regeneration and Christianity its doctrine of resurrection. . . .

Goodbye, my sweet heart. I kiss you and the children many thousand times.

Yours

Karl

(in Padover 1979: 106–7)

If it is legitimate to comment on such a love letter as if it were a philosophical document, it is surely only possible against the contextualization that I have provided here. I offer the interpretation that Marx has drawn on materials from his youthful writings. He had already included a free translation of Ovid's *Libri Tristium* in his 'Book of Love' for Jenny in 1836 (in Marx and Engels 1975a: 57). But more than this, the letter suggests the way that Marx in fact resolved the dilemma indicated by Lifshitz; whether Marx would tend to support Hegel's critique of Christian art as a continuation of sensuous fetishism of the pre-Christian period, or whether he would have purely counterposed sensuous paintings of the Madonna against the pallid fetishes of the Nazarenes. It seems likely that he could have supported both tendencies, arriving at the position of sensuous materialism of Feuerbach. The mention of Feuerbach in the letter is surely not fortuitous, nor is the choice presented (love of the proletariat, or of the woman). Jenny Marx is pure, she has a 'white' heart, and she is elevated to the object of a cult: 'I fall on my knees', I am 'lying at your feet'. Yet the image is also realistic: the photographic image is blackened, his eyes are affected with lamplight and tobacco. It is transformed by the imagination into a living being. Her beauty is ideal but is improved by the effects of reality: time and experience. It suggests how the Madonna portraits can be so adored, since they displace a real longing created by the effect of distance. To kiss the Madonna is to lift the pain of earthly suffering. Perhaps the sacrifice that she has made for him is balanced by the passion he feels for her: a great passion, a giant love. Yet finally it is the transformation in him that she has made which seems most significant: through her he has become a man. It is this experience, likened to the ideas of transubstantiation and metamorphosis of the soul, that, like the revelation of the love of the Madonna, unveils the meaning of world religions: they are magical doctrines of the regeneration of man, and the banishment of pain. Thus Marx does not take the step that Engels took, for example, and combine love of the proletariat and love of proletarian woman. Marx remains very much within the orbit of his early romantic and Feuerbachian philosophical humanistic (but also fetishistic) stage in his relationship with Jenny Marx, and uses all the materials and resources of that stage in his life to divorce his conception of becoming a 'man' from conceptions of the proletarian revolution. Even within the framework of the Feuerbachian position his attitude remains on this score essentially conservative. In his famous 'Theses on Feuerbach', Marx criticizes Feuerbach:

> Feuerbach starts out from the fact of religious self-alienation, the duplication of the world into a religious, imaginary world and a real one. His work consists in the dissolution of the religious world into its secular basis. He overlooks the fact that after completing this work, the chief thing still remains to be done. For the fact that the secular foundation detaches itself and establishes itself in the clouds as an independent realm is really only to be explained by the self-cleavage and self-contradictoriness of this secular basis. The latter must itself, therefore, first be understood in its contradiction and then, by the removal of the contradiction, revolutionised in practice. Thus, for instance, once the earthly family is discovered to be the secret of the holy family, the former must then be criticised in theory and revolutionised in practice.
>
> (Marx and Engels 1968: 29)

Marx's conservativism clearly does not remain, in his own terms, at 'the highest point attained by *contemplative* materialism', a 'materialism which does not understand sensuousness as practical activity' and which is 'the contemplation of single individuals in "civil society" ' (ibid.: 30). For Marx makes love active, sensuous, but *individual and uncritical* and in so doing reproduces the patriarchal holy family.

Part II

Ecstasies of the new man

Chapter 4

In feeling: William Godwin and Mary Wollstonecraft

Very often the received accounts of the early social theorists present a picture of the pure advance of scientific thinking, a mirror of the way in which these thinkers presented themselves. It seems more plausible and interesting to regard the works of the authors discussed in this work more as science which has passed into the domain of literature, or as Barthes has suggested in his analyses of biblical texts, as a religion from which belief has been magically suspended.[1]

Godwin considered himself above all, in the early 1790s, a rigorous theoretician. But the decade of the 1790s was dominated by intense debate, not about social theory in the abstract but about the social and political significance of the French Revolution of 1789 and its course (Butler 1984). A meeting of the Revolution Society in London in November 1789 to hear a political lecture by the radical Protestant Richard Price sparked Edmund Burke to write his famous *Reflections on the Revolution in France, and on the Proceedings in Certain Societies in London Relative to that Event* ((1790) 1969). This indeed provoked a number of immediate critiques, including Tom Paine's *Rights of Man: Being an Answer to Mr Burke's Attack on the French Revolution* (1791–2). Also significant was the extraordinary *A Vindication of the Rights of Men, in a letter to the Right Honourable Edmund Burke: occasioned by His Reflections on the Revolution in France* (1790) by Mary Wollstonecraft, a work followed in 1792 by the *Vindication of the Rights of Woman: with Strictures on Political and Moral Subjects* (1989). William Godwin published his response to these questions in far more abstract form in his *Political Justice* of 1793.

All these works reach different conclusions about the nature of the revolution and the nature of social progress. But what is interesting is the way in which the radicals reproached Burke for playing an ambiguous role, implying, even directly arguing, that his great talents had been corruptly employed by rich patrons (Paine 1949: xix; Godwin 1946: vol. II, 546). Curiously Godwin began *Political Justice* with a discussion whose terminology was derived directly from an essay written by Burke anonymously in 1756 called *A Vindication of Natural Society: Or, A View of The Miseries and Evils Arising to Mankind from Every Species of Artificial Society*. Whole sections and phrases from this work of criticism of aristocratic society are taken by Godwin and woven into the text of his treatise. The problem here arises because in the second edition of his essay, Burke announced that the work was indeed a parody of rationalism, a line of reasoning taken to absurd conclusions in order to ridicule it. Burke says his object was to show that 'the same engines which were employed for the destruction of religion, might be employed with equal success for the subversion of government' (Burke 1883: vol. I, 3).

Godwin's intention was to develop arguments for equality through the withering away, the 'euthanasia' of government; Wollstonecraft's intention was to argue for equality through the subversion of male privilege. The fundamental frameworks and logic of their theories were remarkably similar though both were constructed before they became close friends and then married in 1797. Godwin's essay reveals the effect of long systematic education and intellectual training and discipline in one of the country's leading dissenting academies; Wollstonecraft, on the other hand, was largely self-taught but deeply influenced by the dissenting church tradition. In their different ways they both force a radical logic to extreme conclusions, just as Burke had feared would happen. They each, for Burke, are examples of a mind 'which has no restraint from a sense of its own weakness, of its subordinate rank in creation, and of the extreme danger of letting the imagination loose' (Burke 1883: 4).

The radical analysis of Godwin does not immediately spring from the title, *Political Justice*, though once understood in Godwinian terms, the idea of political justice is completely revolutionary. Justice, not charity, implies the rule of individual liberty to the extent that all action must be judged before the bar of individual conscience. Any institution which claims authority beyond its own technical competence may be obeyed but not esteemed. Thus Godwin refuses all three dominant eighteenth-century models of political authority: authority based on force, on monarchy and aristocracy, and authority based on democratic contract. Unless action is legitimate before reason, it cannot have full-hearted assent. Godwin does not call for a revolution by force (indeed he specifically opposes it) but advocates a long transition to a society without government, a transition brought about through the action of the application of reason and persuasion; not a levelling down, but a true equalization by levelling towards a higher ideal. Through all his many examples he does not, however, discuss the position of women, though he does discuss the institution of marriage. Here he consistently applies his doctrine of individual reason and virtue and proposes an end to what he sees as a pernicious institution: marriage as a contractual legal institution.

Having adjudged co-operation as leading to a certain cramping of the free individual 'to eat or to work in conjunction . . . at a time most convenient to me, or to him, or to neither of us' (Godwin 1946: vol. II, 502), cohabitation is perhaps even worse: 'we should avoid such practices as are calculated to melt our opinions into a common mould . . . (and produce) thwarting, bickering and unhappiness' (ibid.: 506). But the prevailing system of courtship and marriage is absurd at the bar of reason: 'a thoughtless and romantic youth of each sex, to come together, to see each other for a few times, and under circumstances of delusion, and then to vow eternal attachment . . . and add to this marriage . . . is a monopoly' (507–8). If the marriage system was abolished there would be no rush of depravity, quite the reverse, since repressive laws 'irritate' vices; with the rule of justice, all would 'prefer the pleasures of intellect to the pleasure of the sense' (ibid.: 508). Friendship will come to play a predominant role, 'come in aid of the sexual intercourse, to refine its grossness, and increase its delight'. What makes infidelity 'particularly loathesome, is its being practised in a clandestine manner. It leads to a train of falsehood and a concerted hypocrisy' (ibid.: 510). Godwin, astonishingly, states his own direct appeal to the modern woman, and in contrast to Rousseau, makes it plain that he seeks 'a woman whose moral and intellectual accomplishment', strikes in the 'most powerful fashion' since he would feel 'kindness in exact proportion to . . . apprehension of . . . worth' (ibid.: 511).

What of the situation where there is competition over a woman? 'this will create no difficulty' said Godwin: 'her choice being declared, we shall all be wise enough to consider the sexual commerce as unessential to our regard' (ibid.: 511). Indeed Godwin immediately condemned 'the extreme depravity of . . . present habits [which] are inclined to suppose the sexual commerce necessary to the advantages arising from the purest friendship' (ibid.: 511). Coupled with that is the fact that many 'seek by despotic and artificial means, to maintain . . . possession of a woman' (ibid.: 508). It is to the power of individual intellectual judgement and virtue that Godwin appeals, since despotism and sensualism corrupt and deprave.

In relation to education, Godwin proposes that the infant be looked after by the mother, but at the level of 'instruction', he notes that ideally it 'will scarcely be thought necessary to make boys slaves, than to make men so . . . no creature in human form will be expected to learn any thing, but because he desires it' (ibid.: 512–3). It seems that Godwin simply omitted to mention the education of girls or women, except as they were subsumed under boys or men. In this particular case this subsumption has specific consequences, since in the eighteenth century, education was strictly segregated. Wollstonecraft was to pick this up, but Godwin did not follow through his egalitarian logic.

Although Godwin discusses the problem of the division of labour at this point, he does not touch upon the problem of the sexual division of labour, and nowhere else in the work does he discuss the social position of women. This is also true of the work of Edmund Burke, though Burke's orientation was altogether more conservative in demanding submissiveness from women (he refused to read Wollstonecraft).

Wollstonecraft is altogether different on this point and pursues, as I have shown, a specific application, unforeseen by either Burke or Godwin, of the theory of virtue, power and corruption in relation to sexual and gender differentiation. It is nonetheless developed within a framework which, like Godwin's, stresses the notion of the production of virtue through the work of the individual's own intellectual capacities. Where Godwin simply assumes he can judge, without qualification, a woman's level of 'moral and intellectual' accomplishment, Wollstonecraft raises a question: given that women are not educated and are deprived of access from the very means by which men produce virtue, the relation between men and women will be unequal even when the relation is based on moral or intellectual and not sexual attraction.

Godwin sought to argue that institutions tend to usurp the function of individual initiative and independent judgement; Wollstonecraft develops the thesis that institutions in which power differentials become severe have the effect of corrupting both the powerful and the powerless. The 'very elevation' of a man to power 'is an insuperable bar to the attainment of either wisdom or virtue, when all the feelings of a man are stifled by flattery, and reflection shut out by pleasure!' (Wollstonecraft 1983: 96). She develops this thesis at length in *Vindication*, in order to show that 'all power inebriates weak man' (ibid.: 96) through the system of dissimulation that the powerless are forced to create and the delusions of grandeur which the powerful are tempted to harbour.

Wollstonecraft, like Godwin, follows the logic insistently to conclusions that are in many respects quite different from his, though they apparently start from the same initial principles. Where Godwin advocates less institutionalized education, Wollstonecraft advocates the institutional co-education of the two sexes. Where Godwin advocates the abolition of marriage, even the abolition of surnames, Wollstonecraft suggests companionate marriage based on friendship, not love, and the recognition that an unhappy marriage might be in a woman's and her children's best interest. But it is necessary now to examine the outcome of the actual meeting of Wollstonecraft and Godwin, for very rapidly Godwin's intellectual position changed fundamentally.

Following the brief meeting with Godwin in 1791, Wollstonecraft soon found herself (after a disastrous attempt to live *à trois* with Henri Fuseli and his wife) in revolutionary Paris. Here she encountered British and American sympathizers of the revolution among whom was Gilbert Imlay who formed an attachment with Mary Wollstonecraft. Although they were not married, Wollstonecraft adopted the name Imlay and gave birth to a daughter (Fanny Imlay). Gilbert Imlay soon abandoned them. It was as mother with daughter that Godwin encountered Mary Wollstonecraft again in 1796. This second time they became lovers, Mary became pregnant and in spite of the ridicule which fell on Godwin, who had publically criticized the institution, they married soon after; she however was, to die in childbirth, in August 1797. Thus Godwin, having been a bachelor, found himself a widower with a young child (Fanny) and a baby only days old (Mary, later Mary Shelley), and literary executor to Mary Wollstonecraft's manuscripts. He decided to look after the children himself, to publish the remaining manuscripts, and to write the *Memoirs of The Author of a Vindication of the Rights of Woman* (1798). The latter was a detailed and accurate account of the details of Wollstonecraft's life in as completely honest a form as he could achieve, with revelations of her relation with Fuseli, with Imlay, and her suicide attempts. He even included her letters to Imlay in the *Posthumous Works*. The tide of revolutionary sympathy had turned to reaction and the effect of this attempt at complete honesty was to turn Wollstonecraft into a figure of ridicule. Only much later was this judgement reversed. But as William St Clair argues, 'For Mary Wollstonecraft sentiment had neither reinforced reason nor militated against it. In the *Memoirs* the long tradition of rationalism from Locke and Hartley through Hume and the French *philosophes* to its culmination in *Political Justice* is implicitly acknowledged to have rested on an incomplete understanding.' (St Clair 1989: 183–4). In 1798 Godwin wrote a memorandum suggesting that some of the ideas in *Political Justice* were 'defective in the circumstance of not yielding a proper attention to the empire of feeling' (see Tysdahl 1981: 103).

Concretely, the encounter with Wollstonecraft seemed to have considerable consequences, even if in their totality it is difficult to assess them. First of all in the first edition of the *Memoirs*, Godwin notes that the formal convention of marriage makes public in a ludicrous way something that is simply an interpersonal bond. But within a year, the second edition had added to it the qualification that, as the convention has the support of a majority of the population, the negative consequences of abolition (at the present time) outweigh other advantages (see Clark 1977: 119). This line of thought was continued later, particularly in the novel *Fleetwood: Or, The New Man of Feeling* (1805),[2] but in a strange variation. Fleetwood's own education is solitary, but instead of this leading to moral strength, the outcome is suffered, when it comes to relations with the other sex, as a torment of jealousy: Fleetwood has wax models of his wife and presumed lover constructed, then he mocks them and finally smashes them to pieces. This empire of feeling is powerful but does not develop links with reason. Indeed, as Tysdahl points out 'the husband's (Fleetwood's) misgivings are a result only of his own sad lack of inner security' (Tysdahl 1981: 122). Godwin says in the preface to the novel that 'multitudes of readers have themselves passed through the very incidents I relate; but, for the most part, no work has hitherto recorded them. . . . If I had forseen from the first all the difficulty of my project, my courage would have failed me to undertake the execution of it' (Godwin 1832: xvi). In a sense the new man of feeling is not one who is in control (rather the reverse), but who reveals the extent of the domination of feeling.

It is possible to argue, as Don Locke has shown, that Godwin's reaction to the influence of Mary Wollstonecraft involved a revolution in his intellectual system, for, once the logic of the empire of feeling breaks the connection between the motivation for, and the reason for, progress, justice becomes a more complex goal. Godwin says 'if reason be frequently inadequate to its task, if there be an opposite principle in man resting upon its own ground, and maintaining a separate jurisdiction, the most rational principles of society may be rendered abortive, it may be necessary to call in mere sensible causes to encounter causes of the same nature' (cited in Locke 1980: 142). The 'abstract principle' does not any longer by itself move the world.

This line of argument that Mary Wollstonecraft had a 'profound impact' on Godwin has been challenged by Mark Philp (1986: 175–92). Philp attempts to argue that Godwin's changes of opinion can be regarded as either a pure intellectual logic, a concession to public opinion, or to changing social conditions. His account tends to remain close to the various versions of the text of *Political Justice*. The one real exception is his treatment of Godwin's views on marriage. Here he traces the ideological context of the period, and concludes, not that there was on this point any dramatic reversal of view on Godwin's part, but that his 'marriage was an affair of prudence rather than principle' (ibid.: 190). However, from the moment that Philp announces this argument, almost the whole of his subsequent discussion subverts it in the most curious way. Within the space of a few lines, he concludes that 'Godwin's revised attitude to marriage in the 1798 edition might be seen as an indication that the experiment [i.e. his marriage to Mary Wollstonecraft] was successful' (ibid.: 190).

But more than this, Philp points out that Godwin had begun to alter his position just before his involvement with Mary Wollstonecraft, and had in particular begun to tone down the fierce and extreme rationalism of 1793. But it was only in 1798 that the changed notion of truth, which in Philp's words 'is clearly related to his attempt to integrate feeling and emotion into his account of moral action' emerged. On the difference between 1793 and 1798 Philp concludes 'in the first edition [of *Political Justice*] Godwin's confidence in the power of truth left his theory of moral motivation rather undeveloped; in the third edition, although his attention to feeling allows him to develop a more persuasive account of motive and action, it now becomes difficult to see where truth fits into the picture' (ibid.: 202–3). The more Philp examines these differences the more it becomes clear that a complete revolution in theory has occurred. 'Feeling has become all important' says Philp, quoting Godwin to the effect that 'in subjects connected with the happiness of mankind, the feeling is the essense' (ibid.: 203).

Yet there are further changes. The first, which Philp traces to Godwin's *Memoirs* of Mary Wollstonecraft, is Godwin's rejection of the role of reason in 'selecting or recognising which objects are most productive of pleasure' (ibid.: 212). Second, Godwin changes his view of personal affections: 'The benefits we can confer upon those with whom we are closely connected, are of great magnitude or continual occurrence (Godwin, cited in Philp 1986: 213). Philp's discussion of these changes, which he describes as 'crucial', makes a great argumentative 'leap', involves the complete 'destruction' of his earlier position, avoids all consideration of Wollstonecraft's writings and ideas, even the personal history of their relation, and instead concludes 'Godwin thus seems to take on a very crude version of Hume' (ibid.: 213) as though the coincidence of the sharp break in view and the passionate episode and then death of Wollstonecraft, the fact that Godwin had become a father in such circumstances, had no effective reality. Philp seems to be aware of the deficiency of his account and in a final section of his book, he seeks to suggest sociological factors for such a dramatic change of view. He provides evidence that Godwin's social circles became more insular, his contacts during this period became centred on friends and relatives, and finally there was increasingly less opportunity for 'serious intellectual discussion and debate' (ibid.: 220). Clearly Philp implies that the new position, which 'vitiates [Godwin's] entire moral and political theory' (1986: 219), is entirely regressive.

Chapter 5

In sexuality: Prosper Enfantin, the 'sons-in-Saint-Simon' and *la femme libre*

The aftermath of the French Revolution was marked by a period of intense utopian collective experimentation (Fourier, Owen, Cabet, etc.) and a new theoretical investigation of the 'social' (as opposed to the eighteenth-century interest in political and moral science). Most of the discussion has centred, correctly, on the pivotal influence of the writings of Henri de Saint-Simon (1760–1825) which was wide, but highly contradictory: from the revolutionary communism of Marx and Engels, to the later appeals to conservatives of Comte. But this influence was also important for feminism itself since, it has been claimed, the first consciously feminist journal associated with a feminist movement, was born at the same moment as Saint-Simonian doctrine was developed into socialist forms.

Saint-Simon himself was accused in his lifetime of living the life of a libertine, of being an immoral, to which he replied 'the taste for pleasure has never been my dominant passion . . . [that] is the desire to make scientific discoveries' (Saint-Simon 1956: 97). Indeed he contracted a curious marriage which he insisted with shattering honesty was conceived purely as an auxiliary to his scientific pursuits. 'I used marriage as a means of studying the scientists, something that to me appeared necessary for the execution of my enterprise, for to improve the organisation of the scientific system it was not enough to be thoroughly acquainted with the status of human knowledge, it was also necessary to know what effect the cultivation of the sciences produces on those who are devoted to it' (ibid.: 56; see different translation, Taylor 1975: 19). Saint-Simon had sheltered the destitute daughter (Sophie Champgrand) of a friend, then he married and provided her with an annuity in order to make the arrangement appear respectable. Within a year (1802) he proposed divorce, as she seemed unwilling to join with him in his projects for social reform. He deplored the narrowness, which, he said, 'prevented her from soaring with him beyond all hitherto known bounds' (Manuel 1956: 55). After their divorce, which was still a simple matter at that time and at which he was distraught (officials thought he was the one who wanted to

remain married), they never met again. The legend has it that he wished to
be free from Sophie Champgrand to propose marriage to the most emi-
nent woman intellectual of the period, Madame de Stael, and that, true
to the idea of soaring into new spheres, he proposed their first night be
spent in a balloon. Nothing came of the project.

Saint-Simon's thought was a remarkable synthesis of French and British
Enlightenment science and rationalist philosophy. The dominant idea was
that the Enlightenment was a critical moment which had now to give way
to a period of positive social construction. This period also needed its
own new beliefs as well as institutions. His philosophy was marked decisively by the aim of applying scientific methodology to social reconstruction, and the recognition of the importance of social function taken
largely from the utilitarian tradition. The philosophy evolved in the first
instance into a scientistic programme of social meritocracy, with the
watchword, later taken up by Engels: 'from each according to his
capacity, to each according to his work'. As Mill noted, this implied a
continuation of a rational critique of property and inheritance, leading
directly to the idea of the triumph of reason in the withering away of
the State and politics. Liberalism, however, was defined as a form of
revolutionary sickness. Education should be based on the observational
sciences not on the literary classics. It has been claimed that 'if no one
today reads Saint-Simon or refers to him, it is because we are living in
the midst of his system' (Calvino 1989: 223). This is perhaps an over-
simplification. Saint-Simon realized, in his later work, that a strictly
scientistic appeal to reason alone would be insufficient to carry through
his social programme. He developed, therefore, a reinvigorated but
revised, New Christianity as an essential component of the new social
order.

Auguste Comte, himself once a close collaborator with Saint-Simon,
had, at the time of Saint-Simon's death, become estranged from him. At
his death Saint-Simon was surrounded by a young group of intellectuals
who took up his ideas enthusiastically and within a short period had
begun to elaborate a new and systematic social doctrine (see Carlisle
1987: 41–71). Along with similar projects influential and popular at the
time (cf. Fourier, Owen) this movement was keen to see that the elaboration of theory had practical social consequences. Many of the results of
the first exposition of the new doctrine were originally delivered in lectures to large audiences in 1828–9 (Iggers 1972). The new religion and
hierarchy was established in December 1828 (see Carlisle 1987: 88) and
was taken up in a secular form in Marx and Engels. But the second
exposition, little known in English-speaking countries as it has not been
made available in translation, involved a doctrine of collective sexual
revolution and with it, as Offen notes 'the free play of passion, of erotic
forces with the demonstrated capability of undermining the institution of

legal and indissoluble marriage . . . thereby eroding the monogamous familial structure' (Offen 1986: 463).

Of the leaders who took part in this discussion, Philippe Buchez supported the notion that women should be encouraged to enter, as individuals, into a free society.[1] Buchez was to lose out decisively in this argument to Prosper Enfantin and his notion of the couple as the true 'social individual' (he was to claim that Enfantin was simply ambitious for his own interest) (Carlisle 1987: 121). The doctrine of *la femme libre* was promulgated by Enfantin in 1831, in the context of the New Christianity's conception of an androgynous God, a God with distinct male and female attributes. The organization of the social hierarchy, Enfantin insisted, was to be headed by a priestly couple, himself and a woman yet to be named (although he was a father – he had a liaison with Adèle Morlane who had borne a son (Arthur)). The organization was a mixture of pseudo-Catholicism, pseudo-Judaism, and pseudo-Masonism, with priests, popes, and a hierarchy of 'degrees', with confessionals and a catechism, fused into an enlarged family grouping conceived as a working commune. Authority was, in the absence of a popess, vested in the 'living law' of the founding 'fathers', at first the male couple Enfantin and Bazard, and later simply the single father 'pope' Enfantin. The basic idea of this organization was that for a genuine overcoming of the traditional separations, a true sexual liberation, or a rehabilitation of the flesh, the power of a priesthood was a necessary institutional control over appetite and the workings of the new morality: a controlled collective desublimation.

Enfantin suggested first that the spheres and contributions of each sex were different, though of equal value. Thus the male would come to contribute intelligence and reflection, and the female sympathy and sentiment. The male pope would be complemented by the female one, and together they would form a 'papal-couple': in this system, in theory influenced by the later writings of Saint-Simon, but radicalized in the socialist context of the Saint-Simonian experiment, it was sentiment and love which would form the basis of the order and would guide reflection. This implied the full participation of women in all aspects of social life, a participation legitimated on the basis of the unique contribution that women could make. Enfantin argued in 1831 that there were three basic moralities; those of the 'constants', those of the 'mobiles', and those of the new 'papal-couple'. The latter could harmonize the combinations of the other two in a process he described as 'rekindling the numbed feelings' of the first and controlling the 'unruly appetites' of the second (cited in Moses 1982: 245). Enfantin 'equated maleness with activity, femaleness with passivity, maleness with the search for love, and femaleness with the offering of love' (Carlisle 1987: 161). But his theory of personality implied that there were in fact not only 'constant' and 'mobile' natures, but also oriental and Christian natures, and other basic symbolic structures, the 'Othello' and the 'Don Juan', indicating that each human personality was made up of both sides of the complex whole. In the past, one of the sides in each of the sexes had been repressed, in the future, he argued, new combinations of a more balanced and open form could be established (ibid.: 167).

He wrote to his mother at this time, saying

> I ask myself how LIVELY, FLIRTATIOUS, SEDUCTIVE, ATTRACTIVE, CHANGING, ARDENT, PASSIONATE, EXALTED beings ought to be directed, considered, USED in the FUTURE so that their character may be for them and for humanity a source of joy, not of sadness, of fêtes and not of mourning [The highest form of love will be that of the priest and priestess, loved by others for their] beauty, grace, amiability, flirtatiousness, their ardour, their burning and tender eyes. . . . How far will the carnal expression . . . go? . . . I conceive CERTAIN CIRCUMSTANCES where I would judge that my wife alone would be capable of giving happiness, health, life to one of my sons in Saint-Simon; to recall him to social sympathies, to warm him when some profound sadness demands a diversion, when his broken heart would bleed with disgust with life.
>
> (cited in Carlisle 1987: 166)

Unions are not eternal, unless the couple is constant. Other unions may be changed under the guidance of the papal-couple. In the debates around these themes, Enfantin added another element, that of the unlimited independence of women, which involved the right of women to control completely the knowledge of the paternity of the child. As children were to be adopted into the larger social family, in a context where individual inheritance was non-existent, this proposal would solve many questions of jealousy and power. It also points to a new conception of paternity linked to the wider social structure of the group. Bazard, one of the two leading 'fathers', objected to this, and against the background of suspicion that Claire Bazard and Enfantin were aiming to become themselves the papal-couple, had a stroke (on 25 August 1831). In October an intermediary position was adopted and by November, when Bazard had made some recovery, it was announced that there would be three 'fathers, Enfantin, Bazard, and Rodrigues, each with a different function. This solution only lasted a few hours, for almost immediately Bazard rejected his new role, and Claire Bazard, surprised at being excluded from the new papal-couple, left, writing to Enfantin 'Today you have broken me without pity', indicating that she would also leave Bazard (ibid.: 170).

There was a form of regroupment, and the project continued with more lectures from Enfantin, culminating in a lecture on women in December 1831. Here the parallel of oppression of the proletariat and women was drawn in full, with the specific feature of prostitution as the principal social problem. This was now directly linked to the Christian repression of pleasure and hypocritical monogamy. The new regime could provide both a liberation of the flesh and a liberation of women from prostitution; this was made possible by the wise supervision and discipline exercised by the new priestly couple. Some of the phrases used by Enfantin in his letter to his mother found their way into the lecture: the love for the priestly couple is due to their outstanding liveliness, ardour and gaiety. It is this ability to mediate, as they do, between reason and senses more generally, which enables them to control the harmonic evolution of such sensual liberation. Enfantin begins to make his interpellation of woman: 'And now, if one asks what limit I place on the priest and priestess, I answer "none". Women will speak . . . I call to her in the name of the poorest and most numerous class . . . in the name of all these men and all the women who throw the brilliant veil of lies or the dirty wrap of debauchery over their secret or public prostitution, in the name of Saint-Simon I conjure her to reply to me' (cited in Carlisle 1987: 182).

But the background to this is curious. Up until early 1831 the male and female hierarchies in the movement had been separate. After they were merged there were women on the advisory council beside Enfantin and Bazard, as well as in the superior, the second and the third degrees of the hierarchy of the organization. But, as Claire Moses points out, 'as the theoretical power of women was rising . . . the actual power of women was declining' (Moses 1982: 249). And when Enfantin gave his lectures at the end of 1831, he also dismissed the whole female hierarchy:

> Man and woman, this is the social individual, but woman is still a slave; we must set her free. Before reaching a state of equality with man, she [first] must be free. We must then create for Saint-Simonian women a condition of freedom by destroying the hierarchy . . . and have them participate in the law of equality among themselves. THERE ARE NO LONGER ANY WOMEN IN THE DEGREES OF THE HIERARCHY. Our apostolate which is *l'appel de la femme* is an apostolate of men.
>
> (21 November 1831)

Within a short period of time the leaders of this movement were under threat of prosecution for offences against public morality and embezzlement. Under this threat Enfantin led the men in April into chaste retreat, a more or less closed community at Menilmontant, where all were involved in a formal daily ritual and a closely articulated division of labour (Enfantin did the gardening), and in June the men adopted Saint-Simonian costume (red, blue and white) thought by many an attempt to develop a religious habit signifying commitment to celibacy. Acquitted on the charge of embezzlement, Enfantin was nonetheless imprisoned on the charge of offending public morality. Even before his imprisonment the commune began to break up; after the trial many of the remaining followers went to search for *La Femme*, the Jewish female Messiah, in Egypt. But the effect on the women involved in the movement in Paris was remarkable in many respects, especially at the conjuncture at which Enfantin was imprisoned and the women had been separated from the male hierarchy.

Thus there appeared in 1832 the first feminist journal, the *Tribune des Femmes*. As Claire Moses has shown there was to be a remarkable divergence between the direction in which discussion tended to develop in this journal and the direction of Enfantin's thought. There was, among the women, little enthusiasm for the 'rehabilitation of the flesh'; after an initial debate, the issue dropped out of discussion altogether. Economic conditions tended to make independence even more difficult in subsequent years. But a key objection was to the double standards evident in Enfantin's practice. One of the leading female participants Suzanne Voilquin noted that when she made a confession of infidelity in front of her husband and Enfantin, the latter actually comforted the husband, revealing a clear, unconscious bond between the men, the presence of which, said Voilquin, would never encourage her again to make any such confessions. Such confessions would only be made to a woman (Moses 1982: 262). Moses concludes 'Their concern was to achieve autonomy . . . seemingly more conservative than Enfantin, they were in fact more radical. They had enlarged the feminist vision of sexual emancipation, for by linking it to the economic, intellectual, and legal emancipation, they had placed the sexual question into the larger context' (ibid.: 265).

And Susan Grogan's recent account (Grogan 1992: 106) concludes:

Women's attempts to develop both the theory and practice of Saint-Simonianism according to their own insights challenged the neatness of the men's theoretical overview, and the male right to define the identity and the social roles of women.

Chapter 6

In worship: Auguste Comte and Clotilde de Vaux

Auguste Comte who had broken with Saint-Simon before his death, nevertheless rivalled the other Saint-Simonians in trying to work out the logic of the master's thought, even running courses of lectures concurrently with those of the other group. His famous *Cours* beginning in 1829 had a prestigious audience of mathematicians, scientists and philosophers. And it was Comte who expressed Saint-Simon's ideas in a rigorous academic manner, coining the word sociology in the process. The Saint-Simonian group's rival course of 1828–9 criticized Comte (Session xv) for misunderstanding the religious implications of the master's thought, that is, for conceiving the law of the three stages as a movement to atheism. In their critique the Saint-Simonians claimed that in the later positive phases the scientific and the divine were reunited: in such periods 'obedience is sweet and faith easy' (cited in Iggers 1972: 261). Comte's intellectual career falls into two separate periods, and in the later one his thought rejoins that of the Saint-Simonians, not only in giving privilege to religion (the religion of humanity), but also to the symbolic precedence of the feminine principle of feeling over that of the masculine one of intellect and reflection.

Certainly there is a remarkable parallel with Saint-Simon himself in the fact that Comte also married in part to rescue a woman, in this case Caroline Massin, a prostitute who had asked Comte for algebra lessons. 'He gloried in his own generosity' said Littre (1864: 115). They began to live together, and after a scene in a restaurant when a policeman recognized her and attempted to arrest her on grounds of being a registered prostitute who had not kept up with fortnightly medical checks, Comte eventually got her off the charge through marrying her. But their relationship was a difficult one, and Comte at the end of his life blamed her for provoking his mental breakdown (1826–7), for diverting his attention from his true social mission (costing him, he claimed, up to four years of lost time that might have been spent writing), and for being meretricious, unworthy, heartless, and ungrateful. In an attempt to try to prevent her inheriting his property he wrote an elaborate testament, with a secret addition of great bitterness, which vilified her (Comte 1910: 469–539).

On the other hand, Comte met Clotilde de Vaux, a married woman abandoned by her husband, with whom he developed an intense platonic relationship.[1] The whole of his second period he conceived as developing under her influence and the influence of feeling and sympathy. They exchanged many letters, and Comte later codified Clotilde's sayings into maxims and words of general wisdom for the new religion. At Clotilde's death the de Vaux family tried to exclude him as he attempted to control the proceedings; but he tricked the family into leaving the room and Comte locked them out ensuring that she died in his presence (Manuel 1962: 262). After her death he transfigured her into a saint, writing twelve homages known as 'Saint Clotildes'; other manuscripts of de Vaux were kept from Comte by her family (see Comte 1973a: vol. I, xvi). Comte turned himself into a priest of humanity in his *Catechism of Positive Religion* of 1852, which was written as a set of 'thirteen systematic conversations' with an 'imaginary woman'. The principal aim of this work was to reveal the importance of incorporating women 'into the western revolution' (ibid.: 23), which meant a universal emancipation from prostitution by releasing women from the necessity to work outside the home, and at the same time elevating their status into guardian angels. Comtean theory vindicates the duties, not the rights of women, for it is duty (not reason) which engenders feeling (ibid.: 229) and which in turn complements and softens the cool capacities of men. Curiously, the account of Comte as a person, provided by an English mathematics student, presented a picture of the man, at first in the 1830s, as very impersonal: 'only twice did I succeed in gaining proof that he had something mortal in his composition'. Comte was 'invariably dressed in a suit of the most spotless black, as if going to a dinner party . . . his hat shining like a racer's coat.' But by 1851 all had changed, 'he was no longer the rigid thinker, regular and passionless as a mechanism' (in Hutton 1890: 125–33).

But there is something of a covering up of Comte's earlier character by the orthodox positivists, and Comte himself, having become priest of humanity and the founder of a church, wanted to veil much of the story of his relation with Caroline Massin. Works in this tradition, such as Jane Style's *August Comte: Thinker and Lover* (1928) are extremely hostile to Massin, accusing her of manipulating Comte from beginning to end, even of having prepared the episode in the restaurant. But Massin found friendly support from writer Emile Littre whose perspective on Comte takes her position. Indeed, at the end of Comte's life, Littre tried to play the role of intermediary between the two, inducing Comte to write a detailed account of the history of the relation. Henri Gouhier's later biography of Comte ([1931] 1965) provides an account which generally supports Littre and Massin. The elements of Comte's encounter with Massin are complex, and instead of being Comte's downfall, Massin seems to have been his saviour. Citing evidence from Comte himself, Littre shows that the union between them seems at first to have been happy and passionate, even the journey of the couple to visit Comte's parents in July 1825 (Littre 1864: 34). But in 1826 a number of circumstances coincided to induce a serious breakdown in Comte, leading in 1827 to a suicide attempt.

After his civil marriage to Caroline Massin, a marriage profoundly unacceptable to his devoutly Catholic mother, Comte found himself with considerable intellectual problems in his work and confrontation with the Saint-Simonians; he also had financial problems which caused a rift between himself and his new wife. In the 'secret addition' to his testament (published in 1896), Comte revealed that she had been abandoned as a child by her parents, and brought up only to be sold into prostitution. A well-known young lawyer, Cerclet, paid 1,000 ecus for her when she was aged sixteen. Comte was also a client, and far from being anonymous, Cerclet kept a relation with them both, and was even a witness at the civil marriage in February 1825 as well as being instrumental in getting Caroline's name off the register of prostitutes. Comte insisted on, and received, a promise that Cerclet would be excluded from their lives, but when economic difficulties arose, the name of Cerclet was again suggested by Caroline, now Madame Comte; she suggested that Comte was not able to support the marriage. It was this attempt to 'impose' the visits of Cerclet on him, and the first separation of the couple, which, said Comte, later provoked 'mon explosion cerebral' (in Littre 1864: 128). Comte was found wandering near the Enghien Lake, into which he tried to drag and drown Caroline. She escaped and sought aid. Comte was confined to the care of Dr Esquirol in a secure regime, but even so attacked an employee of the clinic, plunging a fork into his cheek. On learning her son was incarcerated, Comte's mother arrived in Paris believing that the problem had arisen out of Comte's secular marriage. But Esquirol would not give permission for an 'uncured' Comte to leave. Eventually Caroline persuaded Esquirol that she would nurse him at their apartment, now made secure after, to satisfy the mother, immediately completing a Catholic marriage. At the marriage Comte muttered his own disbelief as the words of the service were pronounced, and on the register signed his name 'Brutus, Bonaparte Comte'. Under the care of Caroline he made a recovery, but not before he made a final suicide attempt by throwing himself in the Seine. When well enough, he undertook a journey home to Montpellier only to disappear at Nîmes for some days: he wanted to see Caroline again he explained. Later medical evidence to Littre suggested that, had not Caroline taken Comte to Esquirol, he may not have survived at the Enghien Lake (Dr Robin, in Littre 1864: 141–2). But certainly Comte's mother, and Comte himself, began to blame Caroline for all that had happened, with increasing bitterness ('the only capital mistake of my whole life', he wrote (1910: 513)), and the suicide attempt(s) were never mentioned again.

The final separation came after seventeen years, Comte wrote in his testament, but there were earlier temporary separations in 1826, 1828, and 1833. These were unhappy occasions which induced in Comte periods of crisis and depression, but they only interrupted years of what he called 'unseemly daily strife'. What he had hoped for, he said, was a moral calm, in which he could work and write, and engage in his 'supreme labour'. They agreed, finally, to separate and that he would support her, but because of his work he agreed that she would not leave until the beginning of August 1842, but she left on 15 June, throwing him again into a personal crisis. She was persuaded to remain with him, but she complained of his continuing tyranny. He, on the other hand, constantly complained that she was part of the 'western malady' an emphasis on rights and liberty, on revolution, without a respect for duties (she had a fear, he claimed, of moral discipline, and she was frivolous). Above all 'she never appreciated my intellect' he said; she even claimed the writer Armand Marrast was a superior writer, and, he insisted, she never 'understood my heart' (Comte 1910: 517).

In October 1844 Comte met Clotilde de Vaux. Their encounter was brief: she died in April 1846. The effect on Comte of this meeting, he claimed, was a 'deep moral revolution, which brought out the true emotional character of positivism' (ibid.: 506). In the Preface (March 1851) to the *System of Positive Polity*, he outlined the effect de Vaux had had upon him. In his earlier relation he had been 'hopelessly cut off from any affection that could satisfy the heart'. When the final separation occurred he had 'two years of indispensible calm' before meeting de Vaux, who had also been abandoned by her husband. 'Untainted purity gave stability to our affection, and this during one incomparable year of objective union, was the principal instrument on my moral regeneration', he wrote, beginning to describe the Comtean version of the new man. The love he felt previously for his mother was 'never sufficiently shown, owing to the false shame of seeming too fond'. The influence of de Vaux was to make this veneration possible, as it was to appreciate the moral virtues of his housekeeper Sophie Biot, whose 'unfortunate inability to read only brings out more strikingly not merely the excellence of her feelings, but also the clearness and penetration of her mind' (Comte 1973a: vol. I, xix). His preface is followed by a dedication of the work to de Vaux in which he announces that he wishes to

systematise human life as a whole on the principle of the subordination of the intellect to the heart. The chief difficulty of my task is doubtless

to induce the intellect to accept this position voluntarily. . . . Here
. . . it was that the reaction of pure personal love upon philosophic
thought was so specially valuable.

(Ibid.: xxxv)

The new doctrine is announced: 'no intellectual reform can truly regener-
ate society until the transformation of ideas has been followed by that of
feelings: this last alone is decisive of its social power, and without it
Philosophy could never be a substitute for Religion' (ibid.: xxxvii).

Soon after the meeting with de Vaux, Comte had become convinced
that it was necessary to adopt the 'whole Catholic programme of the
Middle Ages' (ibid.: vol. II, xlviii) but with 'proved religion' supplanting
'revealed religion' in a new neo-gothic sociology. It is the 'silent regret'
on the part of women for the chivalrous system of the Middle Ages which
has to be overcome: in fact 'the only way to make them cordial fellow-
workers in the movement is to offer them a philosophy as satisfying to
the needs of the heart as to those of the mind . . . but women can only
be convinced of it by a woman' (ibid.: vol. I, xl). The route to the heart,
for a man, is, however, through the mind, and love the 'sole antidote
for the oppressive barrenness of scientific study' (ibid.: xliii); not love as
egoistic personal passion, but rather the 'systematic prominence, both in
private and in public life, [of] the worship of woman, which in the Middle
Ages had been faintly foreshadowed' (ibid.: xliv). Indeed, so important
were the Middle Ages to Comte, that he was, later in the work, to
suggest that it was mediaeval chivalry that had brought about the first
emancipation of women (ibid.: vol. II, 106).

The project enunciated in the later Comte then, is the theory and
organization of the 'positive polity' conceived as the reintroduction and
updating of the Catholic mediaeval polity, that is, with an element of
fetishism (worship of idols) added to positive social science as the substance of the new belief system: reason and action (masculine) under the
domination of the influence of (feminine) feeling. It was the profound
feeling of 'regret' for the loss of the feudal system of chivalry by women
that maintained an essential link with the possibilities of a unified society.
The high point of the mediaeval synthesis was also marked, said Comte,
by the importance of the worship of the virgin. This was no accident, for
'humanity can never be adequately represented in any masculine form'
(ibid.: vol. I, 167). With the new positive religion it will be essential for
women to withdraw into the family, and for the cult of women to be
systematically elaborated so that the moral influence of women can regen-
erate religion itself. Comte was not uncritical of Catholicism, in the
Catholic Middle Ages the priests separated themselves from women in
their celibate orders, and Catholic doctrine actually became anti-social:
in consequence 'the heart crushed the intellect' (ibid.: 177). Under the

influence of women in the new positive order (with Comte as pope) the heart will nourish the intellect.[2]

This doctrine rests on the assumption that 'women's minds . . . are less capable of generalising very wisely, or of carrying on long processes of deduction . . . less capable . . . of abstract intellectual exertion'. But women are more alive to reality and to emotion (ibid.: 180).[3] It is the family that women must take as the centre of their sphere, and he ardently claims revolutionary attacks on marriage are always opposed by women, since these ideas come from the head and not the heart (ibid.: 185). Yet women's influence extends beyond the family, as is shown in the importance of *salons*, which will make their appearance again. But the crucial contribution of positivism, says Comte, is that unlike the Church, it offers a systematic justification for indissoluble marriage and 'eternal widowhood'. The positive theory suggests that it is women who ennoble the otherwise coarse sexual instinct in man, and render it the basis of a union more beautiful than friendship. If man is force and woman feeling, their union is a complementarity which aims at the 'perfection of each other' – the first step to universal love (ibid.: 188).

In order to have its full emotional and moral effect this union must be as strong as possible. Thus it must not only be exclusive and indissoluble, based also on the principle of eternal widowhood, but it must also acknowledge the principle of the 'union in the tomb' (a principle to be promised at each positivist marriage). Again Comte criticizes Christianity which tends to accept the principle of second marriages, which weakens the institution and its moral effect. The moral results of marriage are most elevated and effective when it is purely chaste. Purity does not only lead to deepening human affection, it is also physically beneficial (207–8). Marriage therefore must be conceived by the new positivist man as the 'voluntary subordination to woman for the rest of his life' (ibid.: 196). Yet the moral position of women is always highest in the poorest classes, he argues. One can deduce therefore that power is 'injurious to delicacy', and indeed the acquisition of power by women would have disastrous consequences for society as a whole. Women, if active in society outside the home, would suffer morally, and 'their social position would be endangered' as a result of the corruption of the power of love, brought about by rivalry, and competition. The basic solution to the problem, he argues, is that 'men should provide for women' (ibid.: 199). At the same time, to prevent the corrupting practice of the dowry, and to separate women from the corrupting power of wealth, only men will inherit (ibid.: 201). Thus the Comtean doctrine on new women asserts that they are 'born to love and be loved, relieved of the burdens of practical life, free in the sacred retirement of their homes'. The (re)newed man 'will kneel to Woman, and to Woman alone' (ibid.: 208).

The new religion will systematically construct the forms of worship of women, and this worship may be morally of 'greater efficacy than the worship of God' (ibid.: 209). It will be based on a pattern of idealization, just as it was in the Middle Ages, and will perfect it. Comte himself cites his own letters to Clotilde de Vaux as his attempt to practise this new form of worship and thus morally transform himself. The elaboration of the theory of the soul, the forms of worship, prayer and ritual, are all precisely constructed and total, involving a reformulation of the calendar into thirteen months, a renaming of the months, days and years, the institution of rituals of the life-cycle (the nine sacraments), and a new system of the naming of individuals. The specifically Comtean inspiration here is to find a continuation with the spiritual forces close to the individual in the historical period of fetishism and polytheism: 'the guardian angels of Catholicism were but a feeble substitute for the household gods of Fetishism . . . gods who stood in a more direct and individual relation to their worshipper, gods exercising a stronger influence . . . one which appealed more sensibly to the feelings' (ibid.: vol. IV, 101). Positive religion therefore identifies the guardian angels of the new men: woman, mother, wife, daughter, sister. The mother inspires veneration, the wife attachment, the daughter benevolence, a 'triple representation of the Great Being' (ibid.: vol. IV, 97). Comte details a round of daily prayers, individual, family and community prayers, the forms and techniques of prayers, even whether the eyes should be open or closed during prayer, etc., as the male side of a completely organized sociolatry.[4]

But the most surprising aspect of this later theory concerns women and sexual reproduction, where Comte introduces what he calls a 'daring hypothesis' (ibid.: 60); this is completely consistent with his notion of the positive completion of the emancipation of woman, or rather what Comte calls her new independence. The change envisaged 'does not merely involve the placing her moral higher than her physical function, hitherto coarsely held paramount. It implies in addition the previous correction of the existing opinions as to this physical function, originally held to be essentially a masculine attribute.' (ibid.: 59). There is, he says, a growing tendency in history for humans to be viewed as the offspring of women. Comte supports the tendency from a scientific point of view, and concedes that in reproduction the predominant role is woman's. The share of the man's is 'much smaller than might be expected from the activity of his generative system' (ibid.: 59). (He argues later that this system has a different purpose.) Then he claims to revive an older tradition to suggest that the action of the mother's brain on the foetus during pregnancy plays a more preponderant role as civilization progresses, and hence the whole reproductive cycle becomes more under the influence of social forces. Indeed the male 'stimulus', not even, according to Comte, the main function of his generative organs, becomes less and less significant in procreation itself. Here it is conceivable, says Comte, 'that we might substitute for this stimulus one or more which should be at women's free disposal' (ibid.: 60). This hypothesis represents an indication, a presentiment, of the possible degree of independence from men within the feminine sphere that women might attain.

Comte put this in the most directly physical terms: physically 'woman is superior to man, by virtue of a more complete development of the nervous and vascular systems. Woman is naturally qualified to be the highest type of the mutual influence of the cerebral and bodily life'. Woman's share in reproduction will increase as women are freed from activity, and 'if so, the Utopia of the Virgin Mother will become, for the purer and nobler women, an ideal limit' (ibid.: 212). It will represent the development of 'a power of which as yet we have only witnessed the faint beginnings' (ibid.: 213). Comte looks forward to the realization of the 'Utopia of the Middle Ages, by presenting all the members of the great family as the offspring of a spouseless mother' (ibid.: 358). In his final testament he was insistent that he share a common tomb with his three guardian angels, or, in their physical absence, significant tokens of their existence (Comte 1910: 480).

Chapter 7

In liberty: John Stuart Mill and Harriet Taylor

In his autobiography John Stuart Mill noted that 'The writers by whom, more than by any others, a new political mode of political thinking was brought home to me, were those of the St Simonian school in France. . . . I was greatly struck with the connected view which they for the first time presented to me, of the natural order of human progress, and especially with their division of all history into organic periods and critical periods.' (Mill 1924: 138). Most significantly, Mill stresses the importance of Comte's early, Saint-Simonian-inspired essays outlining the 'Law of the Three Stages' which 'harmonized well with my existing notions', he says (ibid.: 140). Very dramatically Mill briefly sketched his utopian hopes for a period of 'unbounded freedom of individual action' and a unity of conviction and sentiment 'so firmly grounded in reason and the true exigencies of life, that they shall not, like all former and present creeds . . . require to be periodically thrown off and replaced by others' (ibid.: 141). Common to many European intellectuals at that moment Mill was tempted by the possibility and promise of the end of political discourse and the end of political strife.

He notes that he lost contact with Comte 'for a number of years' but continued in touch with the Saint-Simonians through Gustave d'Eichthal, and was introduced to the leaders of the Enfantin and Bazard group in 1830. It was through their criticism of individualist political economy and their ideas suggesting that labour and capital should be 'managed for the general account' and that individuals be 'classed by their capacity and remunerated according to their work' that a new vision emerged offering 'a far superior description' than any other of what could be done (ibid.: 141). Mill's support only went so far, and in hoping that these doctrines pass into popular forms it was not that he 'thought these doctrines true, or desired they be acted upon, but in order that the higher classes might be made to see that they had more to fear from the poor when uneducated, than when educated' (ibid.: 146). Mill was also to adopt a completely different position on the question of the relation of the sexes than either the Saint-Simonians or Comte, positions which he continuously debated in correspondence for many years.

It has been argued that J. S. Mill (b. 1806) was predisposed to a positive response to feminism from an early age. One writer has recently drawn attention to Mill's conception of egalitarian marriage; as early as 1833 he had written that 'the highest masculine and highest feminine' characters were without significant distinction (Shanley and Pateman 1991: 173, and see the review of Mill's early feminism in Tulloch 1989: 73–88); another has suggested that 'at the age of 17 he had been arrested for giving vaginal sponges to maid-servants in public and to the wives and daughters of tradesmen and mechanics in market places' (Kandal 1988: 23). Other accounts note that Mill was arrested for dispensing tracts about limiting family size: the argument 'Why bear children you cannot feed, cannot educate? Better not bear them at all,' and because the 'practical information concerned women principally, [Mill] strewed it in their way, down area steps where maids were scrubbing dumbly, at factory gates at the close of the sixteen hour day' (Packe 1954: 57). The charge in this court case was obscenity and the corruption of public morals. He was apparently soon released but this significant episode has remained obscure.

Mill came from a milieu steeped in a rationalist social and philosophical culture. In his early life he was introduced to many of the leading social analysts on the continent, including Saint-Simon himself. He corresponded widely with continental thinkers, and with Comte (Thompson 1976: 189–210). In return, continental thinkers and groups of activists tried specifically to influence his opinion and to gain his allegiance in moral causes (see Pankhurst's discussion 'The wooing of John Stuart Mill', Pankhurst 1957: 6–28). Evidently Mill was deeply marked by his contact with the Saint-Simonians and by Comte's first *Cours*. Comte refers, in his correspondence with Mill, to the 'one important difference' between them – the question of women – and to his strong negative reaction on the work of 'Miss Mary Woolstonscraft' (*sic*) (Comte, 1877: 184). Mill followed Comte's development in great detail, eventually writing a devastating critique of the later doctrine in *Auguste Comte and Positivism* (1865).

The importance of Harriet Taylor's influence on Mill was not in any way disguised: in his autobiography, he gave a full account of 'the most valuable friendship of my life' (Mill 1924: ch. 6). The autobiography remained unfinished on Mill's death, and was put together for publication by Harriet's daughter by her former husband John Taylor, and Mary Colman. There exist numerous versions and 'rejected pages', as well as additions and deletions by Mill and Helen Taylor (see *The Collected Works* vol. I, (1981) which provides the published text, an early draft and the 'rejected leaves of the early draft'; it also identifies the various hands at work in making deletions etc.).

Mill's account begins with their meeting in 1839 (Mill was twenty-five, she was already married at twenty-three). Mill writes that she was 'married at an early age, to a most upright, brave, and honourable man . . . but without the intellectual or artistic tastes which would have made him a companion for her' (Mill 1981: 193). Mill immediately recognized, he says, her true qualities and the effect on him was profound. In his own way, his attitude is not altogether unlike that of Comte to Caroline Massin, he was to rescue her from her situation. He paints a glowing portrait of her: 'she possessed in combination, the qualities which in all other persons I had known I had been only too happy to find singly.' Indeed,

> in her, complete emancipation from every kind of superstition . . . and an earnest protest against many things . . . resulted not from the hard intellect but from strength of noble and elevated feelings, and coincided with a highly reverential nature. . . . Shelley was but a child compared with what she ultimately became.
>
> (Ibid.: 195)

In the 'rejected leaves' he wrote of his complete devotion, admiration, and education under her influence.

> To me, so inferior in nature and so widely different in all previous discipline, a complete or adequate appreciation of her is impossible, and such approach to it as I have made has only been the effect of the long course of education derived from the knowledge and contemplation of her.
>
> (Ibid.: 617)

It is clear that Mill writes of a change involving the complete character of his own work under her influence, and through this influence the transformation of himself as a man. At the formal level this close worship was very much in line with the projects of the Saint-Simonians and Comte.

Mill's eulogy in the autobiography to his dead wife deserves to be examined in detail, and here in comparison with the ideas of Enfantin and Comte. Clearly unlike the latter, Mill is attracted to and gives great value to Harriet's moral rebellion against, and her criticism of, contemporary social relations: she had, he says, 'the utmost scorn of whatever was mean and cowardly, and a burning indignation at everything brutal or tyrannical, faithless or dishonourable in conduct and character' (ibid.: 195). This moral earnestness, Mill points out, was not at all simplistic or unreflective; it is based on the distinction 'between *mal in se* and *mala prohibita*' that is 'instinctive badness' and 'wrongs . . . committed by persons in every respect loveable' (ibid.: 197). But, said Mill, his debt to her was incalculable: there was great 'rapidity of her intellectual growth' and what he owed 'even intellectually, to her, was, in its detail almost infinite'. Mill says that from her, both in reflection on 'ultimate aims' and on practicalities, he had 'acquired more from her teaching, than from all other sources taken together' (ibid.: 197). In fact, 'her intellect is supreme and her judgement infallible' (Helen Taylor tried to modify this, deleted infallible, and inserted 'unerring', but it is clear that Mill pointed to an absolute).

The ultimate logic of Mill's eulogy is driven home: 'Everything in my later writings to which any serious value can be attached, everything either far reaching in speculation or genial in tone and feeling and sympathetic with humanity . . . is in all essentials not my writing but hers' (ibid.: 620–1). Thus although Mill had evidently been predisposed to take up a radical position on the question of women's equality, it was, he emphasized, only through her that his thoughts had been able adequately to evolve. Harriet's thought was not motivated, he insisted, by any bitter animus, but 'from two essential features of her character, her love of justice and her sense of dignity' (ibid.: 621). What developed into a 'fusion' of two minds on this subject was the complementarity of their two approaches: she had 'reached her opinions by the moral intuition of a character of strong feeling' and he had reached them by 'study and reasoning' (ibid.). At this point Mill, once called the 'high priest of rationalism', enters into his own most mystical evocation of their mental fusion, in the form of the strangest critique of the exploitation of women:

> Those most capable of the abnegation of any separate self, and merging of the entire being with that of another, which is characteristic of strong passion, or rather, which strong passion in its most passionate moments strives to realise [a phrase deleted by H.T.] are precisely those who would disclaim to be the objects of this self-annihilating feeling unless the renunciation of any separate existence is equally complete on both sides.

> (Ibid.: 621–2)

The precisely delineated twofold influence of Harriet Taylor was described as falling first on his conception of the human ideal, on the 'ideal standard of character'. The argument is rounded out as involving both an evolution of the ideal, and the presence, in her, of a concrete realization: the 'larger ideal was filled and satisfied by her' (ibid.: 622). Thus he was morally and aesthetically transformed by being presented with both a 'new experience' in terms of 'thoughts and feelings', but also the emergence of 'new objects of contemplation' (a phrase changed by H.T. to 'subjects of contemplation' (ibid.: 622)).

The second effect was related to what Mill had always wanted in his life; his own ideal of womanhood, he reflected was an 'object of my admiration' which would be of a type different from his own, a 'character pre-eminently of feeling, combined however . . . with a vigorous and bold speculative intellect' (ibid.: 623) a formula which closely resembles that of William Godwin. This is what he had discovered in her and it was further combined with 'the perfection of a poetic and artistic nature' (ibid.: 623). His whole self-conception and identity began to change into a new being so that 'the best thing I could do for the world, would be to serve as a sort of prose interpreter of her poetry.' (ibid.). This self-transformation in itself could only be achieved on the basis of the recognition that he was giving 'a logical expression' to another being who had realized a higher meaning 'by experience or divined by the intuition' (ibid.). In the end, the precise effect of this transformation was that his 'faculties . . . became more and more attuned to the beautiful and elevated, in all kinds, and especially in human feeling and character and more capable of vibrating in unison with it' (ibid.). The gradual transfiguration through which this was achieved had as its consequence the fact that he 'gradually withdrew . . . from much of the society' which he had hitherto frequented (a comment which does not appear in the early draft, or the final version where the emphasis is placed on the fact that his encounter with Harriet gave a positive stimulus to his 'activity in all the modes of exertion for public objects' as he became 'more involved than before in political as well as literary relations' (ibid.: 198)).

This evocation of devotion, or rather this account of a process of female deification and self-transformation under the impress of feminine principles, seems to have been internalized by Mill as a fundamental revolution, yet curiously in the autobiography, he also says that this revolution was of secondary importance, since in substance the revolution in his modes of thought 'was already complete' before the encounter; the path had already been chosen. In the end what occurred in the course of his life, was that Harriet's influence was realized as the 'presiding principle' of his mental progress (ibid.: 199). But what was this the effect precisely?

Certainly many of the leading commentaries on Mill's development argue an extreme case, that is they not only suggest that everything was written under her guidance, but that this involved the definition of the basic issues of his philosophy, even the immediate reversal of key cognate substantive conclusions of his earlier work. Packe (1954) takes the example of *Political Economy*, the first draft of which was completed in 1847. Harriet Taylor urged Mill to alter his account of the ultimate aim of socialism, his current effort being too bourgeois in orientation. And she wanted a further chapter which was indeed 'taken almost from her lips, outlining the means for the reformation of the working classes' (Packe 1954: 307). The future depended now, said Mill, on the degree to which the labouring classes could 'be made rational beings.' Schemes for social development should enable human beings to 'work with or for one another in relations not involving dependence' (in Packe 1954: 307). Harriet Taylor's response to the social and political crisis of 1848 radicalized her views considerably, and quickly Mill was persuaded to eliminate his objection to socialism and communism. As Packe notes, a 'work which set out to expose all schemes of communal ownership . . . came within a year to regard them as 'the most valuable elements of human improvement now existing' (ibid.: 313). Even the schemes of Fourier, hitherto rejected, under the vision now became a noble objective: socialism should be made an immediate objective in view of its marked and profound beneficial educational effects.

In the third edition, 1852, new sections on women were introduced to *Political Economy* as Harriet achieved, says Packe, an 'astounding, almost hypnotic control of Mill's mind' (ibid.: 315), as the 'influence she had gradually extended over him now ended in complete ascendancy' (ibid.: 316). His works now became registered, explicitly, as 'joint productions'. Mill wrote to Harriet Taylor in 1849 that, on key points, coming over to her point of view 'is only the progress we have always been making, and by thinking sufficiently I should probably come to think the same – as is almost always the case, I believe always when we think long enough' (in Hayek 1951: 135), and again, 'I never should long continue of an opinion different from yours on a subject which you have fully considered' (in ibid.: 137).

Living in a kind of serial *ménage à trois* as Eugene August has called it (August 1975: 48), Mill developed an intense platonic imaginative relationship with Harriet Taylor against considerable opposition from relations and friends. But when her husband John Taylor died, in July 1849, Mill evidently became even more dependent on her (Packe 1954: 346). Their marriage in April 1851, took place in the absence of Mill's family, who were not informed or invited. He cut dead his own mother ('no other episode in his life shows his character to less advantage' says August (1975: 134)), while at the same time, notes August, Harriet became 'his Saint in his Religion of Humanity' (ibid.: 134). Hayek's famous study of Mill and Taylor concluded that 'her influence on his thought and outlook, whatever her capacities may have been, were quite as great as Mill asserts . . . [but] far from having been the sentimental it was the rationalist element in Mill's thought which was mainly strengthened by her influence' (August 1951: 17), and certainly this influence was continued and deepened even after her death in 1858.

There is one strand of the debate on Mill and Taylor, however, which focuses on an apparent difference of emphasis on the question of the emancipation of women,[1] as revealed in a close scrutiny of Taylor's 'On the enfranchisement of women' (1851) and Mill's *Subjection of Women* (1869). Taylor violently objected to the notion of a special 'sphere' for women (Taylor 1983: 13), and to the imposition of one group's definition of a 'proper sphere' onto another group. What she demanded was the 'complete liberty of choice' in this matter of self-definition, her argument based broadly on what she could see happening in the American women's movement. There could be no *a priori* restriction on the supposed capacities of any one group, all that could be assumed is that, in relation to women, they 'have shown fitness for the highest social functions, exactly in proportion as they have been admitted to them' (ibid.: 15). Her argumentative strategy is one of detailing objections to women's participation and analysing them carefully on their merits one by one. She provides a very brief history of the progress of women in society which leads her to the view that

> Those who are so careful that women should not become men, do not see that men are becoming, what they have decided women should be – are falling into the feebleness which they have so long cultivated in their companions . . . in the present closeness of association between the sexes, men cannot retain manliness unless women want it.
>
> (Ibid.: 28)

Harriet Taylor's argument does not rest on women's inferiority, in fact she disclaims 'the belief that women are even now inferior in intellect to men' (ibid.: 28). Men with strong minds would be greatly benefitted by a meeting with women who had intellectual training and education. And, she admits, in common opinion, it is the moral influence of women which is acknowledged 'almost salutary' (ibid.: 32). But this can only be illusory as a genuine influence in existing patriarchal society, since the husband has always the

> propensity to make himself the first and foremost object of consideration . . . if there is any self-will in the man, he becomes either the conscious or unconscious despot of his household. The wife, indeed often succeeds in gaining her objects, but it is by some of the many various forms of indirectness and management . . . [and] the position is corrupting equally to both . . . in one it produces the vices of power, in the other those of artifice.
>
> (Ibid.: 33)

Thus even if women are indeed softer in character than men, they are still forced to become 'artful and dissembling', and in their own way are not less selfish, and no compensatory force is offered to society as public virtues are not developed in women. In marriage, as constituted, the husband tends indeed to become conservative, he 'begins to sympathise with the holders of power, more than with its victims' (ibid.: 36). Yet there is a striking contradiction in encouraging women to follow their inclinations. In literature this contradiction is manifested in women writers exhibiting 'a studied display of submission' in order to counter the view that 'learning makes women unfeminine' (ibid.: 41). Thus, she notes, against Comte, what is required is 'equal rights, equal admission to all social privileges; not a position apart, a sort of sentimental priesthood' (ibid.: 42). Harriet Taylor does not present an elaborate theory of power, only the briefest, tentative remarks. But evident is much of Mary Wollstonecraft's insistence on the route for women's liberation in the rejection of separate spheres, not here through a theory of gallantry–coquetry, but here through the couple power–artificiality. The emphasis is placed on a claim for women's intelligence and the benefits to man not simply of moral regeneration, but also of new intellectual resources.

Mill himself in *The Subjection of Women* approached the question of women's position in society through an examination of the pivotal role of marriage. Within it the situation of women approximated to slavery, indeed in some respects it was worse than slavery, with no recourse or defence for the woman against rape, and no legitimate avenue of escape. Outside marriage, the paths to education and employment were so systematically blocked that there was no meaningful choice for a life outside marital relations, which were thus structurally very similar to slavery. Thus Mill's strategy was to attempt to define the conditions under which the marriage relationship could be conceived as being one of genuine choice, and a place where mutual reciprocal equal statuses could be established. The new men would be those who could begin to establish controls on their power and their passions, as new fields of individual liberty for women were opened up. Outside the family all the barriers to equal opportunity would have to be removed. Yet, curiously, there was still room in Mill's own thought for different spheres and balances. Like Comte he was against the tendency for women to work outside the home once married; the man should be the sole breadwinner. In the family context, the wife should superintend the domestic milieu. It has been emphasized recently by Stanley, for instance, that Mill's solution to the problem was essentially to stress that the 'end of the subjection of women was not equal opportunity but spousal friendship' (in Shanley and Pateman 1991: 175). She speculates that Mill's approach here was not dogmatic, and was purely experimental, so that should the sexual division of labour prove to be inimical to the equality of spouses, he would have reconstructed his position. But it seems clear that there is a difference of emphasis on this point between Taylor and Mill, the former interested in the question of rights and equality, the latter interested in independence, liberty and choice.

Strangely, Mill's *The Subjection of Women* has been largely ignored in the discussion of gender until relatively recently when there has been renewed interest.[2] The 'Enfranchisement of women' (Mill 1851) was translated into German by Freud in 1880, and the *Subjection* was widely known on the continent (even to Nietzsche). It has generally been seen as an archetypal statement of liberalism, but its argument in detail is not widely appreciated or known, often being reduced to the argument that women's nature will remain a mystery until full equality of conditions are established between the sexes. In fact the argument is considerably richer, and highly calculated from a political point of view. The argument is developed in four sections: the first looks at the nature of the prejudices against women's equality and the enormous logical difficulty of facing up to them; it looks at the history of women's subjection and the means enforcing it in modern times, leading to the immense discrepancy between the caste-like status of women in a meritocratic society; the second section looks at the legal side of women's enforced inferiority; the third examines the question of suffrage and the reasons why this should be advocated, especially overcoming the inferiority of intellect and a specific form of injustice, but, he says, women should remain in the home, and it would not be desirable for them to contribute by their income (Mill 1983: 91). The fourth part examines the benefit for society of increasing the domain of liberty, and equalizing the women's social position in conditions of the ineffectiveness of chivalry, while not remaining altogether uncritical before the idea of women's supposed virtues.

Mill develops, then, a complex social critique and political strategy based on certain fundamental presuppositions and historical perspectives. The basic theoretical element turns on his conception of power and liberty, but also, importantly, on equality. His account of the nature and history of women's subjection rests on man's superior force, tradition and elaboration of a vast interlocking network of techniques of social exclusion. He presents a fundamental assault on the fanciful notions of women's 'natural place' and inferior capacities. If women were so naturally different, he suggests, no such elaborate and systematic net of repressive devices would be necessary to maintain women apart from men. In Mill's language on women's social position, the terminology draws on notions of feudal bondage, direct slavery, caste stratification, or just victimization. But Mill does not restrain himself in the discussion, arguing that in modern society 'the wife is the actual bond-servant of her husband' (ibid.: 57). But further: 'the wife's position under the common law of England is worse than that of slaves' (ibid.: 57). Indeed, 'though it may be his daily pleasure to torture her, and though she may feel it impossible not to loathe him – he can claim from her and enforce the lowest degradation of a human being' (ibid.: 59–60). The couple's children are his children. Legally, he concluded, she is the 'body-servant of a despot' (ibid.: 61). Mill extends the argument by suggesting ironically that:

> since her all in life depends upon obtaining a good master, she should be allowed to change again and again until she finds one . . . to those

to whom nothing but servitude is allowed, the free choice of servitude is the only, though a most insufficient alleviation. Its refusal completes the assimilation of the wife to the slave – and the slave under not the mildest form of salvery: for in some slave codes the slave could, under certain circumstances of ill usage, legally compel the master to sell.

(Ibid.: 61–2)

Mill was prepared to take this bitter line of argument to the limit on this point: 'the vilest malefactor has some wretched woman tied to him, against whom he can commit any atrocity except killing her, and, if tolerably cautious, can do that without much danger of the legal penalty'. What exists, he claims, is a form of society which permits the 'utmost habitual excesses of bodily violence towards the unhappy wife, who alone, at least of grown persons, can neither repel nor escape their brutality' (ibid.: 66). Mill talks of the existence of brutal men as 'absolute monsters', 'absolute fiends', and 'ferocious savages' (ibid.: 67–8), which he links directly to the form of domestic tyranny found at this period, an extreme form of the concentration of power.

Following Harriet Taylor's remarks he notes that the counterweight of a power in women is also disastrous, since the woman can only act indirectly, by establishing a 'counter tyranny', the weapon of 'irritable and self-willed women', the power of the 'scold' and the 'shrew'. This has fatal defects: it is rarely effective. But against Wollstonecraft, Mill argues that 'female blandishments' have very little effective force, a 'power [which] only lasts while her charm is new, and not dimmed by familiarity' (ibid.: 71). Male sexual demands are not the driving force of this oppression. Thus, in consequence, the real power at the disposal of women, says Mill, is 'personal affection which is the growth of time insofar as the man's nature is susceptible to it' (ibid.: 71). It grows out of common interests, children, daily comforts, and the 'insensible contagion of their feelings and dispositions'. Actually says Mill, the latter may be the basis by which women 'obtain a degree of command over the conduct of the superior, altogether excessive and unreasonable . . . the wife frequently exercises even too much power over the man', so that curiously, 'her power often gives her what she has no right to, but does not enable her to assert her own rights' (ibid.: 72–3).

Thus Mill also takes this line of thought to logical extremes: 'as things now are, those who act most kindly to their wives, are quite as often made worse, as better by the wife's influence'. And again: 'if she is treated with indulgence, and permitted to assume power, there is no rule to set limits to her encroachments'. So, in the absence of a set of specific rights, the law 'practically declares that the measure of what she has a right to, is what she can contrive to get' (ibid.: 81). Consequently at the moment, the family is a 'school of despotism', while genuine citizenship requires a 'school of society in equality'. Mill suggests that 'what is needed, is that [the family] should be a school of sympathy in equality, of living together in love, without power on one side or obedience on the other' (ibid.: 85). The immense drawback of tyrannical relations is that a vicious circle is established in which women undergo a simple 'physical subjection to [men's] will as an instrument', and this 'causes them to feel a sort of disrespect and contempt towards their own wife which they do not feel towards any other women, or any other human being' (ibid.: 87). It is interesting to the course of this work that Mill never discusses prostitution; I will enquire why this is the case in a moment. The basic dilemma arises acutely in that if the woman does work outside the home, given current balances of power, it is possible that she falls into an even worse position yet 'the *power* of earning is essential to the dignity of a woman, if she has not independent property' (ibid.: 92, Mill's emphasis). Thus the argument that there is a difference between Taylor and Mill, must be qualified on this point, since Mill's position is carefully calculated, and not based on the notion of an absolute, though he often appears to respect the reality and ideal of separate spheres.

There are some important misconceptions created in a situation where women, he says, are still in feudal conditions. One central one is that the nature of woman becomes curiously mystified as essentially virtuous, echoing Harriet Taylor's notion of the sentimental priesthood (in fact women can be 'drags' (ibid.: 171)). Another is that they appear as less criminally inclined, yet nothing is sure on this ground, and nothing less ridiculous he suggests than 'panegyrics of women's essential nature' (ibid.: 147). More liberty and greater function of intelligence, says Mill, mean that substantial benefits become available to men who want greater civiliz- ation, especially who respect reciprocity in marriage. Here Mill becomes lyrical in the most daring of suggestions to Victorians:

> What marriage may be in the case of two persons of cultivated facul- ties, identical in opinions and purposes, between whom exists that best kind of quality, similarity of powers and capacities with reciprocal superiority in them – so that each can enjoy the luxury of looking up to the other, and can have alternately the pleasure of leading and being led in the path of development.
>
> (Ibid.: 183)

A daring proposition implying that his position is not really about a static equilibrium of social identity, but one of dynamic interchangeability of authority, where the new man must be willing to see that it may well be in his overall interest to put himself in an inferior position with respect to his companion, so that he can, but without the Comtean formalities, 'enjoy the luxury of looking up to the other'.

The basic features of Mill's analysis are now clear for the most part. The gender system is driven by the physical and social power of men, not by sexual desire. The intensification of power in the hands of a tyrannical ruling strata corrupts both sides of the relationship, and Mill follows the eighteenth-century view that royalty and aristocratic elites had become corrupt in exactly the same way. The gender system is a survival of feudal and slave relations in a society now based on completely different principles, and therefore it will come under increasing pressure to change. It offends the basic elements of the modern conscience, it creates a complete system of artificial forms, and it restricts the free movement of essential human resources. The specific means of resistance to oppression open to women are also considered. They are few, Mill thought, except the very real power of the affective unity of the couple, but this could lead to women, paradoxically, usurping too much power. The development of a new man capable of establishing a marriage of equals could only be achieved when there was sufficient likeness between the two members of the couple, and this required greater availability of education for women, greater respect developed for each side in a marriage based on the effective independence of both the man and the woman. In this way, marriage would genuinely become the free choice of each side.

But it is clear that Mill refused to use one of the arguments often available to Victorian reformers. He does not say that such changes would alleviate the vast problem of Victorian prostitution, nor does he mention prostitution at any point. Indeed it is difficult to find in any of the major essays on Mill any mention of prostitution or Mill's attitude to it. But in fact Mill had very definite views on the problem and took a coherent view of why the suffrage movement should remain quite distinct from the movements trying to deal with issues around prostitution. One issue which perhaps dominated in the 1860s and 1870s was the problem of diseases spread by prostitution and the attempt in the Contagious Diseases Acts to remedy or mitigate a problem which was severe in the military services. The Acts made it necessary for anyone suspected of prostitution to be registered for compulsory examination. In the apparent failure of these Acts to stem the problem, a Royal Commission was established, and Mill was called to give evidence in May 1871.

Mill on the whole had worked out a very clear-cut line of answers to wide-ranging questioning, except on one or two points, such as whether brothel-keepers should be prosecuted, to which he replied 'this is a very difficult question . . . so many *pros* and *cons* have occurred to me . . . that I have found it very difficult to make up my mind' (Mill 1970: 837). But in the main his position was incisive: his answers were dominated by the question of resolving the issue in ways which were most technically effective without infringement of individual liberty. Thus he was against the compulsory examination and registration of women thought to be prostitutes, but not against the organization of hospitals, as long as these hospitals provided no privileged treatment for these specific diseases. The main victims were the indirectly infected wives and possibly children, and these groups must be given utmost protection; here making the passage of such disease a ground for divorce and for this, penalties would be necessary. The state should not provide facilities for legal prostitution, indeed he went so far as to say 'I do not think that prostitution should be classed and recognized as such by the state' (ibid.: 833). There was a statement of principle enunciated at this point: 'the question of the regulation of brothels, whether they should be systematically put down, or let alone to a certain degree, enters into very wide-reaching considerations as to the degree in which the law should interfere in questions of simple morality, and also how far it should attack one portion of the persons who conspire to do a particular act, while it tolerates others' (ibid.: 833). He was against the state playing any role in attempting to make prostitution safe; against penalties inflicted only on women; against compulsory examination of suspected prostitutes which would have the danger of forcing women to undergo these examinations as well (he noted that the attempts to enforce the obligatory examination produced 'very demoralising effects on many women' (ibid.: 837). If there was to be any compulsion it should be against the men involved; but any involvement of the state which would make prostitution more safe would be bound to increase the extent of prostitution. What was most degrading in the whole set of relations, was not prostitution but 'that which is compulsory' (ibid.: 836). But as far as control of soliciting on the streets was concerned, Mill did not think surveillance here was an infringement of individual liberty: 'No. I think that is the duty of the police, in order to preserve the order of the streets' (ibid.: 837).

Chapter 8

In communism: Friedrich Engels and Mary Burns

Marx and Engels have often seemed inseparable, but rarely indistinguishable. But in respect to the question of the 'new man' and as to their responses to the new challenges of the rights of man and the rights of woman, Marx and Engels fall on opposite sides of the fence. Marx accommodated himself as a sensuous romantic patriarch to the traditional role of husband and father, in a family divided into traditional roles. Engels, on the other hand, situated himself, and his relation to the question of women, quite beyond Marx in a specific variation of the possibilities of the 'new man', and indeed of the two writers, though dependent in fundamental respects to Marx in theory, it was Engels who wrote the 'Marxist' contribution to the analysis of the emancipation of women. The analysis, symptomatically, was published after Marx's death.

Friedrich Engels (1820–95) was born into a successful commercial family, and although well educated was, unlike Marx, an 'autodidact' in philosophy. When young, he became, after an initial infatuation with Pietism, an atheist and radical critic of the Prussian state. His life was divided strictly into two: on the one hand the formal social bourgeois milieu of the successful businessman in Barmen, Bremen, and Manchester; on the other his life amongst the left-wing revolutionaries and the working-class community of Manchester. Indeed in Manchester he had two homes: one *pied-a-terre* in each world, bourgeois and proletarian. He met Marx in 1842, while en route for Manchester. While Marx was already living the one passionate affair of his life, Engels was never involved, when young, in any comparable relationship. From his early writings it is possible to read Engels, the young macho male: 'today I have shaved my moustache off again and buried the youthful corpse with much wailing. I look like a woman; it is shameful' (February 1841, in Marx and Engels 1975b: 525). And he admired at this age the 'real man', for example Lizst, who Engels related had ladies fighting over a dropped glove, Liszt 'the man with the *Kamchatka* hair style . . . I tell you he's a real man. He drinks twenty cups of coffee a day' (ibid.: 541).

He was also proudly independent, and certainly did not want to submit to a conventional respectable marriage. He wrote to his sister, Marie, in July 1842:

> the noble young folk [in Barmen] are rushing headlong into marriage, as if they were mad, and so blindly that they are knocking each other over. It is exactly like blindman's-buff and where two of them catch each other, they get engaged, marry and live in blissful contentment. . . . Even Schornstein has got himself engaged – its terrible! And Stucher definitely wants to become a husband. . . . I begin to despair of the human race.
>
> (Ibid.: 544–5)

Like Marx he wrote poetic works in his youth, but none are to women. His emotional life seems to have been worked out in relation to his religious problems.

> I pray daily he wrote in the midst of his turmoil, in July 1839, 'indeed nearly the whole day, for truth, I have done so ever since I began to have doubts. . . . And yet it is written 'seek and ye shall find'. . . . Tears come into my eyes as I write this. I am moved to the core. But I feel I shall not be lost; I shall come to God, for whom my whole heart yearns.
>
> (Ibid.: 461)

In 1844 he reported to Marx having had an unhappy affair, and to his sister he wrote, in 1852, that he would never have a wife (Marx and Engels 1982b: 37); in fact he boasted of his affairs, and within the milieu of revolutionaries he had a central and permanent relationship with an Irish working-class millworker in Manchester, Mary Burns, whom Engels met some time between 1842–4. A recent account suggests that 'she was . . . his sexual partner – or so we presume – and political associate, who accompanied him to Brussels in 1845', but when he visited Paris and Cologne 'she disappears from view' (Carver 1989: 149). In the 1850s she lived with Engels in Ardwick, Manchester, the address maintained discreetly from his official lodgings. His private and public lives in Manchester were strictly held apart. In 1848 his mother found some of his letters, one to 'Madame Engels', another in French to Engels 'from a lady' (cited in Carver 1989: 150). His mother said she burnt the letters unread. In 1848, he was at the same address as Felicie Andre, who, he boasted to Marx, was his mistress as was the 'flemish giantess . . . mademoiselle Josephine' (Marx and Engels 1982b: 166). But the centre of Engels's domestic life was with Mary and her sister Lizzie Burns, who acted as housekeeper, in the Ardwick address of 'Mr Fredrick Boardman'. Engels toured Ireland with Mary in 1856, but she died unexpectedly in 1863 aged forty-one. After this Lizzie became his partner, and he took her, as he had done her sister, on trips to Ireland, and in 1869 Engels retired to London with Lizzie, her niece Mary, and maid Sarah. In 1875, Engels went to Germany with Lizzie, but this relation was, like the earlier one, kept secret from Engels's family; to the revolutionaries she was Mrs Engels. On Lizzie's deathbed in September 1878, they were finally married, and she was buried in a Catholic cemetery. Carver reflects, somewhat cynically, at the end 'the late Frau Engels – would have no claim on the family socially and no chance of inheriting Friedrich's estate' (Carver 1989: 158).

The other important women in Engels's 'secret' life, were housekeepers, Helene Demuth (after Marx's death in 1883 she was Engels's housekeeper till 1890), and Louise Kautsky (who was Engels's housekeeper after 1890); after 1894 she lived there with her new husband, Ludwig Freyberger, and 'Pumps', Mary Ellen, Lizzie's niece. Helene Demuth gave birth to an illegitimate child, Freddy, in 1851 when she was in the Marx household. The child was fostered out and the birth certificate revealed no father. Either Marx or Engels could have been the father, but the episode has gained notoriety since the publication in 1962 of the 'Freyberger letter', a typewritten document of September 1898 from Louise Freyberger to August Bebel in Germany (available in Henderson 1976: vol. II, 833–4). It relates a deathbed revelation from Engels to Eleanor Marx and Louise Freyberger that Karl Marx had been Freddy's father. This was a revelation, says the letter, Engels made in case he was to be accused after his death of 'having treated Freddy (Demuth) badly' in his will (there was nothing in the will of July 1893 for Freddy, though there was for Lizzie's niece 'Pumps').

There has been considerable debate about this letter, but it has become widely accepted as reliable. Terrell Carver has recently attempted to throw some cold water on the contention and has concluded that the letter is, on balance, a forgery (Carver 1989: 169). Carver argues that

> Engels himself is a better candidate than Karl. . . . The younger, unmarried and handsomer a man was the one with a taste for girls, working class ones at that, and Lenchen was his exact contemporary. Writing to Marx from Paris in 1847 Engels let rip about *grisettes* – 'easy' working class girls called after their cheap grey attire: 'it is absolutely essential that you get out of boring Brussels for once and come to Paris, and I for my part have a great desire to go carousing with you. . . . If I had an income of 5,000 Francs I would do nothing but work and amuse myself with women until I went to pieces. If there were no Frenchwomen, life wouldn't be worth living. But so long as there are *grisettes*, well and good!'
>
> (Ibid.)

It may have been the assumption of the Marx family that Engels was the father, and Eleanor was to say in 1892 'that I can't help feeling that

Freddy has had great injustice all through his life . . . how rarely we practise all the fine things we preach' (in Meier et al. 1984: 240). If she was at the deathbed of Engels in 1895, it would have been her opportunity to say something on Freddy's behalf. In the Freyberger letter Engels is reported to have talked of Eleanor's disbelief

> Tussy wants to make an idol of her father, [and at the crucial moment] Engels himself wrote on his slate that Marx was Frederick Demuth's father. Tussy broke down as she left the room. . . . He had agreed to take Marx's place in order to save Marx from serious domestic difficulties. . . . Since his wife was dreadfully jealous Marx was always afraid that she would leave him. He had no affection for the boy. To acknowledge him would precipitate too great a scandal.
>
> (In Henderson 1976: vol. II, 833–4)

But what is clear is that there was considerable apparent hostility from Marx's wife Jenny to Mary Burns.[1] In an important letter of March 1846, she says of Mary Burns that divisions within the Marx–Engels group were due to 'the machinations of that ambitious woman, Lady Macbeth . . . as regards this critical woman, Engels was perfectly right . . . in finding such a woman '*as she ought to be*', as the eternal antithesis, very arrogant and hence in making a great deal of fuss about very LITTLE.' Thus emerges indirectly something of Engels's claim that from the 'communist' point of view Mary Burns represented a new proletarian type of woman. In fact Jenny Marx reacted scathingly, as under direct attack: 'I myself, when confronted with this abstract model, appear truly repulsive in my own eyes.' She was unlikely to accept this passively. She

> would like to be sure of finding out all its faults and weaknesses in return. Moreover, it is quite false, or at any rate very mistaken, to speak, in respect of Engels, of a 'rare exemplar'. Then he is right in maintaining that 'such is not to be found'. But that is precisely where the argument falls to the ground. There is an abundance of lovely, charming, capable women, they are to be found all over the world waiting for a man to liberate and redeem them. Any man can become a redeemer of a woman. Present day women . . . are receptive to all things and very capable of self-sacrifice.
>
> (In Marx and Engels 1982a: 530–1)

Evidently Jenny Marx saw herself under considerable threat from the line Engels was taking in presenting Mary as the woman of the future, as the way the independent proletarian woman prefigured communist woman.

In the late 1840s Jenny and Marx went to a workers' meeting where Engels and Mary Burns were present. Jenny refused to acknowledge or meet Mary. Stephan Born reported the encounter: 'when I greeted Marx he indicated by a significant gesture and a smile that his wife would in no circumstances meet Engels's companion. In matters of honour and morals the noble lady was quite intransigent' (in Henderson 1976: vol. II, 104). Henderson remarks 'Engels was always a welcome guest in Marx's home [but] he was never able to bring Mary Burns with him' (ibid.). Yet this remark must be tempered by the fact that Engels had informally taken responsibility for the paternity of Helene Demuth's child (born in 1851), and that all letters and all relations between Jenny Marx and Engels were icy and extremely curt and formal: she wrote not to Fred, but to Mr F. Engels, and he signed his name F. Engels as he knew she regarded him and his way of life with great moral reprobation and suspicion (until, that is, the late 1860s when she would sign 'best regards to your dear wife [Lizzie], Your Old Friend, Jenny Marx' (Marx and Engels 1989: 556)). Yet Engels was to enjoy, no doubt, writing to Marx in October 1851: is 'Red Wolff [Ferdinand Wolff] married? Is that in the English, respectably bourgeois sense? . . . . That would really beat everything hollow. M. Wolff *bon epoux, peut-etre meme bon pere de famille!*' (Marx and Engels 1982b: 478), indicating once again the general commitment of revolutionaries not to submit to bourgeois marriage forms – despite the position of Jenny Marx and Marx who she called 'my dear master' (ibid.: 532) or 'my liege lord' (Marx and Engels 1983: 567). Astonishingly, when Laura's marriage was being discussed in 1867, Marx wrote to Engels to ask how to go about making the arrangements: 'if the civil wedding is to take place in London, my wife wishes it to be in secret, as she wants to avoid gossip'. Engels took, again no doubt, great pleasure in replying 'the marriage is performed before the Registrar . . . as for the philistine neighbours, your wife can tell them that a civil marriage was due to the fact that Laura is a Protestant and Paul Catholic' (Padover 1979: 240–1). The tone is unmistakable: the philistine is Jenny Marx, and the incompetent, Karl Marx himself.

The most important crisis in the relation of Marx with Engels arose at the time of Mary's death (1863). Engels wrote 'Mary is dead. . . . I cannot tell you how terrible I feel. The poor girl had loved me with all her heart' (ibid.: 163). Marx's only response was: 'the news of Mary's death has surprised and dismayed me. She was very good-natured, witty, and devoted to you. . . . It is extraordinarily difficult for you who had a *home* with Mary, free and withdrawn from all human muck, as often as you pleased'. Marx's letter was otherwise a long account of his own economic plight (ibid.: 163–4). Engels felt in Marx's letter an 'icy conception', and continued with great force 'All my friends, including philistine acquaintances, have shown me, at this moment which hit me deeply, more sympathy and friendship than I expected. You found this moment appropriate to display the superiority of your cool intellect' (ibid.: 165). Marx's reply, another long account of his own economic difficulties, reported that the earlier letter had been written under pressure from Jenny. 'What drove me particularly mad' says Marx, 'was that my wife thought *I* did not report to you adequately our true situation' (ibid.: 165). Engels replied, emphasizing that 'One cannot live with a woman for so many years without feeling her death dreadfully. I feel as if with her I have buried the last piece of my youth' (ibid.: 166). Clearly Engels thought he had had enough of Marx, and of ending his relations with him definitively. Marx wrote another letter saying

> I have repeatedly declared to my wife that I do not care at all about the whole mess compared with the fact that because of these lousy bourgeois troubles and her eccentric excitement I was even capable of assaulting you with my private needs instead of comforting you at such a moment. Consequently domestic peace was greatly upset and the poor woman had to take the whole blame for a thing of which she was in fact innocent to the extent that women are wont to demand the impossible. . . . Women are funny creatures, even those equipped with much intelligence.
>
> (In Raddatz 1980: 107)

The reconciliation was not long in coming, but hidden in this episode is the continuing evidence, not just of the difference between the lifestyle of Engels and that of Marx, but of this difference harbouring considerable ideological problems and antagonisms. Some have hinted that the matter really revolved around the position of Engels: there was suspicion that as a secure businessman, even a *de facto* millowner, his liaison with a millworker was to be seen as a form of exploitation of his position. In addition Carver, for example, writes 'in love [he] does not seem to have gone searching for his intellectual equal' (Carver 1989: 159). Insofar as Jenny was aware of Engels's remarks to the effect that he 'had a great desire to go carousing' with Marx, that he liked having affairs and meeting *les grisettes* it is only to be expected that tension existed, manifest in Jenny's overdetermined avoidance of Mary Burns. But there is a hint of something more in Marx's own letter, which refers to Engels finding with Mary Burns a haven 'free and withdrawn', a 'home'.

This can only really be understood if the full ideological argument of Engels's position are explored in more detail in their own right, for it could be that Engels thought that Marx was living in violation of the *Communist Manifesto* they had written together, and that in the end the hypocrisy was at Marx's, not his door. If this is a correct interpretation of the differences between them, it becomes clear that it is Engels who is, in effect, criticizing Marx for not breaking with the role of the patriarchal traditional man, and its intimate connections with the structure of private property and the dualism of what Engels called monogamy and hetaerism. One of the main early statements of this view is indeed the jointly authored *Manifesto*, which expresses itself as the proletarian position in dialogue with the bourgeois one:

> you communists would introduce a community of women, screams the whole bourgeoisie in chorus. The Bourgeois sees in his wife a mere instrument of production. . . . He has not even a suspicion that the real point aimed at is to do away with the status of women as mere instruments of production. . . . Our bourgeois, not content with having the wives and daughters of the proletarians at their disposal, not to speak of common prostitutes, take the greatest pleasure in seducing each others' wives. Bourgeois marriage is in reality a system of wives in common and thus, at the most, what the communists might possibly be reproached with, is that they desire to introduce, in substitution of a hypocritically concealed, an openly legalised community of women. For the rest, it is self-evident that the abolition of the present system of production must bring with it the abolition of the community of women springing from that system, i.e., of prostitution both public and private.
>
> (Marx and Engels 1968: 50–1)

This position is clearly indebted to the Saint-Simonian critique of bourgeois hypocrisy. The phrase 'community of women' was used against the Saint-Simonians at their trial by Dupin and Maugin the accusers. Marx and Engels had discussed the presentations of the Saint-Simonian doctrine in the *German Ideology* (1845–6) 1965: 554–74) as transposed for the German socialist market by Karl Grun from Lorenz von Stein. (Grun had also argued that the whole of the movement for the emancipation of women emanated from Saint-Simon, drawing on Stein's comment that in Saint-Simon is to be found 'the first idea of the *emancipation of women*': Marx and Engels comment that this claim was indeed childish (ibid.: 526). But in the *Manifesto* the notion of the hypocrisy of bourgeois society (developed by Enfantin), is given an immediate economic reduction, a reduction to the determinations by the structure of private property of capitalist production (something that Engels felt very directly): women are seen not as a simple instrument of pleasure but of production and the reproduction of capital. The Saint-Simonian doctrine had now become infused with dialectical evolutionary thought and critical political economy. This progressive scheme implies the idea that the current struggle of human progress is determined by the proletarian class struggle against the bourgeoisie and capitalism to which the problem of women's oppression was secondary. It could only successfully be fought on the basis of the victories achieved by the proletariat. Evidently, in the *Manifesto*, women do not figure highly, if at all, as a force for social emancipation. The call is to 'working men of all countries'. It could be asked, indeed, if Marx and Engels together ever produced more on the question of women's emancipation than these simplistic axioms and injunctions.

But the fact is that Engels did produce in 1884, a year after Marx's death, the influential work *The Origin of the Family, Private Property and the State*. Even in earlier works there are hints of Engels's emerging position, for example in *Condition* of 1844: and in *Anti-Dühring* of 1878, Engels draws attention to Marx's own comment in *Capital* (vol. I (1867), to the effect that 'modern industry, by assigning as it does an important part in socially organised processes of production, outside the domestic sphere, to women . . . creates the foundation for a higher form of the family and of the relations between the sexes' (happily cited by Engels 1936: 439). This comment must be examined with reference to the interesting and curious formulation found in Engel's early work, *The Condition of the Working Class in England*, ([1845] 1958). Two very remarkable theses are put forward by Engels. The first is that while the Irish workers have introduced a cultural barbarization of the culture of the working class in England (Engels 1958: 104–7), they have also introduced humour, passion, 'a light hearted temperament akin to that of the mediterranean peoples' (ibid.: 106). This excitable character stimulates the English, characterized normally by stolidity, into action. The hot-blooded character of the Irish directly stimulates the 'workers' animosity against their oppressors' (ibid.: 241). The Irish are to the English as the French are to the German characters (ibid.: 139). Thus, after describing the 'filth' of the Irish, Engels comes to the remarkable conclusion that 'in the long run this union of the livelier, more mercurial and more fiery temperament of the Irish with the stolid, patient and sensible character of the English can only be mutually beneficial. The harsh egotism of the English middle classes would have kept its hold much more firmly on the English proletariat, if it had not been for this Irish element' (ibid.: 139). Indeed the generous nature of the Irish has softened the character of the English, and this has occurred 'through inter-marriage and by daily contact' (ibid.: 149). The whole character of the working class is again 'more friendly' than that of the bourgeoisie, who are completely obsessed with money and possession. The second is the fact that factory employment has tended to favour women in factory work: women are 56.5 per cent in cotton, 69.5 per cent in woollen, 70.5 per cent in silk and 70.5 per cent in flax production (ibid.: 160); and 'all this has led to a complete reversal of normal social relations' (ibid.: 160).

This was a crucial section of *Condition* and remained a clearly unresolved question in Engels's mind at the time as the text evidently reveals. On the one hand he says the new situation creates family pathology:

the various members of the family only see each other in the mornings and evenings. . . . Perhaps his wife and the older children go out to work. . . . In these circumstances how can family life exist? . . . there are endless domestic troubles and finally quarrels which are highly demoralising for both children and the parents.

(Ibid.: 145)

He cites a letter of working man Robert Pounder which describes how 'now *t'world is turned up side down*, Mary has to turn out to wark and I have to stop at home to mind Barns' (cited in ibid. my emphasis). Engels's analysis of this reversal deserves to be examined carefully. At first he says the new situation

deprives the husband of his manhood and the wife of all womanly qualities. Yet it cannot thereby turn a man into a woman or a woman into a man. It is a state of affairs shameful and degrading to the human attributes of the sexes. It is the culminating point of our highly-praised civilization. . . . If all that can be achieved by our work and effort is this sort of mockery, then we must truly despair. . . . If not, then we must admit that human society has followed the wrong road in its search for happiness.

(Ibid.: 164)

Very clearly Engels's first response was to condemn the system as fundamentally an attack on manhood:

the wife is the breadwinner. . . . This happens very frequently indeed. In Manchester alone there are many hundreds of men who are condemned to perform household duties. One may well imagine the righteous indignation of the workers at being virtually turned into eunuchs.

(Ibid.: 162)

But Engels does not altogether stop at that point, for he takes his questioning to the point of self-paradox:

We shall have to accept the fact that so complete a reversal of the role of the two sexes can be due only to some radical error in the original relationship between men and women. If the rule of the wife over her husband – a natural consequence of the factory system – is unnatural, then the former rule of the husband over the wife must also have been unnatural.

(Ibid.: 164)

And pressing this logic to the questioning of the basic forms of justification for the family structure, he argues .

such a state of affairs shows clearly that there is no rational or sensible principle at the root of our ideas concerning family income and property. If the family as it exists . . . comes to an end then its disappearance will prove that the real bond holding the family together was not affection but merely self interest engendered by the false concept of family property.

(Ibid.: 165)

This seems to be the high point of the purely logical reflection that Engels could reach in 1844–5, which was to suggest that there was a profound question opened up by the factory system which, while producing a crisis in masculinity, and in the family, also posed the issue as to whether the basic structure of masculinity was not itself an artificial historical construct, without any firm 'rational and sensible principle'.

If Engels used Marx's ethnological notebooks of the late 1870s as a basis for his later book *Origin* (see Krader 1974, who compares the notebooks with Engels's text), published forty years after the *Condition*, it is clear that Engels stamped the argument with his own independent analysis, which drives the comment of Marx (in *Capital*) to surprising conclusions. In *Origin*, Engels bases his understanding of the evolution of Western marriage and property systems on the work of Maine, Bachofen, and most importantly Lewis Morgan, and suggests that the crucial turning point in history was the emergence of male dominance (patriarchy) and individual private property in ancient Greece in a crucial break with a previous social form which based itself on 'mother right'. In Engels's words, out of the kinship groups was born a 'new society, with its control centred in the state, the subordinate units of which are no longer kinship associations but local associations; a society in which the family system is completely dominated by the system of property' (Engels 1972: 72). After the installation of the new regime by men, (constructed in the sequence, savagery, barbarism, civilization), 'mother right' characteristic of barbarism is overthrown as property is passed through men, and women 'become a mere instrument for the production of children' (ibid.: 121). It was at this moment in the formation of classes, that women were annexed to the domestic sphere, and, as individuals, acquired an exchange value. At the same time as this individuation, came a specific form of 'sex love' (ibid.: 132), and, within the domestic sphere, a new condition of 'leaden boredom, known as 'domestic bliss' (ibid.: 134, it is interesting that Engels should use the same word as his youthful letter to his sister on marriage). There was, he claims, a general downgrading of the power of love and affection in the family and the rise of new patterns of calculation of interest and property.[2]

In *Origin of the Family* Engels casts his eyes back to the *German Ideology* (orig. 1845–6, written with Marx) and notes the comment made there that 'the first division of labour is that between man and woman for the propagation of children'. They also wrote 'property: the nucleus, the first form of which lies in the family, where wife and children are the slaves of the husband' (Marx and Engels 1965: 44). This radical

interpretation is developed in 1884 as Engels writes 'the first class opposition that appears in history coincides with the development of the
antagonism between man and woman in monogamous marriage, and the
first class oppression coincides with that of the female sex by the male sex'
(ibid.: 129).[3] None of these remarks can be found in Marx's enthnological
notebooks, and they reveal the nature of the fundamental question of
Marx's position that Engels presents in 1884: indeed, Engels's coupling
of monogamy and class oppression, even the very definition of women
as an oppressed class, represents a definitive break with Marx on this
problem. At first the evolution of monogamy, he says, is accompanied
by sacred prostitution (ibid.: 139), but from its inception monogamy
represents a divided form. Profane prostitution comes everywhere to
accompany it. It is everywhere condemned as immoral, but

> in reality this condemnation never falls on the men concerned, only
> on the women; they are despised and outcast in order that the uncon-
> ditioned supremacy of men of the female sex may be once more
> proclaimed as a fundamental law of society.
>
> (ibid.: 130)

Then emerges, quite uniformly, he suggests, the wife's lover and the
deceived husband in one classic nuclear family structure. Engels is certain
of his prognosis of the situation: the abolition of this condition requires
the overthrow of the system of private property as a whole and with it
the complete structure of capitalist production. This means that women's
emancipation will have to wait for the socialist revolution to do its work,
for the dominance of men is a natural consequence of his 'economic
supremacy' and can only end with the displacement of this supremacy.

Yet there is, he remarks, a crucial difference in the pattern of love in
dominant and subordinate classes:

> sex love in the relationship with a woman becomes and can only
> become the real rule among the oppressed classes, which means today
> among the proletariat . . . here all the foundations of typical mon-
> ogamy are cleared away. Here there is no property, for the preser-
> vation and inheritance of which monogamy and male supremacy were
> established, hence there is no incentive to make this male supremacy
> effective. What is more, there are no means for making it so.
>
> (Ibid.: 135)

His argument, however, is aimed specifically at the new conditions of
industrialism and factory employment of women (and is quite different
in tone here from the scorching attack on the proletarian culture,
especially among the Irish, he had made in 1844). For now, he says,
when

the wife . . . [is] often the breadwinner of the family, no basis for any kind of male supremacy is left in the proletarian household, except, perhaps for something of the brutality toward women that has spread since the introduction of monogamy. . . . The proletarian family is therefore no longer monogamous in the strict sense. . . . The wife has regained the right to dissolve the marriage . . . in short the proletarian marriage is monogamous in the etymological sense of the word. But not at all in its historical sense.

(Ibid.: 135)

Given the emphasis Engels placed on economic conditions, it is clear that although women were exploited and oppressed under conditions of capitalist production, here was an historic gain, perhaps an unprecedented one, in the employment of women outside the home as wage earners; and, given the fact that in working-class communities legal considerations governing marriages were not taken too seriously, the condition of working-class women was completely different in principle from that of aristocratic or bourgeois women in the dominant property-owning classes.

Engels himself, then, rejected the Saint-Simonian communalist experiments of the utopian community. For him the true basis of a new sexuality and equivalent codes of masculinity and femininity, was to be found in the already existing 'proletarian' style, where the 'eternal attendants of monogamy, hetaerism and adultery, play only an almost vanishing part' (ibid.: 135). Thus the component elements of the differences of Engels's thought and practice from that of Marx now come fully into view. He was certainly not, ideologically, attracted to 'bourgeois' women nor was he attracted to the idea of marriage with one. He must surely have been under considerable pressure from his own family to form such a (in his eyes) hypocritical union. He also knew that marriage to a working-class, illiterate Irish millworker would not have been socially acceptable. He genuinely seemed to have found working-class women indispensible ('so long as there are *grisettes* well and good') and with Mary Burns in particular he formed, in his own view, a relationship that was different in kind from any bourgeois union. As Marx pointed out it was a 'union free and withdrawn from all human muck' even if in fact, as Henderson points out 'it is clear that Marx was contemptuous of the illiterate Irish woman who was held in such high esteem by Engels' (Henderson 1976: vol. II, 547).

Is this the 'new man' evolving in relation to the 'new woman' born out of the contradictions at the heart of industrial capitalism? We know that Mary Burns did not have children, while Jenny Marx, in contrast, wrote that women's 'destiny is to have children . . . [in] Germany it still does one credit to have a child, the need and the kitchen spoon still lend one a modicum of grace' (Marx and Engels 1982b: 527–8). The antagonism between Jenny Marx and Mary Burns was intense and is reflected through Marx himself, in his own 'icy' acknowledgement of Mary's death. It is generally assumed (see Padover 1979: 69) that Marx's visit to Manchester in April 1851 was to arrange for Engels to assume paternity for the child of Helene Demuth. Marx wrote 'there comes a secret, which I shall reveal to you *en très peu de mots*. But just now I am being interrupted and called to my wife's sickbed' (31 March 1851). On 2 April, he wrote, 'I will not write to you about the secret. . . . I will in any case visit you'. It seems possible that Marx thought Engels did not take the issue of principle seriously, for Engels was living the free life of the man without children and without domestic burdens, someone indeed who might write suggesting going 'carousing' with him (and probably did), and who might shrug off an encounter with a domestic servant. If this is the case, it seems clear that Engels drew the line, and was not prepared to acknowledge legal paternity – and neither could Marx. Logically, if Marx did ask Engels, or admitted he was himself the father, he was falling into a situation which Engels could only have found theoretically contemptible. It was simply an instance of the archetypal division of monogamy and hetaerism which he himself as a communist had sought to avoid. The hypocrisy involved was now causing a problem in their relationship for he was being perhaps asked to shoulder this hypocrisy himself and the opprobrium of the Marx household, a household he was maintaining financially. Carver suggests that the Marxists thought that Engels 'lacked self-awareness' and thinks 'perhaps there is some truth in this' (Carver 1989: 159). It is certainly not so clear as this, surely, just where awareness was lacking.

It is not surprising that Engels has been criticized for importing into his analysis all kinds of male prejudices.[4] It is easy to point to the convenience of the arrangements in Manchester for Engels, in terms of a sexual relationship which did not involve on his part any risk to the family property. But he must surely have been naive if he thought that from the point of view of a working-class woman an alliance with a wealthy businessman was altogether innocent of considerations of property and income. In his writing on women and liberation he does not cite the case of women who inherit money, though he does surprisingly consider the position of what he calls the 'petticoat pension', a form of 'prostitution' in which it is the man who is supported by a wealthy woman (see Engels 1936: 356). This belonged strictly to the sphere of the bourgeoisie.

Nevertheless, he was insistent that the 'new woman' was not the bourgeois intellectual. She was the working-class mill worker 'outside' the property system, and this made it possible to form relationships which permitted genuine 'sex love' to appear and flourish. It was quite unlike monogamy where the wife [is] the head servant, excluded from all participation in social production. Not until the coming of modern large-scale industry was the road to social production opened to her again – and then only to the proletarian wife. . . . But . . . if she wants to take part in public production and earn independently, she cannot carry out family duties.

(Ibid.: 137)

There were costs in the new liberty. But this new liberty was not, he thought, going to lead to wider sexual promiscuity, the tendency in fact would be in precisely the opposite direction: 'the equality of women . . . will tend infinitely more to make men really monogamous than to make women polyandrous' (Engels 1972: 145). This is a step in the direction of a completely new society. Engels stood for the full equality of rights for women, but this would not solve the basic problem, it would only create a 'clear field on which the fight can be fought' so that the major struggle 'for the liberty of the wife' could develop so as to 'bring the whole female sex back into public industry'. This in turn will mean that, thirdly, the monogamous family as an 'economic unit' would be abolished (ibid.: 137). For Engels then, the new men are those who will not have known 'in their lives . . . what it is to buy a woman's surrender with money or any other social instrument of power'; and the new women are those 'who have never known what it is to give themselves to a man from any other considerations than real love or to refuse to give themselves to their lover from fear of economic consequences' (ibid.: 145).

At the level of the theoretical and personal resolution of the paradox Engels outlined in 1844, he did not, in the end, rush to the support of a besieged proletarian masculinity, to the defence of the 'eunuchs', or to the defence of bourgeois alternatives. He located in the 'reversal' of roles in the family he found pathological in 1844 a revolutionary principle and the transitional form of gender relations which escaped bourgeois hypocrisy and egotism. He found something different in the passionate, mercurial, light-hearted Irish temperament of the newly independent proletarian woman (Mary Burns), who he presented to the revolutionaries as woman 'as she ought to be' (Jenny Marx). There can be little doubt, whatever the degree of self-deception involved that the encounter with Mary Burns was essential to the reversal of Engels's earlier approach to the question of gender, and to the formulation of the theory developed by Engels against Marx, that the fundamental, primary and elementary form of class oppression was that of men over women, and that the alternative to bourgeois marriage based on property and self interest existed close to hand in the forms produced by advanced capitalism iself.

But finally, is Engels himself a 'new man' in the light of these observations? Engels's life was, in virtually all aspects, divided clearly into two parts. He himself was completely aware of this. In replying to a 'questionnaire' devised by his two daughters, Marx was asked 'What was the quality [he] liked best: in men, and in women?' To the first he answered 'strength', to the second 'weakness' (April 1865, Marx and Engels 1987: 567). Engels was asked some three years later (April 1868), similar questions: 'Your favourite virtue in men and in women'. To the first he replied 'to mind his own business'; to the second, 'not to mislay things'. What was his own principal aversion?: 'affected stuck up women'; what was his favourite dish?: 'Irish stew'. He was asked to define his own 'chief characteristic': 'knowing things by halves' (Marx and Engels 1988: 541). Undoubtedly Engels regarded himself as a transitional form, half-way to being a 'new man' but as having taken the crucial step.

Chapter 9

In fate: Max Weber, Marianne Weber and Else von Richthofen

Weber did not write a text on gender or on women or masculinity, or indeed on feminism. His wife Marianne Weber did so and was active in the liberal feminist movement and it was because of this division of labour, perhaps, that the discussion on Max Weber and gender and the problematic connection of his theoretical development with his practical engagement and involvement with women has to be constructed in a largely indirect manner.

In reading accounts of Weber's life (1864–1920), there remains a curious polarity: on the one hand there are direct discussions of Weber's significant encounters with women, and, on the other, accounts which may only be adequately described as coy, clearly practising an evasive distancing from the question. The latter seems to prevail in accounts which claim 'scientificity' in their approach to Weber. A recent example is Dirk Käsler's work *Max Weber* (English translation 1988) which hints at the 'physical problems of his relationship with his wife' (ibid.: 16), which echoes the more direct account in Mitzman. Mitzman, drawing on interviews with those close to Weber, states categorically, that Weber 'never consummated his marriage' (Mitzman 1970: 276). Käsler suggests that up till 1910 Weber 'suppressed his own sexual impulses and polemicised publically . . . against an ethic of sensual pleasure'. He insists in this vein, and notes that

> an intimate relationship gradually developed between Weber and Else von Richthofen, (later Jaffe), Marianne's closest friend. . . . From about 1918, the character of this relationship changed, and from this time it could be regarded as an intimate friendship which lasted until Weber's death. Furthermore, Weber's relationship with Mina Tobler, which from about 1911–12 became important to him, played a significant role . . . and contributed to the relaxation of this moral rigour.
>
> (Käsler 1988: 16)

Käsler notes the existence of hundreds of letters from Weber to Else and to Mina, yet to be published, which will constitute the main basis for these assertions. Mitzman, who knew of these letters, still remained secretive about the second woman, Mina Tobler, and mysteriously referred to her as 'X'.

For some readers and associates of Weber, these revelations came as a surprise, even a shock. John Dreijmanis, for example, on the reliable evidence of Karl Jaspers' assistant, relates that Marianne Weber had suspected Weber of having affairs, though this does not surface in her autobiography, and had asked Jaspers about the possibility. At first 'Jaspers dismissed the idea, declaring "Max Weber was truth itself"'. It was not until 5 May 1967 when Jaspers wrote to Jaffe, that he discovered infidelity' (Dreijmanis, 1989: xix–xx). According to Dreijmanis, Jaspers 'had difficulty in characterising Weber . . . the more he read Weber's works, the more he saw "a titanic trouble in emptiness". Jaspers' discovery caused him considerable distress' (ibid.).

A similar verdict is given by Nicolaus Sombart, who himself was 'for many years in and out of Marianne Weber and Frau Jaffe's house in Heidelberg' who on learning the details of Martin Green's revelations, talked of the other Weber, the Weber for whom a

> monstrous oeuvre of 'objective' knowledge is tirelessly accumulated. No area of history and society remains unexamined. Thousands and thousands of pages are produced so that proof of the 'meaningless eternity of world history' can be discovered again and again . . . Max Weber was authoritarian, overbearing and intolerant. He was a lord without a realm, a father without children, a man without a woman, whose 'substitute kingdom' was science and whose substitute children were students (the only status he allowed women).
>
> (Sombart [1976] 1987: 135)

Sombart pushes the argument to suggest that if Weber did not act, this was not because there were objective reasons but that 'he had forbidden himself to act. His passionate critique of the system must have been directed against himself to the extent that he had internalized it. "Castration" by a "Father" was constantly repeated in self-castration.' (ibid.: 134). Sombart, apparently traumatized by the revelations, opened up a critique of the way that Weber had been turned into the morally and politically pure hero of the post- (1945) war state, 'as the real leader of another better Germany which did not abdicate and did not fail' (ibid.: 135).

So a number of other accounts have begun to discuss the significance of these letters and the relation between them and the work of Weber itself. Weber's nephew, Eduard Baumgarten in his *Max Weber: Werk und Person* (1964) began the discussion, and Arthur Mitzman's *The Iron Cage* (1970) took these ideas up to begin the examination of what their significance might be for Weber's sociological thought. Martin Green's

The Richthofen Sisters: Else and Frieda von Richthofen, Otto Gross, Max Weber and D. H. Lawrence in the years 1870–1970 (1974), initiated the discussion across the disciplines of psychoanalysis, literature and sociology. Baumgarten wrote a brief reply to Sombart's review of Green's book, trying to contain the speculative implications (summarized by Ellen Kennedy, in Sombart 1987: 150–2). Since the period of the early 1970s there has been a lull in the discussion but the return to these themes has been extremely disappointing in analytic terms: J. J. R. Thomas has worked over the non-socialist feminist position implied in the works of the Webers (Thomas 1985), and Rosalind Sydie's discussion of sociological theory and feminism (Sydie 1987) attempts to consider the theoretical problems but avoids discussion of personal involvements in her reflection on Weber. Only with Terry Kandal's consideration of the theoretical implications in the section on Weber in *The Woman Question in Classical Sociological Theory* (1988) is there detailed consideration, but the analysis is merely an extension of Mitzman, and more surprisingly, in Roslyn Bologh's book *Love or Greatness* (1990), which initiates the feminist discussion of Weber, there is no consideration of Weber's life, as if Baumgarten, Mitzman, Green, or Marianne Weber and Else von Richthofen had not existed.

In order to establish the nature and range of these questions, it is essential to return to the discussion initiated in English by Mitzman (1970) who had drawn, immediately, the most extreme conclusions from the new evidence; he even suggested that Weber's own personal breakdown could only be understood as a paralysing guilt relation to his father, and more astonishingly, sexual paranoia, a 'fear of uncontrolled nocturnal emissions' as revealed in a document Weber is alleged to have written about his own psychological problems. Mitzman draws the relevant conclusions in connection with the effects on Weber's theorizing which were

> the gradual change in Weber's theory of the relationship between asceticism and Christian morality . . . crucial to the formation of the concept of charisma in Weber's mature work was the separation of a Christian ethic of compassion from his mother's Calvinist asceticism. In 1907, in a letter on Gross, Weber still saw 'the ethic of *old* unbroken Christianity' in terms of the Kantian ethic of ascetic heroism. The only alternative was some form of self-indulgent hedonism, which he condemned out of hand. By 1910, a dramatic change had occurred in Weber's view of the moral alternatives. Weber then presented ancient Christianity as specifically mystical and saw its tradition as continued in Greek and Russian Orthodoxy. To this mysticism Calvinism was opposed in the same way that *Gesellschaft* was to *Gemeinschaft*.
>
> (Mitzman 1970: 287)

Mitzman suggests that Weber moved to a new position which now saw 'the "interchangeability" of eroticism and mysticism, and the function of eroticism as an escape from the skeletal coldness of reified ascetic rationality'. Indeed, says Mitzman,

> Weber may or may not have been aware of how his changing ideas on the relationship between Christian ethics and asceticism mirrored the profound changes in his ultimate value code that accompanied his friendship with Else Jaffe, his affair with 'X'. . . . But that the mirror, the changes, and the personal involvements were there, is not subject to question.
>
> (Ibid.: 290)

These changes made Weber 'more receptive than previously to antimodernist, erotic, mystical and aristocratic views', says Mitzman who concluded nonetheless that Weber 'tried to keep these conflicting values in separate compartments of his life. . . . Thus, he never breathed a word of his affair with 'X' to Marianne . . . his unconsummated love for Marianne at times appears similar to the acosmic love he mentioned in 1910 and analysed at length' (ibid.: 291). In effect, however, these changes in Weber's perspective were never generalized beyond his sociology of religion and his personal philosophy, even though, according to Mitzman, a number of intellectuals close to Weber imagined it was possible that he might move and sought to push him consistently in the new radical direction.

Max Weber, though coeval with Durkheim, and responding to the generation of Marx, Mill and Nietzsche, nevertheless had a more radical environment of female influences: Weber encouraged Marianne Weber's writings on women (criticized by Durkheim: see Durkheim 1980: 288–9), and even spoke in meetings for liberal feminism. His circle and immediate acquaintances were involved in radical socialism, and in the 'erotic movement' which grew up alongside early psychoanalysis, whereas it seems that Durkheim remained strictly outside these developments. It is well known that Weber, however, also remained consistently attached to the notion of manly honour, and Marianne Weber gives a long account of how her husband, on her behalf, challenged a critic to a duel: the episode eventually ended in court (Marianne Weber 1975: 430). It is clear that both the Webers actively criticized Engels's approach to the question of women's oppression and emancipation, but nevertheless Max Weber supported the entry of women into the professions and universities, and in his later theorizing not only refused to condemn extramarital relations, but actively celebrated extramarital sexual relations as the 'revenge of animality' (Weber 1991: 348) against the increasingly intellectualized world. Thus in his own practice he seems to have adopted something of the position of Lou Salomé's chaste marriage, with eroticism (this time, however, concealed in his own life but not his writing) lying beyond.

There are three recent accounts which can be discussed with profit, those by J. J. R. Thomas, Terry Kandal, and Roslyn Bologh. Thomas imaginatively tries to reconstruct the common doctrine developed jointly by the Webers but expressed most explicitly in the writings of Marianne Weber (and still available only in German). Clearly there may be nuances of difference between the two but, in the main, the central argument suggests that 'it is not that capitalism demands the subjection of women, but the opposite: its emergence as the key phase in the rationalization of the western world is precisely the force engendering women's emancipation' (Thomas 1985: 414).

Kandal's analysis of Weber's sociology and its relation with gender (Kandal 1988: 136–56) begins with Weber's comments on Gross in 1907, and notes that at that moment Weber certainly sided with Freud against the radical sexual revolution which was, with Gross, undertaken with the use of psychoanalytic ideas. At the end of a survey of Weber's work, Kandal returns to Mitzman's judgement that Weber succeeded only in compartmentalizing the competing elements, and to Green's judgement that Weber was essentially a paradox of 'ethically noble hypocrisy', but for Kandal the most apt description is of Weber the 'patriarchal romantic' (ibid.: 156).

Roslyn Bologh has written at length on Weber and feminism, and her theses are summarized at the beginning of her book (Bologh 1990: xvi–xviii). The first basic thesis is that masculinity in Weber is associated with the heroic, and the values of action, conflict and greatness, whereas the feminine is associated with the ethics of the subjugated. Next, Weber's writing on bureaucracy and modern social structure indicates a threat to heroic greatness, but the basic contradiction is that between rationality and ecstasy: for Weber, 'religion represents the nagging and emasculating presence of sublimated desire – a "feminine" desire for love and ecstasy' (ibid.: xvii). Thus the central problem is that posed by the 'ethic of brotherly love' which opposes both action and eroticism, thus the discussion 'addresses Weber's (proto-feminist) interpretation of the coercion and brutality at the heart of (heterosexual) erotic love – imposition of the stronger will (soul) on the weaker.' She concludes that for Weber neither brotherly love nor erotic love 'provide the basis for reforming the world' (ibid.: xvii). Finally, rejecting Weber's analysis, she chooses to oppose Simmel's analysis of sociability to Weber's conception and ends by adopting a position of 'creative generativity'. It can be seen that Bologh is not interested in the development of Weber's thought, or the interaction between a reflection on his experiences and his theory, or indeed in the feminism developed jointly by Weber and Marianne Weber.

The central chapters of Bologh's essay concern at length Weber's essay of 1915 on the 'Religious rejections of the world and their directions' (in Weber 1991: 323–59). Her discussion is inspired by the 'proto-feminism' of part of Weber's analysis. But the whole framework of Weber's discussion is treated in the most unsympathetic manner, and she wishes to refute all the main arguments advanced. Where Weber builds a picture of the impossible project of religions or movements based on strong 'brotherly love', Bologh suggests that it would make no difference to call them movements based on 'love' itself (Bologh 1990: 165), and that these movements have indeed provided instances of great revolutionary practical success.

It seems to me that these discussions do not really get to the heart of Weber's own thinking and practice. But before turning specifically to a different account, a brief indication and outline of the context of Weber's writing is necessary.

Certainly the most authoritative discussion of Max Weber's life is Marianne Weber's biography, which contains quotations from letters and papers in an account which appears to have been directly connected with the sequence of Marianne's diary. It is a strange document written entirely from a position external to herself and their relationship in order to describe herself objectively. It reads as though it had been written by a third person. Of course, it is now known that Max Weber had a secretive side to his character, and that the biography is radically incomplete. Indeed it is highly likely that the biography written by one of the partners would have the tendency to paint the relationship in certain colours, and that representation of the inner nature of the relationship can never be completely open to higher standards of verification. But where the presentation is substantiated by letters and other documents, and in general by close friends (though in this case the close friends are also to some extent involved in different ways in the fragmentation of Weber's life), there seems to be little genuine reason for not proceeding with the discussion of the relationships between this level of experience and Weber's own ideas, even though the analysis proper may only really begin when the many relevant letters have been published, which may not be for many years. Thus it is possible to draw up a characterization of Max Weber's personal formation which reveals reliably the main sources of tension, and the basis for his intellectual and political projects.

WEBER'S LIFE

Marianne Weber's biography is remarkably frank about Weber's personal life, not stopping to censor the fact even that his younger sisters called him 'fatso' on account of his size. There is also a detailed account of Max's early relationship with Emmy Baumgarten, his cousin, which seems to have been intense and ambivalent. Weber wrote of it after it was over as involving the

full weight of responsibility that I assumed when I was still half a boy in my relationship with girls. I did not recognise myself until late, and it is a lifetime responsibility. *She* knew better than I what my situation was.

(Marianne Weber 1975: 178)

Weber thus seems to admit that there was some kind of commitment transcending mere acquaintance, but it is clear that there was a period of many years when Emmy and Max Weber did not meet, although Max did not break off the relationship formally until his proposal to Marianne. Emmy suffered from a serious but unnamed ailment that required medical surveillance, and when, at the very moment he was becoming involved with Marianne, Emmy's condition started to improve, he could not be sure (he wrote to Marianne) that it was either because Emmy still wanted him or because she was free of him. Marianne wrote, curiously, that 'there gradually developed a mysterious feeling, from his innermost being, that it was not given to him to make a woman happy' (ibid.: 160).

Marianne also cites Weber's sister Klara, who, she says somewhat curiously, he loved to 'tease . . . caress . . . spoil . . . educate . . . dominate' (ibid.: 167). Klara recollected that at this time Weber said 'for Emmy's sake he did not feel entitled to marry. Besides, there would be no woman who could love him and whom – given his nature – he could make happy'. Klara also recalled that he even toyed with the idea of a future life solely with her, but he is reported to have concluded that 'for an old bear like me it is best if he trots around in his cage alone' (ibid.: 168). This picture of a sexually tormented personality is reflected in an account of his mother's views: 'she realised that behind the walls with which he had surrounded himself he had to restrain a demonic passionateness which now and then burst forth with destructive blaze' (ibid.: 170). Eventually Marianne gives the decisive letter in which Max proposed, after an episode where he thought he was to lose her to someone else, and it reveals that he certainly did not want to think of it as primarily his own individual choice. 'I shall *never* dare to offer a girl my hand like a free gift. . . . Only if I myself am under the divine compulsion of a complete, unconditional devotion do I have the right to demand it and accept it for myself', he wrote (ibid.: 177). He claimed that she certainly did not know him: 'you do not see how I try, with difficulty and varying success, to tame the elemental passions with which nature has endowed me' (ibid.). He warned her, portentously, that they 'must not tolerate any fanciful surrender to unclear and mystical moods' in their souls. 'For when feeling rises high, you must control it to be able to steer yourself with sobriety' (ibid.). The letter evokes destiny, passion, repression, and there are scarcely veiled hints of warning of unexpected things to come with the astonishing passage, 'ask my mother; I know well her love for me . . . is rooted in the fact that morally I used to be her problem child' (ibid.: 177–8). It is clear that from the way the (auto-) biography is written, Marianne wanted to present the impression that the marriage was the way that Max resolved these problems. It is therefore remarkable that confirmation of the fact that the marriage was unconsummated is universally accepted, as is the fact that he later had affairs (though this could still mean, of course, that even if Weber was technically impotent, these relations could still have been eroticized – though in his description of the erotic relationship Weber later emphasized the physical side of the sexual union).

Weber outlined his conception of the necessary egalitarian modality of marriage shortly after this, for he believed, she reveals, 'that the best way to assure his wife of her equality would be to provide her with a domain of her own within the household that he could not touch' (ibid.: 186). She asked for reading material, and he proposed August Bebel's socialist writing on women and socialism, yet he insisted that even though the question of equality was crucial it was important not to let it lead to a contempt for housewives. He insisted that it was important to have clearly defined spheres of life, for 'the more our very own fields of interest coincide and are identical, the less independent of me and the more vulnerable will you be . . . you must have a definite sphere of activity that is *valuable* to you as such, so that you will not be dependent on the fluctuations of my temperament' (ibid.: 186–7). Yet Weber's mother had considerable doubts that Marianne would make a good *hausfrau* so Marianne took special training and employed a house-servant, Bertha, who lived in the Weber household from 1893 till her death in 1916. Marianne Weber's account then describes in the most curious formulations that 'in accordance with Weber's wishes, his wife now led a full intellectual life. She attended his lectures . . . and she undertook the leadership of a newly founded society for the propagation of modern feminist ideals' (ibid.: 229). Indeed, in this period (1893), he seems to have altered his views from those he held in 1885 when, says Marianne, 'he expressed preference for the traditional type' (ibid.: 111), for now he attended feminist meetings and even supported the cause of the 'new woman': 'he gave some strong admonitions to old-fashioned women, who – so he said – with their intolerance toward the new type were much more vehement opponents of the entire movement than the men. He compared them to hens that mercilessly peck away with their beaks at a strange hen that has strayed into their barnyard' (ibid.: 229). It seems clear that from quite an early period Weber had broken with a partriarchal ideology which insisted on either the strict idealization of women or on the other hand an emancipation conceived as a union with a proletarian, but free, woman. His ideal certainly seems to have involved a relationship with a potential intellectual equal who had a specific independence in a sphere of the division of labour of the household conceived

in the widest sense. He insisted, more than once, that it was the duty of
the woman to resist the oppression of the man in the relationship (ibid.:
112, 230).

After ten years of marriage Marianne Weber describes the Webers'
reactions to what she calls the 'new types of persons, related to the
Romantics . . . [who] questioned the validity of universally binding
norms. . . . [They] were particularly concerned with the liberalization of
sexual morality, for it was in this area that 'law' and 'duty' demanded
the most perceptible sacrifices' (ibid.: 370). Clearly the 'erotic movement'
had begun to have its effects in Weber's domain in Heidelberg. She
makes it clear that at that time the couple had firm convictions that

> in return for the great happiness bestowed by Eros, there was to be
> a readiness for serious tasks: a partnership for life . . . fidelity and
> exclusiveness in the sexual sphere are a matter of course. Such a
> marriage is . . . an *ethical* norm of the sexual union
>
> (Ibid.)

Indeed she insists that their view at this time was that 'sensual enjoyment
. . . must not be an end in itself, not even in the form of aesthetically
sublimated eroticism. In this area there are no *adiaphora* [things morally
different], for no human relationship is as momentous as the sexual kind'
(ibid.: 371). She notes that these were Weber's ideals from the 'Stras-
bourg period' (1883–4) and that he remained loyal to them in the face
of the new women of the erotic movement who 'caricatured chastity as
the morality of monks, and marriage as the state's compulsory institution
for the protection of private property. They demanded the right to 'free
love' and illegitimate children' (ibid.: 373).

In fact it appears that it was Marianne Weber who responded publicly
at this time as the person in the couple who had written on the theory
of marriage, with a lecture in 1907, and she says 'Weber stood by her'
(ibid.: 373). The lecture made the simple concession that it was time to
recognize that a single ascetic morality was absolute and that those who
chose to have multiple relations should not be called 'immoral'. But it is
clear that as the discussion proceeds it is Otto Gross and his new doctrine
of 'the life-enhancing value of eroticism' which caused the Webers problems, for 'under his influence both men and women dared to risk their
own and their companion's spiritual well-being'. In fact, she says they
'were torn by horror and revulsion at the theory' (ibid.: 374). Weber's
own opinion of Gross's theory is available as a note of rejection of an
article submitted by Gross to Weber's journal (ibid.: 375–80), and in a
number of excerpts from letters, in which he makes the important comment: 'is surrender *without* the compulsion of love *not* "dirty"? You see,
theory everywhere enters into the fractional arithmetic' (ibid.: 381). But
according to Marianne, Weber gradually changed 'his attitude to the

people who had abandoned the norms'. First of all (in 1908) 'he . . . concentrated more on their total existence. Whenever he was able to approve of the latter, he was now more interested in its protection and development'. The ethical scale should not impose too heavy a burden: if the highest was simply too costly, sin should be acceptable for some individuals. But then this was quickly developed, and he became able to accept that for some individuals 'lighthearted' affairs could be handled with ease, whereas for others it could not, for 'if playing around led to the deadly seriousness of a great passion and demanded its due alongside the marriage, then he foresaw with horror the moral destruction of the weaker persons'. Marianne Weber cites his attempt to sum up his position at the end of these reflections: 'What I do not like', he said, 'is that if the fate of a great passion comes over a person, he fashions from it a "right" of himself to act in such and such a way, instead of simply taking it "humanly" – simply as a "fate" with which one must cope and often cannot cope, because one is only human' (cited ibid.: 388–9). What was essential in his position, Marianne remarks, was that 'even if nature and fate compel a transgression, a person should nevertheless humbly submit to the supraindividual norm and acknowledge the distance between it and his own action as *guilt*' (ibid.: 388). Certainly Marianne relates all these developments with the comment that they involved the destinies of companions, for Else von Richthofen, a close friend of Marianne and one-time student of Weber was, with her sister Frieda (who had a famous relationship with D. H. Lawrence), involved with Otto Gross. Weber was the godfather of Peter Jaffe (Else's son by Gross), and Weber later was to write that the child was 'somehow connected for me . . . with faded dreams of a child of my own' (Green 1974: 162). Ironically it was Weber who defended in court the interests of Frieda when, in 1913, Otto Gross's father attempted to claim their child Peter (see Green 1974: 67). Later in 1919, after Else and Max Weber were lovers, he wrote 'I think with deep love and thankfulness of this child [Gross's other child by Else], who time and again took us by the hand and led us to each other, brand new and in such loveliness – he gave me the young mother, who shelters and cherishes me'. (ibid.: 162).

What of the relation between these two new women, Marianne Weber and Else Jaffe? Max Weber died in their presence. Baumgarten has written: 'While Max Weber lay dying in Munich both women were in the ante-chamber, and he called for one, then the other. At a certain point Marianne gave way to a fit of jealousy, there was a terrible scene between the two, but in the night Marianne wrote to Else asking for forgiveness. Thirty-three years later Marianne died with her hand in Else's' (in Sombart 1987: 151). But the love letters from Weber to Else remained completely secret with Else during Marianne's lifetime (see Green 1974: 170). We still await the publication of these letters.

Having looked at the context of Weber's work and his significant relationships, it is now possible to return to look at Weber's development and conceptualization once again. Theoretically what is significant is that Weber rejected, at least in his methodological pronouncements, the notion of a social system and its corrollary, functional explanations and evolutionary schemes of social development. He was also opposed to the causalist schemes of both Spencer and Marx, preferring to identify specific and unique historical configurations which had a high degree of 'individuality', which he transformed into 'ideal types'. For him, as for other thinkers at the end of the nineteenth century, the historical schema of European history since the Greeks had been displaced by a world historic scene of comparative civilizations and cultures. Yet curiously, it is possible to think of Weber as far more consistenly evolutionist and comparative in his sociological constructions than for instance Durkheim who provided its explicit methodology. For instance, although Durkheim argued that any complete sociological analysis of religion should follow its course through all the main stages of evolution, he produced an analysis of only one stage in *The Elementary Forms of the Religious Life* ([1912] 1961). Weber's sociology of religion had far greater scope, embracing all the great world religions. On the other hand, the pathos in Weber is not provided by an appeal to a principle like that of Nietzsche's *ressentiment*. Indeed, Weber remarks that Nietzsche's thesis may have relevance, but that its scope is very restricted and some religions are not touched by it at all. Thus there is no temptation in Weber to appeal to any principle of overcoming or overman, since the main problems he seeks to address do not come from, nor are they associated with the will to power.

The crucial pathos in Weber comes from quite another source, and because it is grounded in much wider social analysis than that provided by Nietzsche, it is eventually more powerful. At one level Weber, despite his denials, is quite content to adopt an evolutionary framework as the basis of his thought, and can easily absorb both Marx and Durkheim into his scheme: he uses class analysis as an essential instrument without adopting the principle of economic determinism, and he simply adopts the whole of Durkheim's sociology of religion in the phrase 'in the community cult, the collectivity as such turned to its God' (Weber 1991: 272), and then moves on (Tiryakian (1966) has pointed out that Weber followed the writings of the Année School in France). And after 1910 Weber makes the crucial addition to Durkheim that not only is it a question of social structure (segmentalism, or tribalism) but it is also a question of the sublimation of early forms of orgiastic, or ecstatic, religion in what he calls the 'world religions': Confucianism, Buddhism, Hinduism, Islam, Christianity. The essential and crucial question concerned the specific historical evolution in the West, its economic and social and cultural disenchantment with traditional formations. In other terms, its specific discipline, its rationalization of the military, of the city, of music, of knowledge, of religion.

The bifurcation of the East and West seems ultimately connected with two quite different sacred genealogies: in the East a God reflected in immanence and eternity; in the West, stemming from Iran and the Middle East, a 'supra-mundane', jealous and loving but wrathful God. In the West evolves a specifically redemptive religion turned towards the this-worldly sphere. This results in increasing rationalization of religious action, which is mirrored not only by secular redemptive political move-ments, but also secularization across the social structure and the culture. But at this point, Weber makes a turn that is quite different from that of both Marx and Durkheim: scientific knowledge does not lead to a greater understanding of ultimate values associated with these develop-ments, it tends to destroy belief that these can be determined rationally: only 'big children' believe otherwise. Thus Weber divorces sociology from all attempts in the positivist manner to begin to define social norms on the basis of claims to scientific knowledge of such ends. As Weber shows, there are two consequences. First, religion gradually becomes assigned to the irrational; second, all such ultimate values and aims become regarded by science as the realm of the irrational, or the realm where science is mute. Unlike Nietzsche, however, Weber does not appeal to another form of knowledge, of any transvaluation that might be a form of human self-overcoming. Weber simply says that what is interesting is the significance of the fact that science has nothing to say.

It is in this context that Weber's later analysis of the failure of the Puritan project, or any project based on 'brotherly love', has to be considered. In this sense there is a parallel with Durkheim and the evolutionists, since it is clear that Weber does hold to something of a view which stresses the evolution from primitive, non-sublimated religions, to the great world religions with their forms of sublimation of orgiastic experience, and eventually to the emergence of science and the cultural turn which the conditions where all religions as such fall into the realm of the irrational. But more than that, the erotic also falls into this zone. It is this which has to be faced, and Weber expresses it in the most forceful terms: 'the person who cannot bear the fate of the times like a man [should] return [to] the arms of the old churches [which] are opened widely and compassionately' (cited by Bologh 1990: 193).

Thus what Weber actually provides is an ideology of the division between the chaste, rational marriage, based, in fact, on brotherly, com-passionate, and chivalrous mutual support, and the irrational, fated, pre-destined sphere of Eros and sexual passion. The latter is indeed a mystical sphere, and Bologh cites a conversation between the Webers where 'Max asked Marianne if she could think of herself as a mystic. She replied in the negative and then asked the same of him. He responded, "It could even be that I *am* one" ' (cited ibid.: 165; Mitzman 1970: 218, from Baumgarten 1964: 677).

MAX WEBER'S DOCTRINE OF EXTRAMARITAL EROS

It is therefore highly doubtful whether Weber can in fact be classified with Marx, Durkheim and Freud. Some have claimed that Weber and Freud are very much alike from the point of view of moral temperament. Brubaker has recently argued that 'both reject conceptions of a happy and harmonious social existence as illusory, and disdain the impulse toward reconciliation and reunion as immature. Both combine an unwavering commitment to scientific rationality with a keen awareness of its limited moral significance. Both aim to advance individual autonomy' (Brubaker 1984: 112). But Brubaker overlooks the great gulf between the two thinkers, and between Weber and both Marx and Durkheim, since Weber alone is utterly resistant to the idea that science can determine the aims of individual or social life. Weber even claimed for himself what Durkheim in effect had identified (Brubaker 1982: 86), that this position was ultimately mystical. Weber was content to promote liberal feminism, and in effect supported Marianne's intellectual project and status. He was no simple patriarch, indeed he was radically opposed to his own father's patriarchal modality. He did not seek to establish directly a theoretical or scientific law, or to discover social or psychological invariants from which norms (and thus pathologies) could be deduced. Thus, unlike Marx, Durkheim and Freud, and even Nietzsche, Weber was no nomothete, law-giver in any simple or direct sense, although he is held to be one of the 'fathers' of sociology. This sociology is quite different from the others considered here in the sense that it makes the gesture of the 'great refusal', profound in its consequences compared with Marx or Durkheim, in that, from within itself, and on its own terrain, it will not enunciate social norms: these are entirely beyond the scope of scientific discourse. The Weberian irony is to point to the fact that science itself makes these goals appear entirely irrational.

Thus what Brubaker misses is the fact that Weber does not only call 'reunion' immature, but also the idea that science can illuminate the ultimate meaning of things, or to provide meaning for social life, or indeed any life. There is in Weber, therefore, not the slightest hint of a movement towards a scientifically based practice of therapy, or intervention in social life on the basis of the scientifically established identification of ends. In the sphere of science it is legitimate to discuss process, conjuncture, combination, historical configurations, even regularities. But in no sense is it legitimate, within science, to point to the fact that any social tendency is socially desirable as value: this is to confuse politics with science, to introduce an illegitimate mingling of spheres, to intrude on the isolation essential for science itself in its radical separation from religion. In this way Weber is also quite different from Godwin, Enfantin, Comte, and Engels, who each sought to make the 'new man' the product of the logic of social science. Weber is much closer in this respect to Mill.[1]

It is probably the comparison and contrasts between Mill and Weber which will provide the best, if 'awkward' (Ryan) route to the understanding of Weber's vision and practice of the 'new man' (which he must have conceived as such in contrast to his father's practice). It seems clear that the internal relationship of Harriet Taylor with Mill had less of a division of intellectual labour and individuality than that of the Webers; perhaps it is curious that Harriet Taylor Mill's views are much better known in Britain than the extensive feminist writings of Marianne Weber, and that in a sense it seems clear that Marianne was far more of an accomplished intellectual than Harriet Taylor and thought of herself as both an independent personality and new woman (it is clear that Weber and Marianne Weber spent long periods apart). Max Weber had a distinct notion, right from the start of his relation with Marianne, that she should have a specific and unique sphere of life of her own, and that it was a woman's duty to resist male oppression, but this was never developed to the point that it was in Simmel's theories, for example, where he elaborates the notion of separate gender cultures (a view attacked vigorously by Marianne Weber as completely reactionary (see L. van Vucht Tijssen 1991)). But it is noticeable that the marriages of both Weber and Mill were childless, in one case the relation was for a long period chaste, and in the other completely so. But the difference between the two is very striking. In the case of the Mills it is clear that the ultimate aim is a kind of intellectual and sexual fusion of the couple in a mystical vision of union; in the case of the Webers the individualism is more marked; the relation is companionate and apparently practical, with the erotic 'revenge of animality' celebrated secretly, mystically, outside the marriage by one of the partners, in yet another separated sphere kept apart from the others.

But even in the very modality of this conception, there is still an interesting question: Weber's own repressive Lutheran background. It seems clear that Weber did try to overcome his father's, and indeed the parental, sexual ethos, an ethos he perceived as involving the idea of

> sexual expression within marriage simply as a lesser evil enjoined for the avoidance of whoredom. Luther construed marriage as a legitimate sin which God as contrained not to notice, so to speak, and which . . . was a conseqence of the ineluctable concupiscence resulting from original sin.
>
> (Weber 1978: 606)

The idea of marriage in this perspective he outlined elsewhere as one of the divine ordinations given to man as a creature who is hopelessly wretched by virtue of his 'concupiscence'. Within this divine order it is given to man to live according to the rational purposes laid down by it and only according to them: to procreate and to rear children, and mutually to further one another in the state of grace.

(Weber 1991: 349)

The strategy of rational asceticism, then, collects the elements of natural sexuality and passion only to locate them as the residues of the Fall. 'According to Luther', he continues, 'God, in order to prevent worse, peeks at and is lenient with these elements of passion' (ibid.: 349).

There is clearly a notion in Weber here of suffering and a repressive redemptive project, which recalls his notion that the 'specific character of ressentiment [is only formed] under special circumstances', (Weber 1978: 494) for clearly the phrase 'revenge of animality' even if it carries a certain ironic charge, seems far from the simple return of the repressed. Here, as Weber makes clear, the sexual sphere is completely transformed into the erotic, and is not a transparent return to the naturalistic sexuality of the peasant or to primitive orgiasticism. For,

at the level of the peasant, the sexual act is an everyday occurrence; primitive people do not regard this act as containing anything unusual, and they may indeed enact it before the eyes of onlooking travellers without the slightest feeling of shame. They do not regard this act as having any significance beyond the routine of living. The decisive development . . . is the sublimation of sexual expression into an eroticism that becomes the basis of idiosyncratic sensations, hence generates its own unique values and transcends everyday life.

(Weber 1978: 607)

This leads us directly to the consideration of Weber's short description of the erotic sphere and what he called, not accidentally, the 'greatest irrational force of life: sexual love'. It should be remembered that for Weber Lutheranism brought about the sharpest conflict between sexuality and religion: the highest degree of 'sublimated sexuality' with the 'relentlessly consistent . . . salvation ethic of brotherhood (Weber 1991: 343). Weber himself is utterly consistent and draws the, apparently inevitable, conclusion

under this tension between the erotic sphere and rational everyday life, specifically extramarital sexual life, which had been removed from everyday affairs, could apear as the only tie which still linked man with the natural fountain of all life . . . a joyous triumph over rationality [which] glories all the pure animality of the relation.

(Ibid.: 347)

Is there ressentiment here after all? Weber reveals in detail why this sphere cannot be accepted by religious ethics. And it is clear that Weber's position is that it is the revenge of sexuality through the erotic sphere itself against the ascetic codes which receives his full enthusiasm by the time of writing this text. This is revealed most emphatically in the account (from Weber's male point of view) of the erotic sphere itself:

> the erotic relation seems to offer the unsurpassable peak of the fulfilment of the request for love in the direct fusion of the souls of one to another. This boundless giving of oneself is as radical as possible in its opposition to all functionality, rationality, and generality. It is displayed here as the unique meaning which one creature in his irrationality has for another and only for another, and only for this specific other. . . . It is so overpowering that it is interpreted 'symbolically' as a sacrament. The lover realizes himself to be rooted in the kernel of the truly living, which is eternally inaccessible to any rational endeavour. . . . The experience is by no means communicable. . . . This is not only due to the intensity of the lover's experience, but to the immediacy of the possessed reality. . . .
>
> As the knowing love of the mature man stands to the passionate enthusiasm of the youth, so stands the deadly earnestness of this eroticism of intellectualism to chivalrous love. In contrast to chivalrous love, this mature love of intellectualism reaffirms the natural quality of the sexual sphere, but it does so consciously, as an embodied creative power.
>
> (Ibid.: 347)

As we now know of Max Weber's own secret affairs and the existence of many letters relating to them (which will surely reveal Weber's ideology here when they are published), it is certainly safe to assume that these paragraphs present the outlines of his own view, and contain the doctrine of his later years, even down to making the distinction concerning the intellectual as well as the mature intellectual. In this sphere the rational intellectual finds a way to escape rationality, and indeed even rational communication, and he says 'in this respect it is equivalent to the "having" of the mystic' (ibid.: 347).

Is this modernism, a modern doctrine of a new man in the world where women are equal and emancipated? It is a modernism and a celebration of fragmentation, of multiplicity, of rationality and of heightened irrationality, in Weber's words 'an inner-worldly salvation from rationalization' (ibid.: 346), a kind of flight. What of marriage itself? This seems to remain in the realm of the functional, of the rational; and indeed Weber seems to say just that: 'from a purely inner-worldly point of view, only the linkage of marriage with the thought of ethical responsibility for one another – hence a category heterogeneous to the purely erotic sphere –

can carry the sentiment that something unique and supreme might be embodied in marriage' (ibid.: 350). Thus marriage has its place, and more than this, it carries a 'supreme' something: a 'mutual granting of oneself to another and the becoming indebted to each other (in Goethe's sense). Rarely does life grant such value in pure form' (ibid.). Even here, then, Weber orients the discussion not to any ascetic conception of marriage itself, but rather, in the end, to Goethe, and to mutual dependence not completely based on rational calculation and 'merit', however, (though it is clear in the conjugal sphere, Weber avoids mystical sentiments and treats the relationship in a practical and responsible spirit, but with the very important further justification of the erotic sphere itself). For it is not from the ascetic ethic that marriage can seem sublime; as he has shown, marriage in Luther's conception is a convenience. It is precisely from the point of view of inner-worldly eroticism itself, that marriage can appear as the 'transformation of the feeling of a love which is conscious of responsibility'. Weber emphasizes this by contrasting Luther with the Quakers, who he says 'may well have achieved a genuinely humane interpretation of the inner and religious values of marriage' (ibid.: 350). But Weber's doctrine goes far enough to begin to suggest a necessary alliance between compassionate marriage, perhaps chaste, certainly con-sidered as a life-commitment, a 'responsibility throughout all the nuances of the organic life process' (ibid.: 350), and an external 'eroticism, genu-ine "passion" *per se* [which] constitutes the type of *beauty*' itself (ibid.: 349, the last phrase here apparently derived from Else Jaffe directly (see Green 1974: 171).

Whatever the temptation, however, Weber is no postmodernist, but a curious combination of traditional duelling male and new man willing to face up to the challenge of the new woman, or should it more accurately be, new women? He did not move to a position 'beyond good and evil' or search to transcend traditional sexual morality. What Weber combined was a kind of Quaker humanism, individualism and responsibility, with notions of fate and guilt. This led him to reject the new ideas of sexual rights: for him the sexual sphere was not lighthearted but dangerous.[2] Yet he became involved, not like Marx with his domestic servant, but with a student and friend of his wife; and, as Martin Green has pointed out, her child (called Peter Jaffe, but fathered by Otto Gross) 'became his, by a spiritual paternity of adoption' (Green 1974: 162). Thus, in his own terms, he had to face the fact that, vulnerable, he could not live up to his own highest moral standards and would have had to live with the fact that he could not exonerate himself of his guilt by making a right out of it: 'This I cannot very well have; everything else must be "understood" ' (in Marianne Weber 1975: 389).

Chapter 10

In transcendence: Friedrich Nietzsche and Lou Salomé

In this chapter I turn back from Weber but not far from the developments largely dominated by responses to the French Revolution and its aftermath, either in terms of the claim to the rights of man, or the rights of woman, or the experiment with new collective forms and ideologies. The situation in German-speaking countries is altogether different, and the specific process of *Aufklärung* was very much more complex. On the one side, there was the direct influence of Saint-Simonian radicalism in the work of Marx and Engels, where virtually the whole programme of political strategy was taken directly and uncritically from the doctrines developed in Paris in the late 1820s: in fact Engels was even prepared to make Saint-Simon directly the source of 'almost all the ideas of later socialists which are not economic' (Engels 1936: 286). Saint-Simon's ideas were popularized in Germany through Heine and Lorenz von Stein, who, incidentally, had been sent to Paris curiously as a police agent to investigate the socialists: his report summarizing socialist ideas, when published, found a wide market (see von Stein 1964; and Avineri 1985: 85). But outside of the rather dour socialist debates leading to the famous Gotha congress criticized by Marx (in Marx and Engels 1968: 315–35), the philosophical oppositions produced also the most profound critique of the whole evolution of modernity in the works of Schopenhauer and Nietzsche, with which, as we have seen, Weber in the next generation would attempt to come to terms.

In relation to the question of gender, the German tradition was conservative. Both Kant and Hegel remained in the traditional mode. Schopenhauer himself developed an extremely anti-feminist, even misogynist position (writing which seems so to have embarrassed his modern readers, see Maggee 1983, which contains no reference to the infamous chapter on women in Schopenhauer's *Aphorisms* nor does the word 'woman' appear in the index). In his essay on Schopenhauer, Maggee hints at a problem of 'maternal deprivation' in the philosopher (ibid.: 10); he also relates the famous court case which followed Schopenhauer's throwing a woman down a flight of stairs because her talking had disturbed his working. He lost the case and was forced to compensate her yearly for the rest of her life (which turned out to be twenty-six years); apparently at this time he did have affairs and only later became the 'misogynistic recluse' known to posterity (ibid.: 17). The most significant of the writers who turned against the revolution and the Enlightenment project was Friedrich Nietzsche (1844–1900), whose influence extends to the current cultural shift into the postmodern, and curiously, via Derrida principally to postmodern feminism.

Nietzsche is quite different in character from all the other writers considered here; for he was not impressed with rationalism, progress, liberation movements, socialism or new forms of Christianity. Yet his critique of these tendencies and the influence of the French Revolution developed into an epistemological and philosophical critique which many subsequent different and diverse tendencies have sought to use eclectically to their own advantage. Nietzsche's father, who died at the age of thirty-six, when Nietzsche was four, was a Lutheran minister. His early family milieu was dominated by strongly willed, but highly conservative women (his mother, his father's mother, a sister, and two maiden aunts). Some have maintained that he contracted syphilis as a youth, but this has never actually been confirmed. It is certain that he had poor health and struggled to develop a permanent relationship with any woman outside his family. He was a brilliant classics scholar, being appointed at twenty-four to the post of associate professor, and in 1870 to full professor at Basel. In 1889 he collapsed and spent the remainder of his life unable to work or write.

There are a large number of personal accounts of Nietzsche, an important book by Lou Salomé,[1] and notably a recent long analysis by W. Warner,[2] a considerable, if not altogether reliable, correspondence, and of course his own 'autobiography', *Ecce Homo*. He attempted to develop relations with a number of women including Cosima Wagner, Louise Ott, Mathilde Trampedach, and Lou von Salomé. These women presented obstacles in that they were either attached or married. He proposed to Mathilde and Lou indirectly, either through a letter or through another person. He was rejected by all of them. Of Cosima Wagner he said he above all admired her style: Wagner was unworthy of such a wife – 'in gratitude', he said, 'he became her victim' (cited by Lavrin 1971: 53–4). The disappointment with Mathilde Trampedach (his proposal by letter was rejected), left him very hurt. After his proposal (though some accounts dispute this) to Lou von Salomé through Paul Ree, he was thrown into turmoil, as the relation was soured by the intervention of his sister.

Reports of Nietzsche from the 1880s, when he was regularly visiting a hotel, The Alpine Rose, for his meals and meeting guests, suggest a gentle character. Helen Zimmern was one who met him; she wrote in

1884: 'I know that Nietzsche wrote about women. But according to my experiences I can only say that Nietzsche was the most perfect 'gentilezza' (in Gilman 1987: 166–8). Another was Marie von Bradke, in 1886:

> The hotel began to fill¬up . . . a newly arrived gentleman sat down opposite me – it was Nietzsche. . . . Something in his voice, his look attracted me. We soon got into a lively conversation . . . when my departure was drawing nearer – I resolved to ask him for the title of the work he considered his best . . . finally he named *Zarathustra* . . . 'but I should not read the book' he said: it would only frighten and repel me. . . . Our last meeting revealed to me the pain of his loneliness.
>
> (Ibid.: 188–92)

Another was Meta von Salis-Marschlins, in 1887:

> Nietzsche loved to 'recreate' himself with me as a reprieve from his loneliness . . . we sat for many hours in my flower-decorated room . . . Nietzsche knew how to 'share joy' as few people do, and how to show it tactfully. . . . He sought to make his mother's stance toward him easy and joyous by keeping from her his peculiar knowledge and conclusions, advising her not to read his books . . . [when she left] he remarked with a small sigh 'now I am widowed and orphaned again'.
>
> (Ibid.: 195–207)

It is clear that with many of his women acquaintances, and even his mother, he was not prepared to discuss his philosophy, particularly as it related to women. But there were some women who were exceptional in this regard. Lou von Salomé (1861–1937) was one such woman, who, after leaving Nietzsche, was to play the role of *femme fatale* to a number of leading intellectuals (Rilke, Tausk, Freud). In 1882 Nietzsche planned to set up with Lou and Paul Ree a kind of intellectual *ménage*. It was in the winter of 1882–3 that he wrote Part I of *Zarathustra*, but it was also a period that he called 'the worst in my life', and when 'my whole life . . . crumbled under my gaze' (see Middleton 1969: 184). Evidently Nietzsche and Lou had become close friends in working together, in the summer of 1882, on a poem written by Lou and set to music (later published and performed) by Nietzsche. Nietzsche said at the time that it was 'just one little way in which we could both *together* reach posterity – not discounting other ways' (Middleton: 192). At the time Nietzsche wrote several letters to and about her. In one he ended by saying: 'become the being you are! . . . In fond devotion to your destiny – for in you I love also *my hopes*.' About her he wrote 'there is a deep affinity between us in intellect and taste . . . I have never met anyone who could derive so many *objective insights* from experience . . . I would like to know if there has ever existed such *philosophical candor* as there is between us' (in Middleton: 174). In October 1882 he wrote 'she has fulfilled all my expectations – it is not possible for two people to be more closely related than we are'.

But for Nietzsche things immediately went wrong as the *ménage à trois* broke up, with Lou and Ree leaving. Lou afterwards reported that Nietzsche had proposed to her through Ree. Others have doubted whether this account was completely reliable (see Kaufman 1968). In any event, by December Nietzsche wrote to both Lou and Ree (perhaps again asking Paul Ree to carry his message): 'Do not be upset by the outbreaks of my 'megalomania' or of my 'injured vanity' – and even if I should happen one day to take my life because of some passion or other, there would not be much to grieve about . . . consider me as a semi-lunatic with a sore head who has been totally bewildered by long solitude. . . . Friend Ree, ask Lou to forgive me everything . . .' (ibid.: 198). Whether or not the account of what had occurred is open to question in is specific detail, it is clear that Nietzsche's hopes had been completely dashed. He himself had been thrown into suicidal despair. He wrote to a friend in December. 'I have suffered from the humiliating and tormenting memories of this summer as from a bout of madness. . . . It involves a tension between opposing passions which I cannot cope with. . . . I am being broken, as no other man could be, on the wheel of my own passions. . . . Unless I discover the alchemical trick of turning this – muck into gold, I am lost.' He reports breaking off relations with his mother (who had said that he was a disgrace to his dead father (ibid.: 206)) and 'my relation to Lou is in the last agonizing throes' (ibid.: 199). Shortly after this he broke off relations with his sister Elizabeth for slandering Lou and Ree. There are many elements in Nietzsche's crisis: his own fierce desire to break out of his solitude, to establish an intellectual and sexual relation with Lou, his own lack of ability or courage to talk to Lou at this level without going through Paul Ree, the bitterness of his mother and sister at his apparent failure, directed both at him and at Lou and Paul Ree, and not least his own despair turned into a thinly veiled emotional blackmail against Lou: 'it is harder to forgive one's friends than one's enemies' (ibid. 198). In February 1883 he said, 'My whole life has crumbled before my gaze: this whole eerie, deliberately secluded secret life' (ibid.: 206).

Who was Lou von Salomé? In Nora Wydenbruck's account, she was the archetype of the 'new woman' who 'scorned the conventions and demanded that men should treat her as an intellectual equal and forget her sex'. In the case of meeting Nietzsche, it was her own idea to have Nietzsche as a 'chaperon' for her partnership with Ree. Nietzsche's proposal was a 'primitive reaction' and came as a deadly shock (Wydenbruck 1949: 52–3). In fact, her ideas on relationships were highly unusual for, although thoroughly 'liberated' in ideas and scornful of convention, she had led a life in which, despite appearances, heterosexual love played no part. Unlike Nietzsche's experience of a predominantly female milieu, Lou's milieu was masculine. She herself said 'every man, no matter when I met him in my life, always seemed to conceal a brother' (cited in Prater 1986: 37). She married Friedrich Andreas under the blackmail of his threat of suicide, but the marriage was to remain platonic, as a marriage should simply be a 'kneeling together' she said. When she became lovers with Rilke, she described their relation as being 'like brother and sister, but . . . before incest became a sacrilege' (ibid.: 39). The relationship did not last. She distinguished carefully between physical love, friendship and marriage. The latter involved a 'deeper, loftier' idealized relation, 'the recognition that each belongs *in* and not just *to* the other, in an almost religious or at least ideal sense' (ibid.: 40). After her well-known relations with Nietzsche and Rilke and the publication of her own works, 'Lou Andreas-Salomé became the leading lady of the European intellectual scene' (Zanuso 1986: 43). Her entry into the psychoanalytic scene saw again the formation of a three-cornered relationship, Lou, Tausk and Freud. It was with Tausk that she formed a sexual relation; after his suicide, Lou was surprised to learn that Freud 'had long taken him to be useless' (in Roazen 1976: 326). In 1885 Nietzsche read Lou's book (*Struggling For God* (see Livingstone 1984: 204–6)), and wrote: 'what a contrast between the girlish and sentimental form and the strong-willed and knowledgeable content! There is loftiness in it; even if it is not really the eternal feminine which draws this pseudo-maiden ever forward . . . then perhaps it is – the eternal masculine. . . . And there is a hundred echoes of our . . . conversations in it' (in Middleton 1969: 249).

Nietzsche himself certainly thought of suicide in the winter of 1882–3, his letters reveal, as his emotional life entered into a period of crisis. His mode of escape is made quite clear in his letters: 'I have an *aim* . . . *without this aim* I would take things much more lightly – that is, I would stop living. . . . I must have an absolute victory – that is, the transformation of experience into gold' (ibid.: 214). Nietzsche appears to be very self-conscious in his attempt to deal with the 'muck' of his emotional turmoil as in some way the raw materials of a process of production. Not just a simple or common practice, but rather a question of continuing to live. He wrote to his friend in the summer of 1883, 'I need to survive *through next year* – help me to hold out for another fifteen months' (ibid.: 215). Early in 1883, in ten days, Nietzsche wrote the first part of *Thus Spake Zarathustra*. 'This book . . . now seems to me like my own will and testament. It contains an image of myself in the sharpest focus, as I am, *once* I have thrown off my whole burden. It is poetry' (ibid.: 206–7). In the autobiographical *Ecce Homo* Nietzsche later said 'except for these ten day wonders, the years during and above all after *Zarathustra* were marked by distress without equal. One has to pay dearly for immortality: one has to die several times while still alive' (Nietzsche 1969b: 303). The theme of the work is Zarathustra's journey of rebirth, the journey to the superman: a specific variation, Nietzsche's variation, of the 'new man' whose will to power enables him to overcome himself: 'I tell you one must have chaos in one, to give birth to a dancing star' (Nietzsche 1969a: 46). And Zarathustra is a new kind of man, one who is a dancer, for whom even the 'most abysmal idea is *not* an objection to existence' (Nietzsche 1969b: 306).

But to men 'I am still a cross between a fool and a corpse' says Zarathustra (ibid.: 49). And in the story, he divides himself into the living and dead, carrying the dead part, the corpse, on his back into the forest where he lays the dead man in a hollow tree. After a long sleep he awakens to realize that from now on he needs living companions, not corpses, but other new beings, and although 'with him everything is ripe . . . he lacks his hundred sickles' (ibid.: 52). The narrative of the work is both an account of the transformation of man to 'superman', but also a search for the companions of the new man.[3]

Part III

Images and mirrors

Chapter 11

Towards postmodernism: Nietzsche's (imaginary) lovers

Men have hitherto treated women like birds which have strayed down to them from the heights: as something more delicate, more fragile, more savage, stranger, sweeter, soulful – but as something to be caged up so that it shall not fly away.

(Nietzsche 1973: 147)

Lying at the base of postmodern considerations of Nietzsche are the pioneering arguments of George Bataille (in essays in the 1930s (in Bataille 1985)), Walter Kaufmann ([1950] 1968), and the essays of Deleuze [1962] 1983,[1] Klossowski (1969) and Foucault [1967] (in 1977),[2] but the full emergence of this line of thought crystallized in the seminars of Derrida in the early 1970s (a group which included Pautrat and Kofman) and which led to the most famous statement of the problem in Derrida's short essay *Spurs* ([1973] 1979). Shortly after Derrida's final version, and Baudrillard's Nietzschean *Seduction*, Luce Irigaray published her long poetic epistle to Nietzsche (or rather to the modern imaginary Nietzsche represented in Deleuze and Derrida) called *Marine Lover of Friedrich Nietzsche* ([1980] 1991), which surely represents one of the strangest replies to Nietzsche ever written and one so bizarre and perhaps even embarrassing to English readers that Irigaray's main English inter-locutor, Margaret Whitford, makes scarcely any reference to its con-clusions in her recent account of Irigaray's work (Whitford 1991). It is possible to read Derrida's subsequent discussions of Nietzsche as in part a reply to Irigaray (Derrida 1982; and Ch. 20 in Jardine and Smith 1987). However, since Irigaray, a number of writers have attempted to follow this train of dialogue, or friendly investigation of Nietzsche, in efforts to unravel some of the deeper mysteries of his, by now purely partial or even purely apparent, misogyny. These include David Krell's search for the lineage of Ariadne in Nietzsche's work as a whole (Krell 1986), and Jean Graybeal's interrogation (Graybeal 1990) of key Nietzsche texts under the inspiration, this time, of the thought of Julia Kristeva (a writer herself generally hostile to Nietzsche, thus that essay could be read as a provocation to Kristeva). The general tenor of this whole ever growing corpus of works is a deep sympathy with the power and complexity of Nietzsche's ambiguous creative encounter with women and the feminine, in the face of what appear to be insuperable barriers and unlikely possibilities. In this chapter I will try to specify as clearly as possible what seem to be the issues at stake in this emergence – a hundred years after Nietzsche's texts first appeared and against the traditional right-wing claim to them – of the new left-wing Nietzschean feminism and its paradoxical relation to the debate over postmodernism.

First of all however, before examining the development of the new debate on Nietzsche, it is worth looking at an example of the continuation of the traditional, even pre-Kaufmann, view of Nietzsche as it is still to be found primarily amongst disciplines as yet untouched by the new French styles of analysis. This can be found in the work of the predominantly Germanist approach of Ellen Kennedy in her essay 'Nietzsche: Woman as Untermensch' (in Kennedy and Mendus 1987: 179–201). This essay has the great merit of being innocent, except for a brief reference to Deleuze which points to Nietzsche as still 'controversial', of all the recent re-evaluations deriving largely from Deleuze, Derrida and the 'left-Heideggerians' or 'left-Nietzscheans' (though some, particularly Derrida, are cautious over these terms (see Derrida 1985: 19–38)), and of the subsequent debate in feminist literature itself. Directly, without feint, Kennedy recalls the specific connection of Nazism with Nietzsche and discusses this theme under the rubric of Nietzsche's 'You are going to visit women? Don't forget your whip!' (from *Zarathustra*). Kennedy immediately proceeds to the judgement that Nietzsche was a *Frauenfeind* 'without par', consistent with his opposition to democracy and socialism (Kennedy 1987: 183).

Kennedy, warning against all euphoria, recommends a 'sober reading' of Nietzsche. The problem, she argues, stems fundamentally from Kaufmann's positive re-evaluation of Nietzsche which 'overlooked the role fear plays in Nietzsche's account of the origin of morality', especially in relation to the question of women, where his debt to Schopenhauer's well-known misogyny was decisive. Indeed Nietzsche's conception and evaluation of women 'remained constant'. Inherently they 'lack the will to power' and woman 'cannot be an Übermensch' (ibid.: 185). Kennedy draws on Elisabeth Förster-Nietzsche's accounts of her brother's private conversations to argue that his ideal was rather uncomplicated, a simple assertion that women should be 'beautiful, strong and healthy mothers' (cited ibid.: 186); and for Kennedy this is obviously congruent with the 'mother-aesthetic of National Socialism'. Against modern feminism and the questioning of the simple notion of the woman's role, Nietzsche condemns feminism as a sickness: the modern woman induces 'the deadly hatred of the sexes. Has my answer been heard to the question of how one cures a woman – redeems her? One gives her a child' (Nietzsche, cited ibid.: 189). Thus the hand of biological determinism is played, says Kennedy, producing in its wake all kinds of paradoxes.

What interests Kennedy is the way in which Nietzsche scorns the wife of Socrates, Xanthippe. Nietzsche says

> Actually she drove him deeper into his real calling, in that she made house and home foreign and unbearable for him: she taught him to go back into the back streets and live where one could gossip and be useless, she made him the great alley philosopher.
>
> (Cited, ibid.: 188)

Her interpretation is that, for Nietzsche, women actually frustrate the will to power. If Nietzsche could say women 'scream and mourn and even disturb the sunset peace of the thinker' then 'it is hardly surprising that Nietzsche was one of the most bitter opponents of women's emancipation' (ibid.: 189). Kennedy notes that Nietzsche read Mill, and argues, somewhat speculatively, that his position is an attempt to provide a counter to utilitarian liberalism which he took to be a key problem just as were socialism and feminism, since it meant the break-up of traditional authority structures.

But curiously, Kennedy does acknowledge that Nietzsche has a conception of a better and different society, but one with no politics, no parties, no law courts, the realm of sovereign individuals: but it is clear, she insists, that women cannot participate – as they have already been disqualified on biological grounds and in consequence crucially lack moral sense. She poses the question: why is it Nietzsche never wants to push women's subversiveness to a logical conclusion? Why is the feminine principle not radicalized? The answer, she says, is all too obvious, is 'blindingly simple', it is the fact that for Nietzsche, women's emancipation would never break out of the repressive framework, it 'would reinforce it all, the whole structure'. Thus his philosophy is a total failure: 'instead of pursuing the radical analysis of morality and politics . . . Nietzsche really does have nothing more to offer . . . than the common prejudices of his age and sex' (ibid.: 193–4). Thus the effort of reconsideration is mis-calculated if one reads soberly the 'sections on women as though he meant what he wrote' (ibid.: 197), for in essence Nietzsche is 'the inventor of one of the crassest and most subtle misogynies' (ibid.: 198). Thus Kennedy's reading stands in very great contrast to all the recent French readings which have asserted that there is in the paradoxical writings of Nietzsche the emergence, precisely, of a positive feminine principle, which provides a decisive key to the understanding not just of the formation of gender but also of philosophy.

Whatever the great drawbacks of the essays by Deleuze and Derrida in relation to feminism, they are certainly suggestive of a reading of

Nietzsche on women only rarely hinted at previously (e.g. by Karl Reinhardt, (1935; see Krell 1986: 12–27)). This has argued that Nietzsche's
apparently bitterly hostile writings on women have to be seen in the
context of a broad and extremely heterogeneous, even ingeniously complicated, strategy of gender negations and affirmations; and that on balance
Nietzsche presents an anti-feminism that in the last resort is overturned
by an extraordinary, yet highly paradoxical and incomplete affirmation
of feminism: not just the feminine, but a genuine search for an affirmation
of independent feminine power. Thus Derrida (who arrived at this problem in trying to tackle issues around Nietzsche's critique of Western
philosophy – for this contextualization see Spivak in Derrida 1976: ix–xc,
esp. p. xxxvi) argued both that for Nietzsche 'Feminism is nothing but
the operation of a woman who aspires to be like man. . . . Feminism
. . . seeks to castrate. It wants a castrated woman' (Derrida 1979: 65),
and also, in a point that is often overlooked, that beyond negations,
'woman is recognized and affirmed as an affirmative power. . . . And no
longer is it man who affirms her. She affirms herself, in and of herself,
in man. . . . And anti-feminism, which condemned woman only so long
as she was, so long as she answered to man . . . is in its turn overthrown'
(ibid.: 97). Derrida is even prepared to express the variations in Nietzsche's thought 'in a finite number of typical and matrical propositions'
(ibid.: 95), and these are:

> He was, he dreaded this castrated woman.
> He was, he dreaded this castrating woman.
> He was, he loved this affirming woman.

And Derrida adds 'at once, simultaneously or successively, depending on
the position of his body and the situation of his story, Nietzsche was all
of these' (ibid.: 100). In this way Derrida has directly opened the possibility that Nietzsche's animus is aimed not at women as such, but at
woman, the victim of repression and oppression, who turns the will to
power into *ressentiment*. Two projects are immediately implied: first, the
examination of Nietzsche's apparently misogynist arguments in a new
context, and second, the search for the identity of the affirming woman:
who is she? Ariadne?

Jean Graybeal's *Language and 'the Feminine' in Nietzsche and Heidegger* is an exemplary attempt to reread Nietzsche in the new perspective.
Although her recommendation is that one should apply 'a careful reading
of certain texts of Nietzsche' and this will in itself provide a 'valuable
insight into the process of human self-constitution within language'
(Graybeal 1990: 1), in fact the theoretical instruments used by Graybeal
are explicitly taken, rather uncritically, from Julia Kristeva. The project
is, then, to some extent already constructed in relation to woman as
other, for as she says, citing Kristeva,

to write in relation to this 'other' that 'lies beyond and subverts . . .
logic, mastery, and verisimilitude' is to engage *la mère qui jouit*, to
come into relation with a force which is terrifying, overwhelming,
unsettling, and at the same time unsurpassably exciting and erotic. . . .
Incest wish is then the psychological motive of writing.

(Ibid.: 20–1)

Kristeva's thesis that 'all phantasms, like any attempt to give meaning,
come from the phallic *jouissance* obtained by usurping that unnameable
object . . . which is the archaic mother' (cited ibid.: 21), is taken as the
point of departure for the study of Nietzsche and evidently determines
the 'careful reading'. Graybeal wants to call any feminism which recognizes the necessity for a critique of gender essentialism postmodern; it is
here that 'women must experience their "phallic" character' and resist
the regressive movement of identification with the archaic mother. She
accepts uncritically Kristeva's two conditions for the liberation of women:
the full entry of women into society's contradictions, and the full acceptance of the sexual heterogeneity of the body and language (ibid.: 23).
Yet if Kristeva insists that women (woman does not exist) must live
without God and without Man, there is still the essential moment of
religion at the 'intersection of sublimation and perversion' (Kristeva), or,
as Graybeal suggests, in the mode of 'eluding exclusive self-dedication to
one side or the other of the human double bind' (ibid.: 24). Hence the
importance of Nietzsche, says Graybeal, moving against Kristeva, as a
way of facing the 'full ambiguities of becoming subjects in process, while
at the same time avoiding imagining any simple "way out" ' (ibid.: 25).
Curiously, even though Graybeal wants to rehabilitate Nietzsche in this
perspective, her analysis could be greatly extended.

The major portion of her reading concerns *Zarathustra*, and although
her analysis lacks elegance, sections must be examined closely. Not surprisingly, she spends considerable time over the traditionally infamous
section 'Of old and young women' which ends with the old women's
words 'Are you visiting women? Do not forget your whip!' (Nietzsche
1969b: 93). What is needed here to break the deadlock, says Graybeal,
is an analysis that treats this 'discourse as discourse . . . in a new light'
(Graybeal 1990: 45). First of all Nietzsche's attitude to 'old' women
should be recalled, she says. In the *Gay Science*, written just before
Zarathustra, Nietzsche treats old women as 'debunkers', and 'old women
are more sceptical in their secret heart of hearts than any man' (Nietzsche,
cited ibid.: 46). Nietzsche says to the old woman: 'Everything about
woman is a riddle, and everything about woman has one solution: it is
called pregnancy' (Nietzsche 1969b: 91). This seems, on the face of it,
exactly the kind of enunciation that Kennedy has stigmatized as National
Socialist mother worship. Graybeal resists the temptation. First, she notes

that one should not overlook the positive value involved: Nietzsche's contempt is mainly expressed for the sterile and sterility. Second, she notes that Nietzsche's text continues with the words 'true man [wants] danger and play . . . he wants woman, as the most dangerous plaything'. With this contextualization everything is turned upside down: 'a call to play', and here, against a view that woman must be literally confined to producing babies, Nietzsche suggests a more powerful, indeed the most powerful of all possible cultural images in the notion of pregnancy which must be given an altogether different and quite 'new meaning' (Greybeal 1990: 47). The call to play is not direct: 'A child is concealed in the true man: it wants to play. Come, women, discover the child in man' (Nietzsche 1969b: 92).

And when Nietzsche continues woman, her 'nature is surface, a changeable, stormy film upon shallow waters'. Again it is essential, Graybeal insists, to see that for Nietzsche this implies no criticism, for his whole position has been developed in a critique of depth, and a celebration of appearance. Indeed, says Graybeal, 'surface is what there is; it is appearance, interpretation, mask, relationship, error, dissimulation, art . . .' (ibid.: 49). But finally this section of *Zarathustra* ends with the passage about the whip. Graybeal's reading notes that the whip appears elsewhere in the text as an auxiliary without which 'he will be powerless in their domain', thus the whole image 'is more overdetermined than is usually assumed' and she offers some possibilities:

> might it not also be saying: 'When you go to *Frauen*, to women you will address directly, don't forget all you've said and thought about them, back here, safely out of their influence . . . because you are likely to forget it all there!' Or could it be that Zarathustra is in danger of forgetting his 'whip', his tongue, his ability to speak, at least so fluently and easily about things he knows so little about, when he is in women's presence? Or again, might *die Peitsche* (not *deine Peitsche*) be not Zarathustra's whip at all but women's whip, women's power and influence.
>
> (Ibid.: 55)

Although Graybeal suggests this last possibility here, she quickly moves on, and fails to add the important evidence of the famous photograph Nietzsche had made at some inconvenience at the time he was writing *Zarathustra* and also involved in a disastrous relation à *trois* with Paul Ree and Lou Salomé. The photo shows Lou Salomé, whip in hand, standing in a cart with Nietzsche and Ree in harness. Lavrin comments: 'the whip in Lou's hand seems to indicate her independence of any whims except her own' (Lavrin 1971: 56). Of course the irony is greatly intensified here as it is precisely the old woman who says 'Do not forget your whip'.[3] And as Graybeal asks in applying her Kristevan line of inquiry: 'is the influence of phallic mastery of language to be forgotten in the presence of the mother?'

Finally, Graybeal's examination of the last section of Part II of *Zarathustra* is worth discussing. In this section, called 'The stillest hour', Zarathustra says he has to leave his friends: 'my mistress will have it so . . . have I ever told you her name? Yesterday, towards evening *my stillest hour* spoke to me: that is the name of my terrible mistress' (Nietzsche 1969b: 167). In Graybeal's words 'the "Stillest Hour" orders Zarathustra to speak what he has to say, regardless of the consequences to him, which she acknowledges are drastic: he will *zerbrechen*, break into pieces, or shatter.' (Graybeal 1990: 65) Faced with the questions from this terrible mistress, Zarathustra weeps and trembles, and asks the question 'who am I?'; this is, for Graybeal, crucial, for 'it has thrown his identity into question.' The discussion continues until Zarathustra says 'I lack the lion's voice for command' to which the reply is 'it is the stillest words which bring the storm. Thoughts that come on dove's feet guide the world. . . . You must yet become a child' (Nietzsche 1969b: 168). Implied here, for Graybeal, is a recognition in Zarathustra of a refused process of 'radical, fearless obedience to the commands of *la mère qui jouit*' (Graybeal 1990: 66).

But Zarathustra resists, refuses. The terrible mistress then laughed and 'tore my bowels and slit my heart' (Nietzsche 1969b: 169), and said he was not yet ready; although his 'fruits' were ready, he was yet to 'grow mellow'. And Graybeal suggests 'she diagnoses the problem precisely . . . she sends him back to solitude. . . . He will "give in" to her wishes, but only when he is ready for them, when "he" has become "not-he" ' (Graybeal 1990: 67). Graybeal draws out of this episode the most dramatic conclusions:

> The demands of the Stillest Hour here seem diametrically opposed to the ordinary or usual forms of 'the sacred'. . . . Here the motives of piety and transgression are reversed. To be obedient to the numinous mother and her wishes, Zarathustra must speak . . . his refusal to speak, is punished by laughter that rips his bowels and heart, and by his being sent away to mellow, until he will be ready to speak the unspeakable.
>
> (Ibid.: 68)

What is this unspeakable? In Graybeal's version we have to move to the autobiographical *Ecce Homo* and the problematic variants on Nietzsche's relation to his mother. One variant, so violent in his rejection of his mother, was censored. But Graybeal insists that the two variants must stand as testimony to Nietzsche's problem of coming to terms with, and loving '*la mére qui jouit*, the great unfigurable figure behind all of Nietzsche's experimentation with language, his erotic, insatiable, overflowing

attempts to achieve full expression' (ibid.: 82). Graybeal reflects on the
idea that Nietzsche tried to suggest both that he was his mother, and
that, as his mother, he tried to give birth to himself.

The problem, curiously parallel to the central problem in Kennedy's
approach (but not Derrida's), which severely limits Graybeal's suggestive
analyses is that they never open into a genuine field of the exploration
of various relations between Nietzsche and different imaginary women,
since, having chosen to work from an already given matrix, *la mère qui
jouit*, all female figures are quickly reduced to a single, if paradoxical,
relation.

But the question remains: who is the affirming woman in Nietzsche?
In fact, surveying the recent literature, there is a surprising number of
propositions. In Deleuze and Derrida, there is of course Ariadne, but
also Penthesilia (Derrida 1979: 53; 'Nietzsche's woman-mistress at times
resembles Penthesilia', Penthesilia, queen of the Amazons, killed by
Achilles); Sarah Kofman notes, against this, that Nietzsche once wrote
'Perhaps truth is a woman who has reasons for not letting us see her
reasons? Perhaps her name is, to speak Greek, *Baubo*' . . . Baubo can
appear as the female double of Dionysus' (Kofman, in Gillespie and
Strong 1988: 195–7). When Persephone was abducted, her mother
Demeter searched for her, disguised as an old woman; she stopped to
talk to some women at Eleusis, and was offered and refused nourishment
from Baubo, who then lifted her skirts to reveal her sex; after this
Demeter accepted. On her belly had been drawn the figure of Dionysus,
but Baubo is also Greek for the female sex organs. And personifications
of the sex organs played an important part in Eleusian rituals. Kofman
recalls Nietzsche: 'I know no higher symbolism than this *Greek* symbolism
of the Dionysian festivals. Here the most profound instinct of life, that
directed toward the future of life, the eternity of life, is experienced
religiously. . . . It was Christianity, with its *ressentiment* against life at
the bottom of its heart, which first made something unclean of sexuality'
(cited in Kofman 1988: 197–8), and Kofman adds: 'Baubo and Dionysus
would thus be both names for protean life. Contrary to Baubo, however,
Dionysus is naked. His nakedness does not signify the revelation of a
truth but the unveiled affirmation of appearance.' Yet it is clear, she
argues, that Dionysus is also the god of masks, and, like woman, knows
the value of the control of appearance. Thus for Kofman, Dionysus is
able to cross the threshold, is a god 'anterior to the system of theological
oppositions, crosses himself out of the distinction between the veiled and
unveiled, masculine and feminine, fetishism and castration. Does it still
make sense, then, to speak of misogyny in Nietzsche?' (ibid.: 198).

But the major investigation on this subject is the impressive argument
of David Krell, who traces the lineage of Ariadne through the personages
of Corinna, Pana, and Calina in Nietzsche's notebooks, rightly scornful

of efforts to trace Nietzsche's thought on women simply to his experiences (Krell 1986: 87). But Krell's book begins with an important confrontation with Deleuze, via a return to the argument developed in the 1930s by Karl Reinhardt. This argument suggests that after *Zarathustra*, which acknowledged no God, Nietzsche turns gradually to a new theology and mysterious religion, a tragic turn as the No began to overcome the Yes. Reinhardt notes the important transformation of the dithyramb 'Ariadne's Complaint' (in Nietzsche 1984: 53–9), which appears in *Zarathustra* as 'The sorcerer' (1969b: 262–70) but with fundamental change of context, a change, for Reinhardt, "unparalleled' in the history of literature (Krell 1986: 16), a defeat and failure, as the plaint moves from the sorcerer to Ariadne herself.

But for Deleuze, Nietzsche's development represents a break with Christian values in the mysterious complementarity of Dionysus and Ariadne, and he proclaims: 'There is no Nietzschean misogyny. Ariadne is Nietzsche's uppermost secret, the premier feminine power, the Anima, the fiancee who is inseparable from Dionysian affirmation' (cited in Krell 1986: 28). And Deleuze identifies a second feminine power in the 'terrifying mother, mother of good and evil, who denigrates and negates life . . . our mothers and our sisters' pointing to Nietzsche's comments on Eve in *The Birth of Tragedy* (cited ibid.: 28). For Krell there are grave problems in Deleuze's reading. First, Eve is not Adam's sister or mother. But more importantly, Deleuze has symptomatically inverted the order of the two versions of Ariadne's Complaint, and in the end Ariadne becomes *araignée* (spider) and, 'the *araignée* of interiorized cruelty weaves its dark web across Deleuze's text' (ibid.: 29). In Deleuze it is the sorcerer who seizes Ariadne's song, and everything moves to affirmation. In fact, it was the reverse, and Deleuze is 'naive' in arguing for a second affirmation of Zarathustra in Ariadne-Anima (Eve) on the basis of an Ariadne lost in Dionysus. In reality it is Ariadne who comes to sing the song, and 'in his eagerness to salvage affirmation from negation and nihilism, Deleuze is blithe about, and even blind to, Ariadne's suffering' (ibid.: 30). If Deleuze makes Zarathustra a pure reflection of Dionysus 'what has become of Ariadne's tortured . . . self?' (ibid.: 31).

Krell searches Nietzsche's notes, sketches and outlines. He notes that in the early 1870s Nietzsche was inspired to write a drama, following Laertius and Hölderlin, on the death of Empedocles. A key figure in Nietzsche's sketches not found in the plays of the other writers, is a figure called Corinna, who seems to have been a gifted Boeotian poetess. She says only the word 'Empedocles' and she seems to call from the position of woman as nature. In the notes for *Zarathustra* of 1883, Corinna seems transformed into Pana. The notes say 'when he recognises Pana, Zarathustra dies out of pity for her pity' and 'now only the smallest gap stands between me and you: but woe! who was ever able to span a bridge across the smallest gaps?' (cited in Krell 1986: 62–3). Krell muses, perhaps Pana is Pan-(thei)-a? In further notes, Nietzsche says 'Pana wants to kill him [Zarathustra] . . . but when he sees her lying there, shattered, he laughs'. But by 1884, Pana no longer figures in the plans, 'Pana has vanished forever' (ibid.: 68).

In the notes for *Zarathustra* of 1885–6, Ariadne returns but in a strange form, an 'eerie guise' (ibid.: 73), after Zarathustra stalks the battlements in a scenario marked by new 'notions of hierarchy and domination, garlanded by the imagery of medieval pageantry' (ibid.: 72). Ariadne returns as the 'orgiastic soul of woman'. Nietzsche continues 'I have seen him [ihn], his halcyon smile, his honey-eyes, sometimes deep/ and veiled, sometimes green and slippery, a trembling superficies,/ slippery, sleepy, trembling, hesitating,/ heaves the sea that is his eyes' (cited, ibid.: 73). On route for Naxos to Ariadne, the eyes are those of Dionysus 'iridescent with emerald beauty' (ibid.). Krell suggests two possible readings. One, the words are those of the soul, and the text is an addendum to 'Ariadne's Complaint'; the other might suggest that the word 'him' refers to the soul. Krell argues that Nietzsche 'knows that without the exchange and ringdance of male/female in him he cannot create' (ibid.: 75). In the plans of 1885–6, Zarathustra is to die, and among the friends who abandon him there is no Ariadne, but Calina: 'brown-red, everything to acrid nearby. Highest sun. Ghostlike./ Sipo Matador' (cited, ibid.: 79). Again different lines: one possible reading is that she is the pious woman who kills Zarathustra (a complement of the man who kills God), but then the tone is wrong since she is also seductive, says Krell. Sipo Matador is referred to in *Beyond Good and Evil* (Nietzsche 1973: 174) and defined as 'sun-seeking climbing plants of Java . . . which clasp an oak tree with their tendrils so long and often that at last, high above it but supported by it, they can unfold their crowns in the open light and display their happiness'. But Krell finds no answer, speculating via the Spanish that Calina is a 'feminine noun referring to an atmospheric disturbance caused either by water vapour or dust' (Krell 1986: 81). But 'how can the sun at its apogee be ghostlike? As though midday and midnight were the same. As though Calina's were the ghostly beauty of the sailing ship, the dream and the risk of death' (ibid.: 80).

A plan of 1887 allows, says Krell, a better interpretation of the fate of 'Ariadne's Complaint', as it reveals that at its conception its lines were from a satyr-play, and then 'displaced' in such a way that Ariadne's words 'have lost their tragic pathos' (ibid.: 82). Philosophy for Nietzsche at this moment is transformed from tragedy to farce (defined from the point of view of the satyr). And at the same time a change occurs in Ariadne: 'Ariadne, [said Dionysus], you yourself are the labyrinth: one doesn't ever get out of you again. . . . Dionysus, you flatter me: you are divine' (ibid.: 82). Finally Krell discusses some lines of 1888, which he finds

'lines of weariness, desperation, and postponement beyond recovery'.
They read:

> Truth –
> a woman, nothing better:
> guileful in her shame:
> what she wants
> she refuses to know,
> raises a warning finger . . .
> To whom will she yield? To force alone!
> – So use force,
> be hard, you who are most wise!
> you must compel her,
> the abashed truth . . .
> for her felicity
> compulsion is needed –
> – she is a woman, nothing better.
>
> (Cited ibid.: 84)

Krell is appalled at these lines, and the collapse of the fate of Ariadne
into 'burlesque, satry-play, and farce'. He concludes that there is still a
tension, and the temptation to resolve the issue into Nietzsche's misogynism ('use force') has still to be held in suspension in the 'acrid obscurity
of Calina' (ibid.: 84). The question is postponed in Nietzsche himself: 'to
satyr-play as postponement of the tragedy, but a postponement that is *in
pursuit*, relentlessly? (ibid.: 87).

It is now possible to turn to Irigaray's recently translated text *Marine
Lover of Friedrich Nietzsche*. The jacket of the French edition carries a
message absent from the English version: 'for Christians, to reflect [rumi-
ner] on the "Good News"; God wanted a woman's body in order to
become flesh and live among us. To all the men to ask if the alternations
of dawn and twilight which lighten and darken the earth are a destiny
which will be for ever insurmountable in their world.' Thus one is to
expect a strange book: a Christian epistle to Nietzsche one hundred years
too late. Or is it an epistle to the contemporary Nietzsche?

Here I shall begin with and concentrate on the second section (77–119),
bearing in mind that the text was published partly in response to Deleuze,
Derrida and Kofman by a Lacanian psychoanalyst ruthlessly excommuni-
cated from the Lacanian circle, and forcefully attacked by Nietzschean
writers like Baudrillard (see Gane 1991a: 147).

But the very title of this section, and the way it opens seems to
indicate a response to Derrida's *Spurs* and its reflection on veils.[4] Irigaray,
reproducing the position taken in a long tradition of women's criticism
(see Gane 1992), directly confronts mimesis in the difference between
woman and femininity: woman 'is not to be reduced to mere femininity.

Or to falsehood, or appearance or beauty' (Irigaray 1990: 77). Immediately, Irigaray refers to 'that other of the self to which truth is, from the outset, hostile'; and to the 'so many things . . . attributed to whoever remains foreign to self-definition. Who risks – the abyss' (ibid.: 77–8). The challenge is evident, in the play of definition of the other, something is given yet there can be no debt: she invokes both the theme of alienation, and a refusal of Deleuze's, Baudrillard's and Derrida's claim to a symbolic order of ineluctible symbolic exchange. Whoever defines woman seems to be able to clothe woman in a mask and to 'reserve the right to make use of it from time to time. To take back, when the moment or the desire demands' (Irigaray 1990: 78).

But Irigaray is also tempted to mock the crassness of the high condemnation of the reactive woman, whose 'ressentiment spoils . . . appearance . . . [for] how is one to get through that absence of veils?' (ibid.: 78). The initial division of Dionysus and Apollo, seems to require a restitution of an original unity, and that is why an interminable search begins in the other, but only the other as same. The search must go round in circles because the original unity was never really broken: 'dispersal into fragments that do not tear apart unity, and can therefore never be put back together' (ibid.: 78). In historical terms, she seems to argue, once woman simply becomes subsumed under the phantasy of the other with no control over self-definition, in what she calls 'echonomy', the 'eternal feminine' is displaced, 'goes into exile in another representation: that will find pathos in the crucifixion of Christ, that scion (*rejeton*) of Dionysos' (ibid.: 79).

Irigaray's strategy in this section is to examine the basic concepts of woman and the feminine against the definitions which come from the Greeks and from Nietzscheans, or from what she calls 'the patriarchal order' (ibid.: 96), in which she clearly includes Freud and Lacan (ibid.: 80). Her story is one of the tragedy of woman under the 'ambiance' of masculinity (ibid.: 118, a clear reference to Baudrillard [1979] 1990, see Gane 1991b: ch. 3), and of the Greek tragedy of the separations of woman and mother, and of man and woman. Instead of invoking the search for Ariadne, or writing as Ariadne/Corinna/Pana/Calina or as Baubo, or even as Xanthippe, Irigaray writes more from the position doubled as Persephone and Mary. In this she has defined the superficiality of women as a device of patriarchy, a structural necessity for the ludic pursuits of men in patriarchy, based as it is on the suppression of any depth, or rather, as she expresses it, any 'access' to woman's depth (Irigaray 1990: 89). This is avoided since 'into her depth, the scene might . . . collapse' (ibid.: 88). Irigaray is intransigent, she will not at any point give way to the position in which woman can only be represented as either error or pure appearance. In this system, woman cannot make any independent entry: she is simply crushed out of recognition. Therefore

all theories of the feminine as play in seduction are false, for 'the stake
of woman's ludism has no fixed value. . . . Even though her having no
value may be the cause of her despisal it does not spoil, for her, the
pleasure of endlessly exchanging herself "within herself"; do not cut off
her access to depth'. But once she is defined as feminine 'pleasure comes
to her with no forethought. Unless she gives up that excess of good
fortune: being born a woman. The whole game is set up so that she
should do so. But "within herself" she never signs up' (ibid.: 90).

It is evident, she argues, that in Greek culture the crucial fact is the
tendency, revealed in Apollo, to deny the mother any role in generation
(ibid.: 95). Symptomatically, Athena is the daughter of the father alone
(ibid.: 96). However, intimately connected to this is the fact that, curiously, 'the law of the father needed feminity' as an adjunct of male power
'in order to take the upper hand over the mother's passion, as well as
the woman's pleasure' (ibid.: 97). But it is Apollo who commanded the
'murder of the mother' – Orestes who kills his mother goes for refuge to
the temple. Women who want revenge are thrown out, and the 'rabble'
of women is driven off by Apollo. Irigaray chronicles the tragedy of
women in the wake of these events, in wars, abductions, robberies, rapes.
'There remains' however, she says, 'Hades, to whom mortals must give
an account, under the earth. . . . On the opposite side, the law of the
gods on high. Their truth, their beauty, their immorality. In between –
Athena: horror concealed, wound masked' (ibid.: 101). Here Irigaray
tries to evoke the ambivalent character of Athena, as pure deception,
but in the 'service of the master'. A fundamental treachery to women 'to
the father's advantage'. Hypocritically reducing women to domestic work
while herself playing a public role, the list is long (ibid.: 102). This is the
paradigm of women's deceitfulness, and it is 'merely a projection of the
Father'. Since, as feminity is adorned, it becomes the dominance of the
father over 'female authority' (ibid.: 102).

Irigaray spells this out: as the power of women, the maternal power is
'swallowed' by the father, 'he engenders, produces, this daughter who
(only) gives herself out to be what she is not: a simulacrum borrowed by
the God to help him in his work, establish his empire' (ibid.: 102). She
is the pure product of this strategy, 'knowing nothing but the master's
jouissance'. A distance has been established, however, and it is a distance
Nietzsche recognizes. But it is necessary, she insists, to note that the
distance does not come from her, 'even if it is at a distance that her
seductive charm works' (ibid.: 105). This distance is both established as
a crime and denied as his work, and therefore the abyss opens. But for
the woman, the separation from the mother, and then from herself leads
to a situation, quite unforeseen in Derrida's consideration of the question
of distance, where the distance *to herself* is abolished, she is 'taken over
by proximity' to herself (ibid.: 106). For men, the body of the woman

then comes to represent an ideal, but it is simply a 'double' of man, its 'sublime soul', indeed the very 'music of Ariadne: at last beyond immediate pleasure and pain' is the ideal (ibid.: 109). Here Irigaray is scathing in relation to Ariadne as ideal: she is

> a simulacrum without a hint of deceit . . . nothing underneath, nothing inside, no more depth, split, hole, chasm, abyss. She is infinitely divided from herself. Her secret: she is all webs. She spins all day long. The woman of your dreams. Perfectly 'absent from herself'. . . . She is too ignorant or already too sceptical for pleasure.
>
> (Ibid.: 100)

At this point Irigaray *returns* the famous interrogation 'What do women want?' with 'What do men want?'. Her answer is clear, at least as it arises within systematic patriarchy: power. But in producing it, in relation to women, they produce also the abyss, a 'dis-tance with no possible relations. No lips, since they too now, mark the tempo for distancing to take place' (ibid.: 110). It is no choice that women have made to construct feminity, and here Irigaray cites Nietzsche:

> *Perhaps* our acts of will and our purposes are nothing but . . . throws [of the dice] – and we are only too limited and too vain to comprehend our extreme limitedness: which consists in the fact that we ourselves shake the dice-box with iron hands, that we ourselves in our most intentional actions do no more than play the game of necessity. Perhaps! – to get out of this *perhaps* one would have to have been already a guest in the underworld and beyond all surfaces, sat at Persephone's table and played dice with the goddess herself.
>
> (Cited, ibid.: 111)

Persephone, the daughter of Demeter, was abducted by Hades. Her release was a compromise, since she had already eaten a pomegranate seed in the underworld, thus the seasons reflect the fact that she only spends half the year in each world. Irigaray seeks Persephone's etymology: there is none, it is in 'suspension'. The abductor is the brother to both father and mother, yet it is to the men that she belongs 'as a piece of property' (ibid.: 112). Here even the earth has become the property of men, or at least the 'mother (now) is doubled in Hades' (ibid.: 112). Thus

> the daughter who has been kidnapped away from her mother, from herself, by the father, is taken by the brother, the father's other, despite/without his consent. The *Kore* is given by the heavenly god to the infernal god, who can take her only by raping her. . . . This is the way with exchanges among man/men.
>
> (Ibid.: 112–3)

If Persephone knows both worlds, a woman, alone, who knows how to move from hell to heaven, then to make a bet with her means to take a wager. It means

> to risk seeing the end of the game. For she knows all the rules, and more. . . . Persephone, in effect, does not hold to one (male/female). She can sub-sist with different ones (male/female). . . . More than Athena, who was never a little girl. Than Ariadne, who has not known Hades. [She] has experience of the two veils . . . crossing ceaselessly, aimlessly back through the frontier of those abysses.
>
> (Ibid.: 114–5)

Persephone does not remain still; if she embraces with her lips, and, crucially, she does this 'without ressentiment', she nevertheless 'does not take him *into* her', and she is dependent on the other. Against the emphasis in Nietzsche and Derrida on the ear, especially small ears, Irigaray invokes the unique rhythm of Persephone (the 'ceaselessly engendered . . . expansion of her "world" that does not develop within any square or circle or . . . and remains without limit or boundary') which is 'barely perceptible even to "small ears" . . . bathing everything in light and warmth without appearing to do so . . . [an] affirmation without subject or object' (ibid.: 116). The movement here suggests a music, she argues, and a harmony which emerges out of difference but also movements across boundaries that are not forms of plunder and destruction (ibid.: 117). In Irigaray's final section, 'an epistle to the last Christians' she invokes the powerful image of the Virgin Mary; in this very scenario 'the word made flesh in Mary might mean – might it not? the advent of a divine one who does not burst in violently' (ibid.: 181).

Irigaray examines the Christian tradition in its relation to Mary and Christ, and pursues an inquiry into the Christian notion of the flesh, mediation, into the 'yes' of Mary, against a background of a muted suspicion of patriarchal power. Finally, surprisingly, she returns to Nietzsche, and to a starkly posed alternative: either Christ or Nietzsche (ibid.: 188). Rehearsing again the Nietzschean critique of religion, Irigaray insists on its positive evaluation of Christ, and expresses the possibility of a new interpretation starting from Nietzsche's critique (which has at its base a critique of the distance between self and other). This new interpretation would not be centred on 'the product of the love between Father and son, but the universe already made flesh or capable of becoming flesh, and remaining in excess to the existing world'. Indeed, 'a marriage that has never been consummated and that the spirit, in Mary, would renew' (ibid.: 190).[5]

Derrida's discussions of Nietzsche in the 1980s often seem to be a response to Irigaray (as Krell (1986: 108) has pointed out), but they also feed into the wider discussion of contemporary and postmodern feminism.

But the general tone and substance of Derrida's pronouncements on woman and feminism in the 1980s has been profoundly disappointing, revealing that, in the face of increasing interest from feminist intellectuals, his thought has remained secure in the 'system' he developed in the early 1970s, unable to respond to writers like Irigaray. Against the active involvement of a feminism which might seek mastery, Derrida, like Nietzsche, argues that if women 'constitute men as an object of study, and women become the mastering subjects, they merely recapitulate the same structure' (in Jardine and Smith 1987: 203), a comment which appears inconsistent with his conception of his own project, in which the phase of reversal is essential (see Derrida 1981a: 45). But more than this, he has been tempted to speculate on the excommunication of women in history as indeed precisely women's own choice: she can resist and step back from a certain history (precisely in order to dance) in which the concept of revolution, or at least the "concept" of revolution is generally inscribed . . . a history of women who have – centuries ago – "gone further" by stepping back with their lone dance' (Derrida 1988: 167).

But what indeed is at stake in the debate with Nietzsche as it has evolved over the last two decades? Increasingly Nietzsche's critical attitudes to women and feminism have come under more open and sympathetic treatment insofar as they were seen as contextualized, and subordinated to a scheme in which they were revealed as conditioned, secondary to a conception which was fundamentally affirmative. As Spivak reveals, this opening was essentially an auxiliary to Derrida's questioning of Western philosophy, closely allied to a Nietzschean notion of deconstruction as affirmative (see Derrida, in Jardine and Smith 1987: 197 for a recent statement). Although there are some writers who refuse to become involved in this debate and insist on the Nazi connection of Nietzscheanism (Kennedy), the interest and substantive issues are now really quite beyond this reductive barrier. Yet the problem of Nietzsche's misogynism has not altogether been dispelled as Derrida would have hoped, and as Kofman and Graybeal continue to believe. The work of Irigaray and Krell has produced new problems that still have not been thoroughly digested. First is Krell's argument that a certain element of misogynism seems essential to the inner tensions of Nietzsche's work, and is never resolved or transformed; indeed Nietzsche may even in the later phase have regressed on this issue. Second is Irigaray's argument (quite against Kennedy's view that his values were common prejudices) that Nietzsche is hopelessly caught in the specific features of a Greek culture rapidly undergoing the process of formation of a rigid and tragic patriarchalism that ensnares all who do not question its fundamental axioms. Thus Irigaray is not prepared, as are the Derrideans following Nietzsche, to remain within the enclosed world of the 'others of Dionysus'. Her embracement of Marian values enters into another bizarre aspect of postmodernism, which in its way, however, seems still caught in the patriarchal web. But perhaps her strategy, like those of other feminists (e.g. Kristeva), seeks to develop the symbolic and essentially mysterious power of women at the base of human culture, at the same time making the specific and concrete claims of the feminist movement on the ground, a strategy of combination which never seems to have occurred to Nietzsche (though it has, at an individual level, to Derrida (1988: 169)).

Chapter 12

Conclusion

> The world does not revolve around those who invent new upheavals
> but around those who invent new values; it revolves in silence.
>
> (Nietzsche, in Hassan 1975)

Although this work began with an examination of Durkheim's theory of
woman as outsider and Mary Wollstonecraft's theory of woman as alienated other to man, the principal concern of this book has been to look
at some of the ways in which leading male writers responded to the
new situation opened by the declaration of the rights of man, and the
requirement that institutions be legitimated before the bar of reason.
Some have taken the view that the old pattern of traditional patriarchy
should not be abandoned, and that widespread experimentation was
indicative of a malaise, a period of anomie in conjugal relations. In the
traditonal pattern the individual was sure of the stable and secure places
in the whole structure, and of the hierarchies it entailed. It has been
argued that women were symbolically powerful under the old system, but

> at this time she had no vote, on marriage she and all her possessions
> including her children belonged to the husband under the 'fiction' of
> marital unity. If she left her husband he could force her to return,
> could refuse to support her, could refuse her access to her children.
>
> (Gavron 1966: 4)

As Mill argued in the mid-nineteenth century, the power of the husband
was almost total, including the unfettered right to rape, in one of the
most complete systems of absolute domestic, economic, political and
cultural domination ever organized. But as Wollstonecraft points out, this
pattern of domination also recognized women's power, the power to
attract and seduce: men could be driven to bow down before them, and
to worship them. Marx was serious when he said to Jenny Marx 'I am
destined to play the role of chief lover in a second-class theatre . . . [and
to be] lying at your feet' (cited in Padover 1979: 106).

Durkheim provides theoretical terms to describe the conjugal relation,
the articulation between the domestic milieu and the wider sphere of the
action of sexuality, the pattern of development of the nuclear family, and

the effects of the size of the family on other 'social facts'. But his argument is designed to show that because gender divisions have been so important over such a long period of time, women are different from men in every key respect, that is as 'total social facts'. Given such differences, women should hold on to their domestic role as the central guarantee of what moral authority they do possess. Thus he was against any premature extension of civil rights, or even greater liberty to divorce.

It was Comte who had taken up this general position earlier in the nineteenth century and provided an elaborate programme of social reform involving the organized worship of women on the model of the cult of the Virgin Mary. Comte recognized that such a cult required a co-ordinated effort involving the transfiguration of individual women into saints, and the reordering of the life of every man to acknowledge the holy influence of the women around him: mother, sister, wife, daughter. He evolved the view that man's reason was sterile without the influence of emotion, sympathy and affect, and this influence should come to prevail over intellect. Comte wanted to retain all the institutional powers in the hands of men, to exclude women from society and work, but to elevate the status of women as the source of virtue. He, too, was thus not only against divorce, he wanted to extend divorce into 'eternal widowhood' (with few exceptions – one that applied to himself however – individuals would only ever be allowed to contract one marriage in their life). He thus altered the definition of the last phase of his law of the three stages to suggest that, along with positive knowledge, society would also reinvent forms of fetishism and ritual. The difference between Marx and Comte is that Marx practised a private form of romantic sensual fetishism, whereas Comte practised a public form of idealized spiritual fetishism.

Enfantin and the Saint-Simonians struggled to find a sensual liberation of sexuality in a hierarchical community. Like Marx and Comte they argued that the crucial unit was the conjugal couple not the individual, but maintained that the strict monogamous unit gave rise to severe problems of unhappiness, sexual exploitation and hypocrisy. Thus they sought to break down the barriers between the public and private spheres and to allow public authority to intervene in the life of the couple. Their ambition was to begin to lift the constraints on those members of society whose emotional life was artificially restricted by life-long monogamy. The controlled abandonment of repressive nuclear pairing would undermine the need for prostitution. Established by men, the new institution sought to form a priesthood of couples headed by a papal couple who would have the authority to reorganize the liaisons of the group. As it evolved, no female complement of Enfantin (the pope) was ever acknowledged or appointed. When the group disbanded, the ideal 'female messiah' was sought, but never found, in Egypt by the remaining followers.

Engels found the new woman in the working-class districts of Man-

chester. The exemplar of the new type was made independent economi-
cally by the fact that she was a factory worker with her own income. The
evolution of capitalist production had produced, he argued, a situation
which had completely undermined the traditional patriarchal family. The
effect of such capitalist development had brought women back into society
and public production after many centuries of annexation to the domestic
sphere. The new woman was thus free from practically all the hidden
structures of dependency which corrupted bourgeois conjugality: the corruption and hypocrisy of sexual mores, the calculation of affection
through the power of private property and sexual slavery. Engels found
himself a new man in the sense that he could form a relationship untainted
by ulterior motives of commerce or wealth. But this affected only half
his existence, for he also maintained his place within the bourgeois
system, which, he theorized, would continue to reproduce the bourgeois
patriarchal family as long as it was the dominant economic system. Patriarchal man was defined principally by the fact that he was the economic
provider and controlled the property of the family. The new man required
an economic equal so that the instruments of patriarchy were not available.

John Stuart Mill discovered his ideal new woman in an intellectual
partner, Harriet Taylor. She was a writer and poet and was already
committed to women's emancipation and equality. In dialogue with her,
Mill developed most of the ideas he later published on women's liberation. He claimed he simply elaborated Harriet Taylor's vision. The
conception he developed was one which attacked the principal legal and
institutional restrictions on women. He provided one of the most damning
indictments of the maintenance of the slave-like status of women in a
democratic society, asking the question: if women have a natural place,
are naturally inferior in intelligence etc., why is there a need for systematic institutional forms of exclusion? He presented an inventory of the
forms of control and instruments of power available to men to argue that
they contravened basic canons of liberty of the individual. He campaigned
as a member of parliament for women's suffrage, and for the lifting of
all restrictions on women's liberty. His own view was that there were
separate spheres and that women would choose in the main to remain in
the domestic sphere. He claimed that the new man would enjoy the
luxury of looking up to a woman in the spheres in which she was superior.

Max Weber married a woman committed to liberal feminism, an intellectual in her own right, who specialized in the history and the sociology of
women. Max Weber thus avoided this area in his writing as there seemed
to develop an intellectual division of labour between them. Max Weber
insisted that a woman should have her own completely independent sphere
of power where the man would not intervene; he also spoke at meetings
in favour of women's emancipation and liberty. From a position which

maintained absolute principles of fidelity in monogamous marriage for life, he modified his position to acknowledge the right of others to act in other ways. A liaison with Else Richthofen led him to write of the power of fate in the erotic sphere and the significance of the secret extra-marital relation. The new man was thus one who acknowledged both responsibility and fate, unitary culture and the separation of spheres, but not the simple rule of the pleasure principle or complete openness.

Friedrich Nietzsche's vision of the new man as Zarathustra, superman, was developed at the moment of an intense disappointment in love for Lou Salomé. Lou Salomé was an intellectual, a writer and poet, who wrote one of the first accounts and analyses of Nietzsche's work. Salomé's account is a damning critique of Nietzsche's notion of superman as a self-delusory, as a self-deification. Nietzsche described in letters how the work evolved to deal with and sublimate his inner emotional turmoil. In this period, he says, he turned the tyrannical forces of his will to power against bitterness in order to elevate himself above *ressentiment*. At this level Nietzsche accepts the notion of *amor fati* and the transcendence of good and evil. Yet superman is without a partner: who is Ariadne? he asks.

Clearly some new men found an ideal partner, some looked in vain (Saint-Simonians, Nietzsche). The women who were chosen as ideals (Clotilde de Vaux, Harriet Taylor, Mary Burns) were idealized and transfigured into exemplars. Other women apparently wanted to be idealized but were not chosen (Claire Bazard), or refused to be idealized (Lou Salomé). Some ideal partners were of a lower social class, some were non-intellectuals. Some were adored sensually, some were adored as abstractions. Some women had a clear idea that they were struggling for independence as a new kind of woman, others remained attached to their traditional identity, role and status. These are some of the main variations in the choice and relation toward virtual woman, that is the ideal-object-becoming-Woman.

On the other hand, men became new men by reconstructing the relation between reason and emotion (Godwin), by maintaining and strengthening the difference between them (Comte). Others proceeded by forming a relationship in a new way beyond property (Engels), in liberty (Mill) or in more than one relationship (Weber). Some attempted transformation in a situation controlled by a new moral authority (Enfantin, Comte), others in a framework of individual liberty (Godwin, Mill, Weber, Nietzsche). Some were eroticized (Enfantin, Engels, Weber), others were de-eroticized (Comte, Mill). Most reactions involved an attempt to generate a new moral code based on new convictions, Weber tried to hold on to an ethic of responsibility; for Nietzsche the quest was for self-overcoming and the transcendence of morality itself.

The important patterns which emerge, however, are located essentially on a different dimension. What is clear is that there is a relation between the specific theories developed, the virtual objects which appear in them, and the beings which come to fill the role of icon. First of all there is evidently the largely unconscious formation of a structure of desire, the formation of predisposition. In the cases of the 'new men' I have discussed here this is twofold: a sexual strategy, the search for a sexual partner, and a theoretical strategy, the search for a solution to a theoretical or ideological problem. The encounters I have examined are not wholly controlled or planned as such, but occur and appear as fortuitous or providential or predestined. The search is highly motivated (in the grammatical sense). As an individual's theoretical make-up changes it is possible to see the emergence of dislocations and disjunctions, as well as conjunctions between the two strategies.

Thus, second, there is the moment of the actual 'discovery' of the loved object. Clotilde de Vaux seems genuinely astonished that she has been 'chosen' to play the role of saint in a new religion. Engels had worked out a theory of the exploitative nature of modern capitalism, and had formed a distinct antipathy towards bourgeois women. In his liaison with Mary Burns he discovered the new model of communist woman. Nietzsche had reached the phase in his thinking where he developed an intense ethos of affirmation, and the notion of *vita femina* (life is a woman). He discovered his imaginary partner in meeting the poet Lou Salomé, a meeting he describes as a 'dear coincidence'. At the critical moment of his deepest disappointment and emotional despair he elaborates a practice of self-overcoming. Mill and Weber encounter intellectual women actively supporting the women's cause; Weber also fatefully meets a woman in the 'erotic movement' at the moment he theorizes the erotic sphere and the concept of fate. The cool rationalist thinker Godwin encounters the revolutionary intellectual Mary Wollstonecraft just as he reverses the role of reason and emotion in his theory.

Third, there is an intense process of idealization. This is not only in conformity with the expectations of theory, but also most often in relation to the expectations of significant social groups (of course, in some instances it runs counter to such groups and must remain an idealization in a disguised form). In the relationships described here it is clear that the motivations are sexually overdetermined encounters, often involving long periods where prohibitions and inhibitions have been active, and in some cases the expected sexual encounter did not materialize (Comte, Nietzsche), or where the sexual encounter was not expected it occurred (Weber).

Fourth, the theoretical elaboration evidently uses the forces and the materials from the idealization (of the person, or the experience) so that the way the theory finally takes shape is profoundly affected by the 'choice' of the partner and the direction of the idealization (it can be turned around to the self). This is the case for many varied reasons. The theoretical predisposition of the author leads the theory to such a discovery. But also, such is the ideological character of this elaboration, it is often a dialogic process of the couple concerned at some important rhetorical level of their relationship. There is, obviously, a point at which the partner will agree or not to accept the role which she is being assigned, or perhaps desires.

It is in this sense that the processes of creative idealization and theoretical elaboration are also sexual strategies of the new men. It is important to note that this is not to say that these are the only such sexual strategies, since it is clear that Marx also adopts the most sophisticated form of theory in his love-letter to Jenny Marx, a letter of self-transformation, a letter of adoration and self-humbling, a letter of idealization (a letter which plays the game of fetishism in the Comtean sense). The difference between that letter and the other forms of theoretical writing discussed here is that the latter attempt to transfigure the Other not only into an ideal, but into a solution to a much wider problem, the crisis and failure of the traditional model. And in so doing the formation of the new man is also seen to occur, for he is reflected in the virtual images that he has desired.

Notes

INTRODUCTION

1 The British Sociological Association has condemned this language as implicitly sexist, and recommends a change in terminology by its members.

2 To be exact, he claims it was not strictly speaking an autobiography (1992: 25).

3 In Boutang's biography of Althusser there is an interesting reference to a short manuscript of 1951 found amongst Althusser's papers 'Sur l'obscénité conjugale'. Apparently this text was resorted to in 1978, when Althusser upgraded the manuscript into a longer piece, occasioned by the stormy debate on feminism on the extreme left in that year (Boutang 1992: 328). More detail on Hélène Althusser can be found in the chapter 'La femme et le parti: Hélène Legotien' (pp. 343–436).

4 Boutang describes her letter-writing style as 'tres prolix' (Boutang 1992: 436).

5 Of course there is still much resistance to these developments, and much of it comes from groups formed under the influence of theoretical traditions such as Durkheim's or Althusser's (see, for example, the confrontation between Paul Hirst and the feminists in *Politics and Power* (1981). These oppositions go deep into institutional forms and social and intellectual networks: there are sociology departments without women members, boards of journals without women, all-male conferences on issues such as democracy and citizenship, all of which seem also to evade consideration of the category of experience and gender. The problematics of the private and the public are discussed in Hearn (1987: 1–15), Wolff (1990: 12–33), Pateman (1991: 118–40).

6 Many other individual writers have moved in this same direction in a parallel movement to Althusser. The same tendency can be found in Michel Foucault ('Each of my works is part of my own biography. For one or another reason I had the occasion to feel and live those things' (cited in Martin et al. 1988: 11). The quotation is taken up in Sawicki (1991). Sawicki also says that she met Foucault and 'told him (she) had just finished writing . . . on his critique of humanism. Not surprisingly, he responded with some embarrassment and much seriousness. He suggested that I not spend energy talking about him and, instead, do what he was doing, namely, writing genealogies' (ibid.: 15). Another writer who has attempted in a very different spirit and manner a rapprochement with biography is Jean Baudrillard (Gane 1993: 39). Barthes's strange alphabetically ordered autobiography is also worth noting (Barthes 1975).

7 See this terminology in Connell (1987: 183–8).

8 Remy (in Hearn and Morgan 1990: 43–54), also Hearn (1987) and Walby (1990) for recent discussions. It would also be necessary to explore the other important possibilities here: matriarchy, gynaeocracy, gynarchy, uxorialism/ uxoriarchy. The principle elements: rule by mother (matriarchy), or wife (uxoriarchy), or sisters (sororiarchy?) or woman (gynaeocracy), etc.

9 Freud's relationship to women has recently been studied by Appignanesi and Forrester (1992); but their study rarely examines in detail how Freud's theory emerged within actual relationships; thus Freud's attitudes are discussed (1992: 421) separately from the dynamics of the significant relation of which it was a part (1992: 28–41).

1 EMILE DURKHEIM: WOMAN AS OUTSIDER

1 The former principle is clearly related to the project of establishing a social science, distanced from directly political concerns. This has led some recent commentators like Steven Lukes to claim for example that it is precisely 'the political import of Durkheim's sociology [that] can be in part seen in its systematic neglect of politics' (in Durkheim 1982: 23). Paradoxically, Lukes can then refer to a recent work by Lacroix (1981) which argues that Durkheim's work must above all be seen as a politics. Unfortunately, even Lacroix's work ignores key political problems tackled by Durkheim, as especially the politics of the sexes.

2 See his 'Do Dual Organisations Exist?' (in Lévi-Strauss 1972: 132–63); Lévi-Strauss always makes a detour round Durkheim by appealing directly to Mauss. But Mauss's essays have also been read in a different way, as 'a question not so much of reciprocity, circulation and communication as of collision and violence, power . . .' (Paz 1971: 11–12); Paz mentions Bataille, one could also mention Moret and Davy, etc. See also Meillassoux (1981).

3 Clearly the emphasis of Durkheim in this respect has its parallel in the other influence on Althusser, Gramsci, and the concept of hegemony. In this context it is interesting to compare Perry Anderson's 'The Antinomies of Antonio Gramsci' (NLR 100), with Lacroix's essay on Durkheim (1981: 207–98).

4 Derrida's conception of dissemination seems to be a concept of the same order, thereby perhaps making a connection possible between the Durkheimian idea of the control of contagion, with Gramsci's concept of hegemony. This cannot be developed here however.

5 Lacroix's suggestion (1981: 114) that between Durkheim's The Division of Labour (1893) and Suicide (1896) there was an epistemological break, seems to confuse a change of theory with a change of problematic. Lacroix also almost completely ignores the reorganization of the elements of the theory discussed here. Also misleading is M. Verdon's recent comment that 'once in their "natural place", both Durkheimian individuals and Aristotelian objects do not wish to move' (1982: 346).

6 An attempt to develop some of the ideas in a Durkheimin direction has been made in the works of Roger Caillois (see esp. 1959).

7 Two recent discussions of this question are B. Easlea (1981: ch. 5) and J. Sayers (1982: part one).

8 It is interesting that Steven Lukes in his brief comments on the article on incest simply presents Lévi-Strauss's summary which omits the sections of the article which are of most sociological interest (Lukes 1973: 188–9). A recent remark of Anthony Giddens refers incautiously to Durkheim's theory that in tribal society 'a sexual division of labour task is everywhere the most prominent axis' (1981: 158), and refers to a work by anthropologist E. Freidl

which symptomatically contains no reference at all to Durkheim. Paul Hirst's recent discussion of Freud's ideas on incest fails to notice that Freud's rejection of the eugenic argument is taken from Durkheim, compares Freud's ideas on incest not with Durkheim's on the same issue but with Durkheim's conception of religion, relying solely on Lévi-Strauss's critique of Durkheim's argument from 'states' of consciousness (Hirst and Woolley, 1982: 149–53). Thus from the demolition of the problem of totemism by Lévi-Strauss, through the elimination of the problem of the incest taboo by Needham (1971: 24–9), to the recent announcement by Edmund Leach that 'the fascination of anthropology (lies in the fact that) . . . there are no "laws" of historical process. . . . The fundamental characteristic of human culture is its endless diversity' (1982: 51). It is something of a contemporary paradox that so many proclamations of the discovery of the nonexistence of evolution can at the same time count so naively as positive evolutionary progress in the field of knowledge. There are, however, other works which continue to stress 'the near universal menstrual taboo, associated with the notion of malignant power residing in the menstruating woman and her menstrual discharge; especially the belief that she is dangerous to men' (Stephens 1972: 17). Even essays in Needham (1971) develop this theme.

9 Lévi-Strauss in adopting Bergson's paragraph on the subject of totemism ignores these remarks developed by Durkheim which argue the same point (Lévi-Strauss, 1969).

10 This is still perhaps the general view of anthropologists. See for instance even M. Harris (1977: 65).

11 See the attempt to develop this theme in Moret and Davy (1970: ch. 6).

12 Attempts to analyse Nietzsche's position show that like Durkheim's it is caught in considerable contradictions: cf. Derrida (1979), Irigaray (1990) on the one hand with Easlea (1981: 174–6), and Bentley (1947).

13 Durkheim's idea of the 'sexual fix' seems a mirror inversion of that elaborated by Stephen Heath (1982) as the pure to the impure.

14 There was one problem here, the rates between the sexes in England were much closer, just as they were much lower than elsewhere (1970: 166). But Durkheim dealt with this by arguing in general that the division of labour had not affected English society to the extent that it had in France, a perspective essential to the conception of the Durkheimian project as an intervention, however quaint such an idea appears now. It may be that the whole problem of the differences in types of integration between France and other societies which Durkheim placed at the centre of his work is that same problem treated by Crozier (1964) as a difference between cultures. But if this is the case then the whole structure of the project of *Suicide* could more profitably have been a *comparative* sociology. It would also have suited Durkheim's purpose of treating French society as a leading case, and situated his proposals more concretely. It may be, however, that Durkheim foresaw certain difficulties in this approach.

15 Besnard's article (1973) illuminates many of the problems of Durkheim's treatment of the statistical analysis of the differences between the sexes in these two works, his statistical errors and his inconsistencies.

16 This has led some writers to suggest simply that 'Durkheim seems to be rather mixed up about women' (B. D. Johnson, in Glazer-Malbin and Waehrer 1972: 167).

2 MARY WOLLSTONECRAFT: WOMAN AS OTHER

1 Here are two current editions of *Vindication* (1983 and 1989). The more recent edition is a critical edition which provides details of the variations between the two editions of Wollstonecraft's own lifetime as well as many of the literary and other allusions, though not all, in the text. Here I give references only to the available paperback edition. I would like to draw attention to the analysis of Mary Wollstonecraft by Virginia Sapiro (1992: 117–65), too recent to be discussed here, but which reaches very similar conclusions to my own.

2 There is a brief review of the literature in Spender (1982: 100ff.). I have left out of the discussion reference to Lundberg and Farnham (1947) who argue that Wollstonecraft was not only mentally ill but also induced the feminist movement out of her illness. This is surprisingly and curiously echoed in Todd (1989: 252).

3 There is perhaps a difference between Godwin and Wollstonecraft if the two statements are read carefully. I do not know of any discussion of Wollstone-craft's method as such (it has been described recently as 'proto-structuralist' (Butler in Wollstonecraft 1989: vol. I, 17), but it is clear, as Spender has said, that the work is 'logical, consistent' (1982: 109).

4 Even in Coole's comparison of Rousseau and Wollstonecraft there is only one paragraph on sexual empowerment (Coole 1988), one in Charvet (1982), and in Spender (1982) and Vogel (in Evans et al. 1986) none at all.

5 For the essential background on eighteenth-century sexuality see Porter (in Bouce 1982). On Rousseau's notion of alienation see Merquior (1980: 71). Highly relevant to this analysis is Baudrillard's suggestion (1990: 174–5) of a transition from alienation to seduction as forms of servitude in the period since the eighteenth century (see Gane 1991a, 1991b). Wollstonecraft's text theorizes the coexistence of these forms and their effects.

6 Terry Castle's evocation of the eighteenth-century masquerade has many of the features of Wollstonecraft's representation of the then existing world of women, 'a feminocracy', a festival dedicated to the Goddess of Wantonness – a 'voluptuous midnight of "whores". . .' (Castle 1986: 253–8). Castle writes 'One might argue that the collective transformation of female narcissism is indeed female utopianism – or more simply feminism' (ibid.: 257). An extremely difficult notion to apply to Wollstonecraft, who nonetheless is cited on the same page.

7 Indeed as there is very little about rights in *Vindication*, it is surprising that so many accounts present it as a liberal document.

8 As presently constituted, she says, marriage is an 'absurd unit' (Wollstonecraft 1983: 257), as citizens, women's first duties are to themselves, and secondly as mothers (ibid.: 257). Spacks (1976: 69) correctly notes that in Wollstonecraft there is 'an openly bitter view of the assumption that happiness and marriage bear any relation to one another'.

9 Her critical attitude to authority in the family suggested that 'The father who is blindly obeyed is obeyed from sheer weakness, or from motives that degrade the human character' (Wollstonecraft 1983: 268).

10 Nicholson (1990) is right to refer to this as a liberation theology, a crucial support of Wollstonecraft's whole theory and practice but rarely cited in women's current struggle for equality in the religious establishment, which surely raises crucial questions about the theory, based as it is on the call for progress through virtue. Her theology was highly personal and unconventional; thus she realized the 'cry of irreligion, or even atheism [would] be raised against' her (Wollstonecraft 1983: 174).

11 Differences over Wollstonecraft's understanding of this are intense, ranging from Fige's (1970: 160) recognition of her 'sense of sexual reality', a 'potentially powerful but still muddled analysis of female sexuality' (Todd 1989), to Poovey's thesis that she 'turns away from every potentially dangerous acknowledgement that women have sexual . . . needs' (Poovey 1984: 78).

12 'I discern not a trace of the image of God in either sensation or matter' (Wollstonecraft 1983: 132).

13 Wollstonecraft adopts the word from Hume (Wollstonecraft 1983: 145).

14 This argument is also possibly one of the sources of the view that Wollstonecraft thought sexuality was provoked from the male side, since it was less difficult for women to be chaste. If, however, chastity and its virtue of modesty is an application of reason and humanity, she could have argued that chastity was a sexual discipline in both sexes; but this would have entailed the view that women had access to reason.

15 'It would be proper to familiarize the sexes to an unreserved discussion of those topics which are generally avoided in conversation from a principle of false delicacy; and that it would be right to speak of the organs of generation as freely as we mention our eyes or our hands' (cited in Taylor 1958: 7).

16 Instead of recognizing this as Wollstonecraft's evocation of the feminine, Poovey stigmatizes it as a repressive 'dematerialisation' of sexual desire.

17 A direct if complex challenge to Rousseau's 'a male is only a male now and again, the female is always a female' (cited in Poovey 1984: 71).

3 KARL MARX: WOMAN AS BLACK MADONNA

1 For considerations of Marx and gender see, for example, the recent discussions, MacKinnon (1989) and Hearn ('Gender: biology, nature and capitalism' in Carver (ed.) 1991: 222–45).

4 IN FEELING: WILLIAM GODWIN AND MARY WOLLSTONECRAFT

1 Lepenies (1988: Introduction) draws attention to the fact that there was a strong contrast between the cold science of reason and the literary culture of feeling in the early nineteenth century. As he points out this opposition is 'not confined to the realm of scientific and literary publications: it also sets its stamp on . . . lives, private and public. . . . And this is consistent with the fact that in this contention, which I see as a kind of "secret history" of the modern social sciences, so significant a role is played by women: Clotilde de Vaux, Harriet Taylor' (Lepenies 1988: 14).

2 There is a debate about the genealogy of the man of feeling in England between the 1730s and the 1790s (see Crane 1934, and Greene 1977). It may be that some of Godwin's writings are oriented to the sensibilities discussed in that debate, but the crucial point at issue here is not the 'new man of feeling' as a mode of sensibility, but more as modification in relation to women.

5 IN SEXUALITY: PROSPER ENFANTIN, THE 'SONS OF SAINT-SIMON' AND LA FÉMME LIBRE

1 Moses comments that 'Buchez's feminism derived from French Revolutionary radicalism and its politics of individual rights. Like feminists of that earlier period – . . . Mary Wollstonecraft . . . or Olympe de Gouge – Buchez believed

that both sexes were born similar in capacity and character' (Moses 1982: 244). I have not discovered any evidence to suggest that Buchez had actually read Wollstonecraft.

6 IN WORSHIP: AUGUST COMTE AND CLOTILDE DE VAUX

1 See the recent account of their relationship in Lepenies (1988: 19–46). Lepenies makes the point that one of the crucial changes that occurred was a reconsideration of the role of art and literature which was upgraded at the same time as women were made into a cult.
2 Vernon (1984: 556) argues that it is in part the status given to women in the later Comte that is responsible for his radical view on the state 'it is evidently for the sake of enhancing spiritual authority that the state is required to dissolve itself. But the connections are indirect'.
3 Cohen (1965: 175) rightly points out that 'in the conjugal relation Comte saw the highest type of social sentiment, which finds its clearest expression in the women's cultivation of altruistic love. In its pure form such feeling is unattainable for anyone engaged in productive labour'.
4 This was of course an exchange. Bram Dijkstra (1986: 32) notes that for Comte 'woman in yielding up the active impulses within her to her mate, provided him with additional power to triumph in the supreme realm of Force. Thus as the emissary of "goodness" she contributed to man's power to dominate even as she endeavoured to "modify the harshness with which men exercise their authority".'

7 IN LIBERTY: JOHN STUART MILL AND HARRIET TAYLOR

1 See Eisenstein (1981: ch. 6). A discussion that stresses the differences between Mill and Harriet Taylor is Richard Krouse 'Patriarchal liberalism and beyond' (in Elshtain (ed.) 1982: 144–72). This emphasizes Harriet Taylor's socialist position, and her view that full employment of women outside the home and access to education were essential for women's emancipation. Considered together, says Krouse, their 'liberal feminism is, implicitly, socialist feminism' (ibid.: 171).
2 Mary Shanley has recently noted 'the theoretical force of Mill's condemnation of domestic hierarchy has not yet been sufficiently appreciated' (in Shanley and Pateman 1991: 175).

8 IN COMMUNISM: FRIEDRICH ENGELS AND MARY BURNS

1 And indeed to Engels, Hyndman reported that Marx had discussed this with his wife, and the fact that the Marxes were dependent on Engels. 'The thought of this was intolerable for Frau Marx . . . she disliked the situation and bemoaned his influence on [Marx]. Talking to my wife she more than once referred to him as Marx's 'evil spirit' (cited in Raddatz 1978: 297).
2 It is curious that Janet Sayers in her essay 'For Engels: psychoanalytic perspective' (Sayers et al. 1987), does not psychoanalyse Engels, but simply equates Freud with Engels's judgement that the family is 'double-edged, double-tongued, divided against itself, contradictory' – but Engels, she says, teaches Freud a lesson: emancipation depends on social conditions since the family is an historical product, not an absolute form. It is not altogether clear what the full implication of this is for the theory of the Oedipal complex.

3 Ste Croix (1981: 99) notes that 'Marx and Engels seem hardly to have realised what far-reaching consequences ought to have been drawn from all this particular specialisation of role . . . Engels' *Origin of the Family* deals with the subject very inadequately.' Yet it is difficult to see that Engels did not draw extremely far-reaching conclusions, far more 'far-reaching' than anything in Ste Croix's book written a hundred years later. The essays in Coontz and Henderson (1986) try independently of Ste Croix to work out some of the same issues in a form that is far more sympathetic to Engels.

4 Mary Evans criticizes the passage 'the intense emotion of individual sex love varies very much from one individual to another, especially among men, and if affection definitely comes to an end or is supplanted by a new passionate love, separation is a benefit for both partners as well as for society' as a particularly blatant piece of patriarchal ideology (in Sayers et al. 1987: 86–7), though she does not provide any detailed argument for her opinion.

9 IN FATE: MAX WEBER, MARIANNE WEBER AND ELSE VON RICHTHOFEN

1 Mitzman (1970: 160–2) only likens them insofar as concerns the personal breakdowns of the two; Ryan, in Mommsen and Osterhammel (1987: 170–81), draws out a number of interesting parallels, but not, surprisingly, on the problem of gender and sexuality, a theme absent generally from Ryan's treatment of Mill in any case: elsewhere Mommsen (1989: 173) himself has emphasized the fact that Mill 'must be rated very highly for Weber's intellectual development'.

2 Scaff (1989: 111), however, suggests that 'only a fine line might be seen to separate the escape into eroticism from the nihilistic enjoyment of pure sensuality'.

10 IN TRANSCENDENCE: FRIEDRICH NIETZSCHE AND LOU SALOMÉ

1 Lou Salomé wrote a brilliantly critical account of Nietzsche, published in 1894 (English version/1988). She provides not only the detail of close conversations with him, but a periodization of his work. This periodization notes a transition in 1881–2 from what she calls a 'positivist' phase to a 'mystical philosophy of will' (1988: 81). She focuses attention to the critical work of this transition period, *Daybreak* of 1881 and *The Gay Science* of 1882. She first met Nietzsche in the spring of 1882. Up to the summer of 1882, Nietzsche apparently planned to study the natural sciences and to base his philosophy on them but then the direction changed and 'from then on all of his teachings take on a more personal character . . . their last secret sense is hidden under so many masks that the theories he expresses emerge almost only through images from his inner life' (ibid.: 87). She cites Zarathustra: 'As far as I am concerned, what is there except my self? There is no externality'.

Salomé is not at all convinced by the new vision of the superman as a solution to human problems, it was, she said, a complete 'self-delusion and secret cunning'. She described the process of the transitions involved in the following way:

At first he fashioned the mystical superior-human ideal through self-intoxicated fantasy, dreams, and nature-like visions; and then, in order to save himself from himself, he sought to identify himself with them through one tremendous leap. Finally, he became a dual figure – half-sick and suffering;

half-saved; a laughing and superior human. The one is like a creature and the other a creator; the one assumes a reality and the other a mystical sur-reality.

(Ibid.: 89)

She describes his philosophical development in the same way: 'formerly a *discoverer* of truth, the philosopher now has become . . . an *inventor* of truth' (ibid.: 98). The consequence of this is that there is a pronounced transition to a situation in which there emerges the 'superiority of the emotional over the intellectual life' (ibid.: 99). The middle period is regarded as the most imaginative and creative; the last period is one of decline into a reactionary mystical view of the world (ibid.: 107); as a symptom of this change she notes the change in Nietzsche's attitude to Napoleon: in 1881 he was for Nietzsche a pathological example of ruthless egotism, but later he was to become an example of 'superabundant health' (ibid.: 109). Nevertheless, even the creations of his greatest period, particularly *Thus Spake Zarathustra* are, for Salomé, flawed works. Certainly Zarathustra, she says, 'represents Nietzsche's own transformation' (ibid.: 123) but as a form of 'self-deification' (ibid.: 125). But, she claims, instead of providing salvation for Nietzsche they ultimately 'ravaged' him (ibid.: 158), divided him and led him to the abyss (ibid.: 148). Biddy Martin, I think, correctly concludes 'Salomé's "woman" confounds the structure of the knowing philosopher and the unconscious woman of his philosophy not by laying claim to his position of mastery for women but by occupying both positions in that structure at once' (Martin 1991: 116).

2 William Beatty Warner has written a long and detailed biographical and philosophical account of the birth of Zarathustra (Warner 1986: 115–213). He provides a detailed account of the theoretical developments in Nietzsche's work before the meeting with Lou Salomé, and the phases of Nietzsche's work in relation to this meeting and its aftermath. The reading is long and impressive and once more takes Zarathustra as Nietzsche himself (ibid.: 209), but tends not to interpret Nietzsche's struggle as one to overcome male problems, a struggle for the superman, but rather as raising, astonishingly, 'questions about selfhood' in the gender-neutral sense (ibid.: 129). His reading of the *Vita femina* (life is woman) in an attempt to find the 'special conditions . . . of the affirmative moment' (ibid.: 148). But when he analyses the break-down of the relation with Lou and the breakdown of the ethos of aesthetic affirmation, the discussion turns on two acts of Lou Salomé. First she withdrew from the new living arrangements with Nietzsche and Ree. Second, she refused to withdraw 'accusations she has made about his ulterior motives', that is to say that 'what she expects all men finally want from women – sex' (ibid.: 190). Warner interprets these events as a blow to Nietzsche, not because she has refused his project, but that she 'shatters Nietzsche's image of her'. Nietzsche quickly admits, notes Warner, that he had taken her 'for the earthly apparition' of his 'ideal' (cited ibid.: 190–1). After falling in love (prepared by a theorization of affirmation), he now fell out of love and this 'enabled him to write a sceptical critique of art' (ibid.: 195). It was now also that Nietzsche identified the true failings of modern woman, says Warner, her denial of her aesthetic calling yet her 'daring to will'. Despite the enormous amount of evidence Warner assembles in his discussion about a passionate relationship, nowhere is there a consideration of the specific vision Nietzsche developed of the virtual partner to Zarathustra.

In the end Warner's reading seems to come close to agreement with that of Salomé. He describes Nietzsche's process of coming to terms with his situation:

> first Nietzsche assumes the mask of a god, repeating human desires from a safe position above human entanglements. Then he repeats and interprets the dizzying confusion of his designs upon life and wisdom. He then gives ambivalent expression to his hatred and love in a series of blessings and curses. Finally all these moments – desire, confusion, and ambivalence – issue in the writing of *Zarathustra*.
>
> (Ibid.: 211)

He concludes by saying that this effort had lasting costs for Nietzsche, 'Nietzsche does not again risk a close, passionate friendship' (ibid.: 212).

3 For a study of the genealogy of the superman, see Foster (1981).

11 TOWARDS POSTMODERNISM: NIETZSCHE'S (IMAGINARY) LOVERS

1 For a Discussion of Deleuze's subsequent analyses, see G. Rose (1984: ch. 6), and for Derrida, see Jardine (1985: ch. 9).

2 Foucault's effect on feminist theory is altogether secondary, compared with that of Derrida; but see the discussion in Diamond and Quinby (1988), Rosalyn Diprose (1989), Nancy Fraser (1989), Jane Sawicki (1991) and Michele Barrett (1991).

3 Gillian Rose notes what she calls the emergence of 'gender distinctions' in what she presents as the critique of Kant. She notes 'when Zarathustra goes to visit her with his whip, it is at the crux of gender that philosophy – love of wisdom – the republic, and the legal fictions of personality explode' (Rose 1984: 6). But gender is immediately lost again in Rose's text, never to reappear (thus it is interesting to compare Rose on Derrida (1984: ch. 8) against Jardine (1985: ch. 9).

In relation to the whip, perhaps it is worth noting here, that two hundred years ago Mary Wollstonecraft ended the *Vindication* (1989: 266) with the bitter anti-patriarchal observation: either 'let woman share the rights and she will emulate the virtues . . . or justify the authority that chains such a weak being. . . . If the latter, it will be expedient to open a fresh trade with Russia for whips; a present which a father should always make to his son-in-law on his wedding day'. See also 'Nietzsche, women and the whip', in R. H. Thomas (1983), pp. 132–141.

4 See Derrida (1979: 41–3, and 1988: 11, 33–8); actually it is virtually impossible to tell from the dates given about the texts and their rewriting just where a reply to Irigaray might have been envisaged, since certainly within the texts there is no direct reference to Irigaray. Yet it is clear from the internal structure of references, that Derrida is a target for Irigaray, just as Irigaray's argument, in another context, is a target for Baudrillard.

5 If Irigaray wanted to raise the question of the genuine re-evaluation of the symbolic power of the mother, she had chosen a moment when both Baudrillard and Derrida had begun to elaborate a theory of the emergence of the state in its maternal form (see Gane 1991b: ch. 3; and Derrida 1988: 35).

Bibliography

Alexander, M. (1989) *Women in Romanticism*, Macmillan: London.
Allison, D. (ed.) (1985) *The New Nietzsche*, MIT Press; Cambridge, Mass.
Althusser, L. (1971) *Lenin and Philosophy*, NLB: London.
—— (1992) *L'Avenir dure longtemps*, Stock: Paris.
Althusser, L. and Balibar, E. (1970) *Reading Capital*, NLB: London.
Appignanesi, L. and Forrester, J. (1992) *Freud's Women*, Weidenfeld & Nicolson: London.
Assiter, A. (1990) *Althusser and Feminism*, Pluto: London.
Auerbach, N. (1978) *Communities of Women*, Harvard University Press: London.
August, E. (1975) *John Stuart Mill*, Scribner: New York.
Avineri, S. (1985) *Moses Hess*, New York University Press: New York.
Bakhtin, M. (1981) *The Dialogic Imagination*, University of Texas Press: Austin.
Banks, O. (1981) *The Faces of Feminism*, Martin Robertson: Oxford.
—— (1986) *Becoming a Feminist*, Wheatsheaf: Brighton.
Barrett, M. (1991) *The Politics of Truth*, Polity: Oxford.
Barrett, M. and Phillips, A. (eds) *Destabilizing Theory*, Polity: Oxford.
Barthes, R. (1975) *Roland Barthes*, Seuil: Paris.
Bataille, G. (1985) *Visions of Excess*, Manchester University Press: Manchester.
Baudrillard, J. (1990) *Seduction*, Macmillan: London.
Baumgarten, E. (1964) *Max Weber*, Tübingen: Mohr.
Benhabib, S. and Cornell, D. (1987) *Feminism as Critique*, Polity: Oxford.
Bennet, F., Campbell, B. and Coward, R. (1981) 'Feminists – degenerates of the social?', in *Politics and Power*, 3: 83–92.
Bentley, E. (1947) *The Cult of the Superman*, Hale: London.
Besnard, P. (1973) 'Durkheim et les femmes ou le Suicide inacheve', *Revue Francaise de Sociologie*, 14: 27–61.
—— (1982) 'Durkheim and sexual anomie: a comment on Tiryakian', *Social Forces*, 59: 902–17.
Bologh, R. (1990) *Love or Greatness, Max Weber and Masculine Thinking – A Feminist Inquiry*, Unwin Hyman: London.
Bottomore, T. (1981) 'A Marxist consideration of Durkheim', *Social Forces*, 59: 902–17.
Bott, E. (1964) *Family and Social Network*, Tavistock: London.
Bouce, P. (ed.) (1982) *Sexuality in Eighteenth Century Britain*, Manchester University Press: Manchester.
Boutang, Y. (1992) *Louis Althusser*, Grasset: Paris.
Brailsford, N. (1913) *Shelley, Godwin and their Circle*, Williams & Norgate: London.

Brandon, M. (1991) *The New Women and the Old Men*, Flamingo: London.
Brennan, T. (ed.) *Between Feminism and Psychoanalysis*, Routledge: London.
Brod, H. (1987) *The Making of Masculinities*, Allen & Unwin: London.
Brown, A. (1987) *The 18th Century Mind*, Harvester: Brighton.
Brubaker, R. (1984) *The Limits of Rationality*, Allen & Unwin: London.
Burke, E. (1883) *The Works of Edmund Burke*, Bell: London.
Butler, M. (1984) *Burke, Paine, Godwin and the Revolutionary Controversy*, Cambridge University Press: Cambridge.
Caillois, R. (1959) *Man and the Sacred*, Free Press: Glencoe.
Calvino, I. (1989) *The Literature Machine*, Pan: London.
Carlisle, R. (1987) *The Proffered Crown*, Johns Hopkins University Press: Baltimore.
Carver, T. (1989) *Friedrich Engels*, Macmillan: London.
— (ed.) (1991) *The Cambridge Companion to Marx*, Cambridge University Press: Cambridge.
Castle, T. (1986) *Masquerade and Civilization*, Methuen: London.
Charvet, J. (1982) *Feminism*, Dent: London.
Clark, J. (1977) *The Philosophical Anarchism of William Godwin*, Princeton University Press: Princeton, N.J.
Clark, L. and Lange, L. (eds) (1979) *The Sexism of Social and Political Theory*, University of Toronto Press: Toronto.
Cohen, D. (1965) 'Comte's changing sociology', *American Journal of Sociology*, 71: 168–77.
Comte, A. (1877) *Lettres d' Auguste Comte*, Leroux: Paris.
— (1910) *Confessions and Testament*, Young: Liverpool.
— (1973a) *The System of Positive Polity* (4 vols), Hill: New York.
— (1973b) *The Catechism of Positive Religion*, Kelley: New Jersey.
Connell, R. (1987) *Gender and Power*, Polity: Oxford.
Coole, D. (1988) *Women in Political Theory*, Wheatsheaf: Brighton.
Coontz, S. and Henderson, P. (1986) *Women's Work, Men's Property*, Verso: London.
Coward, R. (1983) *Patriarchal Precedents*, Routledge: London.
Crane, R. (1934) 'Suggestions toward a genealogy of the "Man of Feeling" ', *English Literary History*, 1: 205–30.
Croix, S. (1981) *The Class Struggle in the Ancient Greek World*, Duckworth: London.
Crouter, R. (1988) *Friedrich Scheiermacher on Religion*, Cambridge University Press: London.
Crozier, M. (1964) *The Bureaucratic Phenomenon*, Tavistock: London.
David, D. (1987) *Intellectual Women and Victorian Patriarchy*, Macmillan: London.
Deleuze, G. (1983) *Nietzsche and Philosophy*, Athlone: London.
Derrida, J. (1976) *Of Grammatology*, Johns Hopkins Press: Baltimore.
— (1979) *Spurs: Nietzsche's Styles*, University of Chicago Press: Chicago.
— (1981a) *Positions*, Athlone: London.
— (1981b) *Dissemination*, Athlone, London,.
— (1988) *The Ear of the Other: Otobiography, Transference, Translation*, University of Nebraska Press: Lincoln.
Diamond, I. and Quinby, L. (eds) (1988) *Feminism and Foucault*, Northeastern University Press: Boston.
Dijkstra, B. (1986) *Idols of Perversity*, Oxford University Press: Oxford.

Diprose, R. (1989) 'Nietzsche, Ethics and Sexual Difference', *Radical Philosophy*, 52 (Summer): 27–33.

Dollimore, J. (1991) *Sexual Dissidence*, Clarendon: Oxford.

Dreijmanis, J. (ed.) (1989) *Karl Jaspers on Max Weber*, Paragon: New York.

Durkheim, E. (1956) *Education and Sociology*, Free Press: Glencoe.

— (1957) *Professional Ethics and Civic Morals*, Routledge & Kegan Paul: London.

— (1960) *Le Suicide*, PUF: Paris.

— (1961) *The Elementary Forms of the Religious Life*, Collins: New York.

— (1962) *Socialism*, Collier Macmillan: London.

— (1963) 'Incest: the nature and origin of the taboo', in: Durkheim, E. and Ellis, A. *Incest*, Lyle Stuart: New York.

— (1964) *The Rules of the Sociological Method*, Free Press: New York.

— (1964b) *The Division of Labour in Society*, Free Press: New York.

— (1970) *Suicide*, Routledge & Kegan Paul: London.

— (1973) *Moral Education*, Collier Macmillan: London.

— (1975) *Durkheim on Religion*, Routledge & Kegan Paul: London.

— (1977) *The Evolution of Educational Thought in France*, Routledge & Kegan Paul: London.

— (1978) *On Institutional Analysis*, Chicago University Press: Chicago.

— (1979) *Durkheim: Essays on Morals and Education*, Routledge & Kegan Paul: London.

— (1980) *Contributions to L'Annee Sociologique*, Collier Macmillan: London.

— (1982) *The Rules of Sociological Method*, Macmillan: London.

Durkheim, E. and Ellis, A. (1963) *Incest*, Lyle Stuart: New York.

Durkheim, E. and Mauss, M. (1963) *Primitive Classification*, Cohen & West: London.

Easlea, B. (1981) *Science and Sexual Oppression*, Weidenfeld & Nicolson: London.

Eden, R. (1983) *Political Leadership and Nihilism*, University Presses of Florida: Tampa.

Eisenstein, Z. (1981) *The Radical Future of Liberal Feminism*, Longman: London.

Ellis, K. (1989) *The Contested Castle: Gothic Novels and the Subversion of Domestic Ideology*, University of Illinois Press: Urbana.

Elshtain, J. (ed.) (1982) *The Family in Political Thought*, Harvester: Brighton.

Engels, F. (1936) *AntiDuhring*, Lawrence & Wishart: London.

— (1958) *The Condition of the Working Class in England*, Blackwell: Oxford.

— (1972) *The Origin of the Family, Private Property and the State*, Pathfinder Press: New York.

Evans, J., Hills, J., Hunt, K., Meenan, E., ten Tusscher, T., Vogel, U. and Waylen, G. (1986) *Feminism, and Political Theory*, Sage: London.

Evans-Pritchard, E. E. (1965) *Women in Primitive Society*, Faber: London.

Feuerbach, L. (1957) *The Essence of Christianity*, Harper & Row: New York.

— (1966) *Principles of the Philosophy of the Future*, Bobbs Merrill: New York.

— (1980) *Thoughts on Death and Immortality*, University of California Press: Berkeley.

Figes, E. (1970) *Patriarchal Attitudes*, Faber: London.

Fleischman, E. (1964) 'De Weber a Nietzsche', *European Journal of Sociology*, 5: 190–238.

Fliess, R. (1950) *The Psychoanalytic Reader*, Hogarth: London.

Foreman, A. (1977) *Femininity as Alienation, Women and the Family in Marxism and Psychoanalysis*, Pluto Press: London.

Foreman, J. (1977) *A Romantic Triangle: Scheimacher and Early German Romanticism*, Scholars Press: Missoula.

Foster, J. (1981) *Heirs to Dionysus*, Princeton University Press: New Jersey.

Foucault, M. (1967) 'Nietzsche, Freud, Marx', *Cahiers de Royaumont*, 6, 183–92.

—— (1977) *Language, Counter-Memory, Practice*, Blackwell: London.

Fraser, N. (1989) *Unruly Practices*, Polity: Oxford.

Gallagher, C. and Laqueuer, T. (eds) (1987) *The Making of the Modern Body*, University of California Press: Berkeley.

Gane, M. (ed.) (1989a) *Ideological Representations and Power in Social Relations*, Routledge: London.

—— (1989b) 'Rhetoric', *Economy and Society*, 18 (2): 127–131.

—— (1991a) *Baudrillard: Critical and Fatal Theory*, Routledge: London.

—— (1991b) *Baudrillard's Bestiary: Baudrillard and Culture*, Routledge: London.

—— (ed.) (1992) *The Radical Sociology of Durkheim and Mauss*, Routledge: London.

—— (ed.) (1993) *Baudrillard Live*, Routledge: London.

Gavron, H. (1966) *The Captive Wife*, Routledge & Kegan Paul: London.

Giddens, A. (1978) *Durkheim*, Fontana: London.

Gillespie, M. and Strong, T. (1988) *Nietzsche's New Seas*, University of Chicago Press: Chicago and London.

Gilman, S. (1987) *Conversations with Nietzsche*, Oxford University Press: Oxford.

Glazer-Malbin, N. and Waehrer, H. (eds) (1972) *Woman in a Man-Made World*, Rand McNally: New York.

Godwin, W. (1798, 1969) *Memoirs of Mary Wollstonecraft*, Haskell House: New York.

—— (1832, 1975) *Fleetwood or the New Man of Feeling*, AMS Press: New York.

—— (1946) *Political Justice*, Toronto University Press: Toronto.

Gouhier, H. (1965) *La Vie d'August Comte*, Vrin: Paris.

Gouldner, A. (1975) *For Sociology*, Pelican: Harmondsworth.

Graybeal, J. (1990) *Language and 'The Feminine' in Nietzsche and Heidegger*, Indiana University Press: Bloomington.

Green, M. (1974) *The von Richthofen Sisters*, Basic Books: New York.

Grimshaw, J. (1989) 'Mary Wollstonecraft and the tensions in feminist philosophy', *Radical Philosophy*, 52 (Summer): 11–17.

Grogan, S. K. (1992) *French Socialism and Sexual Difference*, Macmillan: London.

Guattari, F. (1984) *Molecular Revolution*, Penguin: Harmondsworth.

Gunew, S. (ed.) (1990) *Feminist Knowledge*, Routledge: London.

Guralnick, E. (1977) 'Radical politics in Wollstonecraft's *Vindication*', *Studies in Burke and His Time*, 18: 155–66.

Harris, M. (1977) *Cows, Pigs, Wars and Witches*, Fontana: London.

Hassan, I. (1975) *Paracriticisms*, University of Illinois Press: Urbana.

Hayek, F. A. (1951) *John Stuart Mill and Harriet Taylor*, Routledge & Kegan Paul: London.

Hearn, J. (1987) *The Gender of Oppression*, Wheatsheaf: Brighton.

Hearn, J. and Morgan, D. (1990) *Men, Masculinities and Social Theory*, Unwin Hyman: London.

Heath, S. (1982) *The Sexual Fix*, MacMillan: London.

Hegel, G. W. F. (1975) *Aesthetics, Lectures on Fine Art* (2 vols), Clarendon Press: Oxford.

Hekman, S. (1990) *Gender and Knowledge*, Polity: Oxford.

Henderson, W. (1976) *The Life of Friedrich Engels* (2 vols), Cass: London.

Hill, C. (1972) *The World Turned Upside Down*, Temple Smith: London.
Hirst, P. (1979) *On Law and Ideology*, Macmillan: London.
—— (1981) 'Reply', *Politics and Power*, 3: 93–6.
Hirst, P. and Woolley, P. (1982) *Social Relations and Human Attributes*, Macmillan: London.
Hutton, H. (1890) *Lettres D'Auguste Comte a Henry Dix Hutton*, Reeves & Turner: London.
Iggers, G. (1972) *The Doctrine of Saint-Simon*, Schocken Books: New York.
Irigaray, L. (1985) *This Sex Which is Not One*, Cornell University Press: Ithaca.
—— (1990) *Marine Lover of Friedrich Nietzsche*, Columbia University Press: New York.
Jack, M. (1989) *Corruption and Progress*, MAS Press: New York.
James, H. (1932) *Mary Wollstonecraft*, Oxford University Press: Oxford.
Janes, R. (1978) 'On the reception of Mary Wollstonecraft's *Vindication*', *Journal of the History of Ideas*, 39: 293–302.
Jardine, A. (1985) *Gynesis*, Cornell University Press: Ithaca.
Jardine, A. and Smith, P. (eds) (1985) *Men in Feminism*, Methuen: London.
Johnston, M. (1967) 'Karl Marx's verse of 1836–7 as a foreshadowing of his philosophy', *Journal of the History of Ideas*, 28: 259–68.
Kandal, T. (1988) *The Woman Question in Classical Sociological Theory*, Florida International University Press: Miami.
Kaplan, C. (1986) *Sea Changes: Essays on Culture and Feminism*, Verso: London.
Kapp, Y. (1976) *Eleanor Marx: the Crowded Years*, Lawrence & Wishart: London.
Kasler, D. (1988) *Max Weber*, Polity: Oxford.
Kauffman, L. (ed.) (1989) *Gender and Theory: Dialogues on Feminist Criticism*, Blackwell: Oxford.
Kaufmann, W. (1968) *Nietzsche*, Vintage Books: New York.
Kay, C. (1986) 'Canon, ideology and gender', *New Political Science*, 15: 63–76.
Kennedy, E. and Mendus, S. (eds) (1987) *Women in Western Philosophy*, Wheatsheaf: Brighton.
Kierkegaard, S. (1971) 'Diary of a seducer', in *Either/Or* (vol. I), Princeton University Press: Princeton.
Klossowski, P. (1969) *Nietzsche et le Cercle Vicieux*, Mercure: Paris.
Kofman, S. (1972) *Nietzsche et la Metaphor*, Galilee: Paris.
—— (1978) *Aberrations: Le Devenir Femme d'Auguste Comte*, Flammarion: Paris.
—— (1985) *The Enigman of Woman*, Cornell University Press: Ithaca.
Kolb, C. (ed.) (1990) *Nietzsche as Postmodernist*, SUNY: Albany.
Krader, L. (1974) *The Ethnological Notebooks of Karl Marx*, Van Gorcum: Assen.
Krell, D. (1986) *Postponements: Woman, Sensuality and Death in Nietzsche*, Indiana University Press: Bloomington.
Krell, D. and Wood, D.(1988) *Exceedingly Nietzsche*, Routledge: London.
Kirsteva, J. (1983) *Histoires d'Amour*, Denoel: Paris.
Lacan, J. (1982) *Feminine Sexuality*, Macmillan: London.
Lacroix, B. (1981) *Durkheim et la Politique*, Presses de l'Université de Montreal: Montreal.
Lavrin, J. (1971) *Nietzsche*, Studio Vista: London.
Lea, F. (1975) *The Ethics of Reason*, Brentham: London.
Leach, E. (1982) *Social Anthropology*, Fontana: London.
Lepenies, W. (1988) *Between Literature and Science: The Rise of Sociology*, Cambridge University Press: Cambridge.

Lévi-Strauss, E. (1969) *The Elementary Forms of Kinship*, Eyre & Spottiswoode: London.
— (1972) *Structural Anthropology*, Penguin: Harmondsworth.
Lifshitz, M. (1973) *The Philosophy of Art of Karl Marx*, Pluto Press: London.
Linford, M. (1924) *Mary Wollstonecraft*, Parsons: London.
Littre, E. (1864) *Auguste Comte et la Philosophy Positive*, Hachette: Paris.
Livingstone, A. (1984) *Lou Andreas-Salomé*, London: Gordon Fraser.
Locke, D. (1980) *A Fantasy of Reason*, Routledge & Kegan Paul: London.
Lundberg, F. and Farnham, M. (1947) *Modern Woman, The Lost Sex*, Universal Library: New York.
Lukes, S. (1973) *Emile Durkheim*, Allen Lane: London.
Lyotard, F. (1989) *The Lyotard Reader*, Blackwell: Oxford.
MacIntyre, B. (1992) *Forgotten Fatherland*, Macmillan: London.
MacKinnon, C. (1989) *Toward a Feminist Theory of the State*, Harvard University Press: London.
Maggee, B. (1983) *The Philosophy of Schopenhauer*, Clarendon, Oxford.
Manuel, F. (1956) *The New World of Henri Saint-Simon*, Harvard: Cambridge, Mass.
Manuel, F. (1962) *Prophets of Paris*, Harper: New York.
Martin, B. (1991) *Woman and Modernity*, Cornell: Ithaca.
Martin, H. Gutman, H. and Hutton, P. (eds) (1988) *Technologies of the Self*, Tavistock: London.
Marx, K. (1971) *A Contribution to the Critique of Political Economy*, Lawrence & Wishart: London.
— (1973) *Grundrisse*, Penguin: Harmondsworth.
Marx, K. and Engels, F. (1965) *The German Ideology*, Progress: Moscow.
— (1968) *Selected Works*, Lawrence & Wishart: London.
— (1975a) *Collected Works* (vol. 1) Lawrence & Wishart: London.
— (1975b) *Collected Works* (vol. 2) Lawrence & Wishart: London.
— (1982a) *Collected Works* (vol. 18) Lawrence & Wishart: London.
— (1982b) *Collected Works* (vol. 38) Lawrence & Wishart: London.
— (1983) *Collected Works* (vol. 39) Lawrence & Wishart: London.
— (1987) *Collected Works* (vol. 42) Lawrence & Wishart: London.
— (1988) *Collected Works* (vol. 43) Lawrence & Wishart: London.
— (1989) *Collected Works* (vol. 44) Lawrence & Wishart: London.
Mauss, M. (1969) *Oeuvres* (vol. 3) Minuit: Paris.
May, K. (1988) *Nietzsche and Modern Literature*, Macmillan: London.
Meier, O., Evans, F. and Rowbotham, S. (1984) *The Daughters of Karl Marx*, Penguin: London.
Meillasoux, C. (1981) *Maidens, Meal, and Money*, Cambridge University Press: Cambridge.
Mendus, S. (1989) *Sexuality and Subordination*, Routledge: London.
Merquior, J. (1980) *Rousseau and Weber*, Routledge: London.
Mestrovic, S. (1988) *Emile Durkheim and the Reformation of Sociology*, Rowman & Littlefield: New Jersey.
Middleton, C. (ed.) (1969) *Selected Letters of Friedrich Nietzsche*, University of Chicago Press: Chicago and London.
Mill, J. S. (1878) *The Subjection of Women*, Longman: London.
— (1924) *Autobiography*, Oxford University Press: Oxford.
— (1963) *The Early Letters of J. S. Mill, 1812–48*, Routledge & Kegan Paul: London.

—— (1970) 'Evidence to Royal Commission 1871', *British Parliamentary Papers: Infectious Diseases*, 5, 830–7. Irish University Press: Dublin.

—— (1981) *Collected Works: Autobiography and Literary Essays*, University of Toronto Press: Toronto.

Mill, H. T. and Mill, J. S. (1983) *Enfranchisement of Women and The Subjection of Women*, Virago: London.

Mills, P. (1987) *Woman, Nature and Psyche*, Yale University Press: New Haven.

Mintz, S. (1983) *A Prison of Expectations*, New York University Press: New York.

Mitzman, A. (1970) *The Iron Cage*, Grosset & Dunlap: New York.

Mommsen, W. (1989) *The Political and Social Theory of Max Weber*, Polity: Oxford.

Mommsen, W. and Osterhammel, J. (1987) *Max Weber and His Contemporaries*, Unwin Hyman: London.

Moret, A. and Davy, G. (1970) *From Tribe to Empire*, Cooper Square: New York.

Moses, C. (1982) 'Saint-Simonian men/Saint-Simonian women: the transformation of feminist thought in 1830s France', *Journal of Modern History*, 54: 240–67.

—— (1984) *French Feminism in the Nineteenth Century*, State University of New York Press: Albany.

Mullan, J. (1988) *Sentiment and Sociability: The Language of Feeling in the Eighteenth Century*, Oxford University Press: Oxford.

Needham, R. (1966) 'Comments on a translation of Durkheim on incest', *American Anthropologist*, 68: 161–3.

Needham, R. (ed.) (1971) *Rethinking Kinship and Marriage*, Tavistock: London.

Needham, T. (ed.) (1973) *Right and Left*, University of Chicago Press: London.

Nicholson, M. (1990) 'The eleventh Commandment: sex and spirit in Wollstonecraft and Malthus', *Journal of the History of Ideas*, 15: 401–21.

Nietzsche, F. (1960) *The Joyful Wisdom*, Ungar: New York.

—— (1968) *Twilight of the Idols*, Penguin: Harmondsworth.

—— (1969a) *On the Genealogy of Morals and Ecce Homo*, Vintage: New York.

—— (1969b) *Thus Spake Zarathustra*, Penguin: Harmondsworth.

—— (1984) *Dithyrambs of Dionysos*, Anvil: London.

Nye, A. (1988) *Feminist Theory and the Philosophies of Man*, Routledge: London.

O'Brien, C. (1972) *The Suspecting Glance*, Faber: London.

Ochshorn, J. (1981) *The Female Experience and the Nature of the Divine*, Indiana University Press: Bloomington.

Offen, K. (1986) 'Earnest Legouve and the doctrine of "equality in difference" for women: a case study of male feminism in nineteenth century French thought', *Journal of Modern History*, 58: 452–84.

Okin, S. (1979) *Women in Western Political Thought*, Princeton University Press: New Jersey.

Ormiston, G. (1984) 'Traces of Derrida: Nietzsche's image of woman', *Philosophy Today*, (Summer): 178–88.

Packe, M. (1954) *The Life of John Stuart Mill*, Secker & Warburg: London.

Padover, S. (1979) *The Selected Letters of Karl Marx*, Prentice Hall: New York.

Paine, T. (1949) *Rights of Man*, Watts: London.

Pankhurst, R. K. P. (1957) *The Saint Simonians, Mill and Carlyle*, Sidgwick & Jackson: London.

Pateman, C. (1991) *The Disorder of Women*, Polity: Oxford.

Pautrat, B. (1971) *Versions du Soleil: Figures et Systeme de Nietzsche*, Seuil: Paris.

Payne, R. (1968) *Marx*, Allen: London.
— (1973) *The Unknown Marx*, University of London Press: London.
Paz, O. (1971) *Claude Lévi-Strauss*, Cape: London.
Philp, M. (1986) *Godwin's Political Justice*, Duckworth: London.
Poovey, M. (1984) *The Proper Lady and the Woman Writer*, University of Chicago Press: London.
Prater, D. (1986) *A Ringing Glass*, Clarendon Press: Oxford.
Prawer, S. (1976) *Karl Marx and World Literature*, Clarendon Press: Oxford.
Preedy, G. (1937) *This Shining Woman*, Collins: London.
Raddatz, F. (1978) *Karl Marx*, Weidenfeld & Nicolson: London.
— (1980) *The Marx-Engels Correspondence*, Weidenfeld & Nicolson: London.
Reik, T. (1931) *Ritual*, Hogarth: London.
Reiss, T. (1989) 'Revolution in bounds: Wollstonecraft, women and reason', in Kauffman (ed.) *Gender and Theory: Dialogues on Feminist Criticism*, Blackwell: Oxford, pp. 11–50.
Ricci, N. (1987) 'The End/s of Woman', *Canadian Journal of Political and Social Theory*, 11 (3): 11–27.
Roazen, P. (1968) *Freud, Political and Social Thought*, Knopf: New York.
— (1976) *Freud and His Followers*, Allen Lane: London.
Roheim, G. (1930) *Animism, Magic and the Divine King*, Kegan Paul, Trench, Trubner: London.
Rose, G. (1984) *Dialectic of Nihilism*, Blackwell: Oxford.
Rose, M. (1984) *Marx's Lost Aesthetic*, Cambridge University Press: Cambridge.
Rose, P. (1984) *Parallel Lives: Five Victorian Marriages*, Knopf: New York.
Rousseau, E. (1956) *Emile*, Heinemann: London.
Ryan, A. (1974) *J. S. Mill*, Routledge & Kegan Paul: London.
St Clair, W. (1989) *The Godwins and the Shelleys*, Faber & Faber: London.
Saint-Simon, H. (1976) *Selected Writings*, Croom Helm: London.
Salomé, L. (1988) *Nietzsche*, Black Swan: Redding Ridge.
Sapiro, V. (1992) *A Vindication of Political Virtue*, University of Chicago Press: Chicago and London.
Sawicki, J. (1991) *Disciplining Foucault*, Routledge: London.
Sayers, J. (1982) *Biological Politics*, Tavistock: London.
— (1991) *Mothering Psychoanalysis*, Hamish Hamilton: London.
Sayers, J., Evans, M. and Redclift, N. (eds) (1987) *Engels Revisited*, Tavistock: London.
Scaff, L. (1989) *Fleeing the Iron Cage*, University of California Press: Berkeley.
Schaeffle, A. (1892) *The Impossibility of Social Democracy*, Swan Sonnenschein: London.
Schofield, M. (1990) *Masking and Unmasking the Female Mind*, Associated University Presses: London.
Shanley, L. and Pateman, C. (eds) (1991) Feminist Interpretations and Political Theory, Polity: Oxford.
Shorter, E. (1977) *The Making of the Modern Family*, Fontana: London.
— (1984) *A History of Women's Bodies*, Pelican: London.
Sombart, N. (1987) 'Max Weber and Otto Gross: on the relationship between science, politics and Eros in Wilhemine Germany', *History of Political Thought*, 8 (1): 131–52.
Spacks, P. (1976) *Imagining a Self*, Harvard University Press: London.
Spencer, K. (1986) *The Rise of the Woman Novelist*, Blackwell: Oxford.
Spencer, S. (ed.) *French Women and the Age of Enlightenment*, Indiana University Press: Bloomington.

Spender, D. (1982) *Women of Ideas*, Routledge: London.
Stanley, L. and Pateman, C. (1991) *Feminist Interpretations and Political Theory*, Polity: Oxford.
Stephens, W. (1972) 'A cross-cultural study of modesty', *Behavioural Science Notes*, 7: 1–28.
Strong, S. (1975) *Friedrich Nietzsche and the Politics of Transfiguration*, University of California Press: Berkeley.
Sunstein, E. (1975) *A Different Face*, Harper & Row: London.
Swart, K. (1964) *The Sense of Decadence in 19th Century France*, Nijhoff: The Hague.
Sydie, R. (1987) *Natural Women, Cultured Men: A Feminist Perspective on Sociological Theory*, Open University Press: Milton Keynes.
Taylor, B. (1983) *Eve and the New Jerusalem*, Virago: London.
Taylor, G. R. (1958) *The Angel-Makers*, Heinemann: London.
Taylor, K. (ed.) (1975) *Henri de Saint Simon*, Croom Helm: London.
Therborn, G. (1976) *Science, Class and Society*, NLB: London.
—— (1980) *The Power of Ideology*, NLB: London.
Thomas, J. H. (1983) *Nietzsche and German Politics and Society*, Manchester University Press: Manchester.
Thomas, J. J. R. (1986) 'Rationalization and the status of gender divisions', *Sociology*, 19 (3): 409–20.
Thomas, K. (1959) 'The double standard', *Journal of the History of Ideas*, 195–216.
Thompson, K. (1976) *Auguste Comte*, Nelson: London.
—— (1982) *Emile Durkheim*, Tavistock: London.
Tijssen, L. van V. (1991) 'Women and objective culture: Georg Simmel and Marianne Weber', *Theory, Culture & Society*, 8 (3): 203–18.
Tiryakian, E. (1966) 'A problem for the sociology of knowledge', *European Journal of Sociology*, 7: 330–6.
—— (1981) 'Sexual anomie, social structure, societal change', *Social Forces*, 59: 1025–53.
—— (1982) 'A sop to Cerberus: response to Bernard', *Social Forces*, 61: 287–9.
Todd, K. (1989) *The Sign of Angelica*, Virago: London.
Toews, J. (1980) *Hegelianism, The Path Towards Dialectical Humanism*, Cambridge University Press: Cambridge.
Tomalin, C. (1974) *The Life and Death of Mary Wollstonecraft*, Harcourt Brace Jovanovich.
Tulloch, G. (1989) *Mill and Sexual Equality*, Harvester: Hemel Hempstead.
Tysdahl, B. (1981) *William Godwin as Novelist*, Athlone: London.
Veeder, W. (1986) *Mary Shelley and Frankenstein: the Fate of Androgyny*, University of Chicago Press: London.
Verdon, M. (1982) 'Durkheim and Aristotle: some incongruous congruences', *Studies in History and Philosophy of Science*, 13(4): 333–52.
Vernon, R. (1984) 'Auguste Comte and the withering away of the state', *Journal Of the History of Ideas*, 45: 549–66.
von Stein, L. (1964) *The History of the Socialist Movements in France, 1789–1850*, Bedminster Press: New York.
Walby, S. (1990) *Theorizing Patriarchy*, Blackwell: Oxford.
Walters, M. (1976) 'The rights and wrongs of women: Mary Wollstonecraft, Harriet Martineau, Simone de Beauvoir', in J. Mitchell and A. Oakley (eds) *The Rights and Wrongs of Women*, Penguin: Harmondsworth.

Warner, W. B. (1986) *Chance and the Text of Experience*, Cornell University Press: Ithaca.
Weber, Max (1965) *The Protestant Ethic*, Unwin: London.
—— (1978) *Economy and Society* (2 vols) University of California Press: Berkeley.
—— (1991) *From Max Weber* (ed. by H. Gerth and C. W. Mills), Routledge: London.
Weber, Marianne (1975) *Max Weber: a Biography*, Wiley: London.
Wessell, L. (1979) *Karl Marx, Romantic Irony and the Proletariat*, Louisian State University: Baton Rouge.
Whitford, M. (1991) *Luce Irigaray: Philosophy in the Feminine*, Routledge: London.
Wolff, J. (1990) *Feminine Sentences*, Polity: Oxford.
Wollstonecraft, M. (1983) *A Vindication of the Rights of Woman*, Penguin: Harmondsworth.
—— (1989) *The Works of Mary Wollstonecraft* (5 vols), Pickering: London.
Wydenbruck, N. (1949) *Rilke, Man and Poet*, Lehmann: London.
Zanuso, B. (1986) *The Young Freud*, Blackwell: Oxford.

Name index

Subject index

acosmic love 159
affection 31, 81, 123
alienation 65, 87
Althusserianism 2ff
ambience 61
androgyny 24, 25
animality, revenge of 159, 169
anomie: conjugal 11, 16, 24, 47; Mill on 137; sexual 24ff
anti-erotic ethic 68
asexual reproduction 126–7

biography 15; reduction to 15ff
blood 41ff
body 37f, 62, 64, 69, 78, 81
British constitution 70
brotherly love 160ff, 167, 170

capitalism: and women's liberation 152, 160
carousing 146, 153
Catholicism 10, 85, 124ff
cause: of female oppression, not sexual 137ff; sexual 62ff
chaste love 73
chaste women 65
chastity, inner 81
chivalry 124, 171
citizenship 138
classification 42ff
collective representation 27, 31
communist organization 88ff
community of women 147
compulsion of love 164
conjugal sentiment 54
conscience collective 35, 41
contraception 129
controlled desublimation 116

coquettry 135
couple, the 116ff
crisis of masculinity 11
cult: of women 124; of Virgin Mary 124f, 195ff, 199

daughter 73, 193ff
desire 33, 203
destiny 162
divorce 58, 136–7, 199
domestic: division of labour 135, 162; sphere 150, 162
dowry 31, 125

education, moral 53, 109
emancipation of women 133, 147
equality 38, 134ff
eroticism 115, 159, 167, 171
erotic movement, the 164ff
erotic sphere 169
eternal masculine 177
eternal widowhood 125, 199
evolution, of family 33ff
extramarital eros 52ff, 168ff

family: pathology 148; proletarian 148; property 150; school of despotism 137
fate 165, 172
feeling 71ff; empire of 111ff; Mill and 131; and reform 124; women and 120
feminism 63ff, 115ff, 124ff
fetishism 89ff, 126, 199, 203
friendship 73, 76, 135
fusion, masculine and feminine 131, 169

gallantry 135